The Community College Library

ASSESSMENT

edited by
Janet Pinkley *and*
Kaela Casey

Association of College and Research Libraries
A division of the American Library Association
Chicago, Illinois 2022

The paper used in this publication meets the minimum requirements of American National Standard for Information Sciences–Permanence of Paper for Printed Library Materials, ANSI Z39.48-1992. ∞

Library of Congress Control Number: 2022932474

Printed in the United States of America.

26 25 24 23 22 5 4 3 2 1

Contents

Introduction

Community colleges are a cornerstone of higher education and have long aimed to serve the unique needs of the communities in which they reside. While each community college has its own programs and culture, they share a common set of values and goals:

- serving all segments of society through an open-access admissions policy that offers equal and fair treatment to all students
- providing a comprehensive educational program
- serving the community as a community-based institution of higher education
- teaching and learning
- fostering lifelong learning[1]

Community college libraries and librarians are integral to achieving these goals as they aim to provide equitable access to information and resources for all students while promoting information literacy. Additionally, and most importantly, community college libraries and librarians support student success by meeting the information and research needs of their college population both in person and remotely, all while providing a safe, inclusive space for students to explore and learn.

In 2019, community colleges accounted for 41 percent of all undergraduate students in the United States.[2] Despite their significant contributions to in higher education, community college libraries and librarians are not equitably represented in professional literature. This series aims to change that.

Goals of the Series

As information professionals, librarians often look to literature to inform their practice. Following this approach, the editors of this series found the conversations on assessment were primarily from the perspective of a four-year institution. However, we knew that our colleagues in community college libraries across the nation were engaging in meaningful work across all aspects of library programs and services to serve the needs of their diverse populations and to support student learning. We wanted to find a way to lift the voices of community college librarians and highlight their innovation, creativity, tenacity, and commitment to students; thus, *The Community College Library* series was born.

We believe that the titles within this series will inspire community college librarians to reflect on their own practices, develop new programs or enhance existing ones, and serve students with renewed dedication and passion. Additionally, we hope that they will encourage community college librarians to share their own experiences and endeavors to serve students through publications in order to allow the dynamic, passionate, innovative work taking place at community college libraries to become more abundant in professional library literature.

Assessment

Each community college library provides a unique set of services, programs, and resources to meet the needs of its campus community. Assessment allows us to measure, evaluate, and reflect upon the services we provide and is a way for libraries to document the challenges encountered and improvements made and to demonstrate the value and impact of library services and resources. While assessment is sometimes viewed as a mandatory activity that must be included as part of program review or statistics reporting, going beyond that to build intentional assessment projects and programs can give community college libraries and librarians a comprehensive view of the performance and quality of their services. Additionally, it allows for proactive and anticipatory means for requesting funding and additional resources to support the unique needs of a library and the population it serves. Assessment is critical in order to ensure that library services are truly serving campus needs, meeting the mission and goals of the library, and keeping the library's focus on improvement and innovation.

The chapters in this book highlight the research, comprehensive plans, and new approaches to assessment done by community college librarians around the country. We hope that it informs and inspires our readers to reflect on their own libraries and professional practice and perhaps embark on a new assessment project.

The COVID-19 pandemic hit the United States early in this project. We would be remiss if we did not take a moment to highlight the commitment that all of the contributors had to this project. They all faced unique challenges and circumstances, shifting all of their professional responsibilities online, while also juggling the demands that COVID-19 made on their personal lives, such as assisting elderly parents, helping their children shift to virtual schooling, and much more. We were humbled by the perseverance and dedication of our community college colleagues as they continued to draft and edit their chapters during the global pandemic, which was fraught with so many unknowns and challenges on a daily basis.

Notes

1.   George B. Vaughan, *The Community College Story*, 2nd ed. (Washington DC: Community College Press, 2000), 3.
2.   "Fast Facts 2021," American Association of Community Colleges, accessed June 1, 2021, https://www.aacc.nche.edu/research-trends/fast-facts/.

Bibliography

American Association of Community College. "Fast Facts 2021." Accessed June 1, 2021. https://www.aacc.nche.edu/research-trends/fast-facts/.

Vaughan, George B. *The Community College Story*, 2nd ed. Washington, DC: Community College Press, 2000.

CHAPTER 1

Where to Begin?

Constructing an Assessment Plan from the Ground Up

Bryan Clark and Amy Glass

Assessment planning at the Illinois Central College (ICC) Library had been discussed for years, but very little had been accomplished by the beginning of 2010. Part of this, of course, was because of time; working with students on research projects and technology issues consumed planning time. However, there was also a sense of "Where do we even begin? This is an overwhelming project!" Through some hard work and experimentation (plus a little bit of luck, thanks to the American Library Association), assessment began to take shape at the ICC Library.

The Association of College and Research Libraries (ACRL) division of the American Library Association (ALA) received a National Leadership Demonstration grant to establish Assessment in Action: Academic Libraries and Student Success (AiA) in 2012.[1] This program was designed to show the value of academic libraries and the part they play in student success, using data-driven methods. The ICC Library applied to this program and was selected in 2013 as one of the first seventy-five college libraries in the nation to take part. ICC's project assessed the value of library instruction in several sections of ENG 111 (Composition II) as compared to sections of the same class with no library instruction.[2] Through participation in this program, librarians learned how to gather data for assessment and how to use this data. The collected data and the information learned through the program resulted in the first professional presentation on library assessment for the ICC Library, a poster session at the 2014 ALA Annual Conference in Las Vegas. Faculty members who were asked to submit artifacts for AiA also saw that the library was invested in assessment data, which strengthened relationships between certain faculty and librarians. As a result of this, the library was invited to be part of the ICC College-wide Assessment Committee.

Also in 2013, a colleague attended the Association of College and Research Libraries Conference, held in Indianapolis. At this conference, the ICC Library learned about ALLI (Active Learning in Library Instruction), created by Kevin Seeber.[3] After contacting Mr. Seeber for permission to adapt ALLI for ICC needs, librarians started incorporating ALLI worksheets into instruction sessions. These sheets were distributed to students during instruction sessions, either as a supplement to instruction or as part of classroom discussion on library resources. The incorporation of ALLI also resulted in the library forming an instruction committee. This committee guided all librarians in the use of ALLI and other instructional methods.

One of the ALLI worksheets adapted discussed the selection of keywords (see appendix 1A). This worksheet became the building block for the first group effort at assessment in the ICC Library. During instruction sessions in spring semester 2015, librarians discussed procedures for selecting keywords to students. At the end of a session, a worksheet was given to students for completion. As seen in appendix 1A, students were asked to write down their research question, select keywords from that question, and locate an article from Academic Search Complete using those keywords as their search terms. Data from these sheets was analyzed at the end of the semester, using a rubric created by ICC librarians (table 1.1).

Table 1.1
Keyword assessment rubric, 2015

	Not Evident = 0	Beginning = 1	Developing = 2	Accomplished = 3
Identify keywords for a topic	• No keywords identified	• Minimal keywords provided • Keywords unclear, unrelated to topic	• Keywords related to topic • Synonyms too general or vague	• Variety of specific, precise keywords related to topic
Select a relevant article on the topic	• No article	• Article not relevant to topic	• Article tangentially relevant to topic	• Article relevant to topic

The results showed that this first effort at assessment did not promote qualitative results of a student's ability to do research. Of the students sampled, 65 percent were not able to identify a keyword for their topic or would provide only an unclear keyword. Yet, 60 percent of the same sample were able to provide one article that was at least tangentially related to their research question. At the same time, though, librarians realized that since students' grades were most often not tied to the handouts, they did not put their best effort forward. Librarians then repeated this same assessment project in fall semester 2015, with few changes in assessment practice. They wanted to see if there would be similar results and found that there were.

At this point, library staff knew that there were flaws in their approach, due to the inconsistencies between unsuccessful keyword selection and discovery of a relevant article. Because of the new participation in the College-wide Assessment Committee, it was decided to talk to the chairs of that committee for advice. The meetings with these experts in assessment at ICC provided a crucial turning point in our assessment plan. In our conversation with these faculty members, librarians realized the goal of our assessment work was to prove our value to students through our instruction sessions. Therefore, librarians changed the emphasis of our assessment work. The starting point became the contrast between students in classes having embedded library instruction and one-shot library instruction.

For this assessment, *embedded instruction* was defined as a collaboration between librarian and faculty over the course of multiple instruction sessions with the students of one class, while *one-shot instruction* was defined as a single instruction session per class where the faculty and librarian do not collaborate as fully to integrate the librarian into the class as a whole. Librarians at ICC have tried to expand the embedded instruction program to more faculty, believing it would engage students and improve their knowledge and usage of library resources. Assessment data on embedded librarianship could potentially prove its effectiveness toward student success.

The next step was to draft documentation to guide staff in the assessment process. Librarians held meetings to determine which college instructors worked with the ICC Library on a regular basis, putting them in the embedded or one-shot group. A draft e-mail was created for the faculty identified, explaining our new plan for assessing library instruction and asking if they would be part of this process. Most of the faculty contacted agreed to work with us on this project. In this e-mail, sent in September/October of 2016, librarians specified the following criteria for submissions for assignments:

- a minimum of three sources
- papers of 1,000–2,500 words in length OR
- recorded presentations of three to five minutes in length
- a works cited page required, using a professional style for the type of presentation or paper
- instructors to submit student artifacts via an online drop service, which connected to the library's Google Drive
- instructors asked to send a copy of their assignment along with the student submissions

The first three criteria were selected as representative of many assignments given to ICC students. The number of sources also ensured that librarians had a sample of types of sources for each artifact. By asking instructors to provide a copy of the assignment, librarians knew whether the students met the basic requirements, as well as whether the instructor required library resources.

ICC librarians decided to focus on the student's ability to incorporate sources into their research papers or projects. In order to assess this information, staff needed to create a new rubric. Fortunately, Illinois Central College created rubrics for general education assessments, and librarians were able to adapt this rubric (table 1.2).

Table 1.2
ICC Assessment of Library Instruction Rubric

	0	1	2	3
Incorporate credible sources appropriate to the topic	• No sources used to support claims.	• Some attempt at engaging with sources, but information does not support their claims.	• Some attempt at engaging with sources, and information occasionally supports their claims.	• Engages and fully incorporates sources with evidence that fully supports their claims.
Integrate information ethically and legally	• No citations or attributions. • Plagiarism—writer cuts and pastes without appearing to recognize the sources or the content of the sources.	• Sources cannot be located due to poor/inconsistent citations, and attribution is provided with numerous errors.	• Sources can be located, but citation and attribution contain a few errors.	• All citations are complete and consistent, and information is fully attributed.

At the end of the semester, the library received eighty-four artifacts from ICC faculty. Once the artifacts were submitted, all the student information was stripped from the papers. Each artifact was given a number and labeled to indicate whether it was part of an embedded class or a one-shot instruction session. At this point, random numbers were chosen (using an online random number generator) for a sample size of forty artifacts. Five librarians assessed a total of sixteen artifacts each so that every artifact was assessed by two librarians. If the librarians disagreed on the rubric score, a third librarian was brought in to assess those specific artifacts.

Initial assessment results showed 10 percent more students in embedded librarian sessions were able to incorporate credible sources into the papers than students in the one-shot sessions. However, when librarians analyzed the integration of sources ethically in student's work, 10 percent more succeeded with one-shot instructions as compared to the embedded work. The results suggest embedded librarian work had an effect on students' sources, but not necessarily on their ethical use of those sources. Librarians also realized that other factors could affect these results. To that end, the submission requirements for future assessment periods were reworked. Limiting the number of sources required and word count did not contribute to our research. Librarians also felt that limiting by level of course (100 versus 200) and the actual time spent in instruction should be addressed.

After changing the method for instruction assessment in fall 2016, librarians met to expand the Illinois Central College Library assessment beyond instruction. Cate Kaufman, the library director at ICC, tasked fellow librarians with researching external library assessment plans with the goal of finding examples of how other colleges assess the different avenues of impact and incorporate the information into one document.

An open Google search produced assessment plans from two institutions: California State University, Northridge, and City College of San Francisco. While other reports existed, these two best represented the concept the library envisioned. California State University's document creates a complete picture of how assessment areas are tied to measurement tools and time frames.[4] The document from City College of San Francisco demonstrates how the assessment is tied to student learning outcomes and that each outcome has a different assessment method.[5] Illinois Central College reviewed these and merged these strengths to create a framework for its own assessment plan.

Once the library found these two example assessment plans, the librarians also looked to the *Standards for Libraries in Higher Education* from ACRL. These *Standards* guide library policy and procedure, so ICC focused on the structure of these *Standards* when creating its assessment plan:

> The core of the Standards is the section titled "Principles and Performance Indicators." *The nine principles and their related performance indicators are intended to be expectations—standards—that apply to all types of academic libraries* [italics in original]. Nonetheless, each library must respond to its unique user population and institutional environment.[6]

To that end, ICC focused on creating this same base structure of principles and performance indicators for its assessment.

Finally, before constructing the plan, librarians needed to determine which assessment model to follow. The ACRL *Standards* provide an assessment model based on their structure, an outcome-based model (figure 1.1).

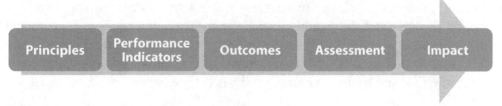

Figure 1.1

Outcomes-based Assessment Model (Source: Association of College and Research Libraries, *Standards for Libraries in Higher Education* [Chicago: Association of College and Research Libraries, 2011, rev. 2018], 7)

By combining the example assessment plans with the ACRL *Standards* structure and student learning outcomes, ICC was ready to start drafting an overall assessment plan using the model in figure 1.1. Putting this all together took all of the fall 2016 semester and most of the spring 2017 semester. The work paid off with a completed product,

"Assessment of Library Impact", dated May 8, 2017 (see appendix 1B). How ICC combined the pieces is a big part of the story to come.

Following this groundwork, ICC began by formalizing the principles to use for this assessment plan. The ACRL *Standards* use nine different principles in their structure. However, the librarians did not see the need to use all nine. After deliberation, three principles were selected: resources (which the library curates), services (what the library provides), and instruction (that which the library teaches). Once the librarians picked the principles, the next step was creating definitions for them:

- *Resources:* Libraries curate resources for the college community to assist students with coursework and support overall learning.
- *Services:* Libraries provide services to the college community that allow students to prepare for college and lifelong learning.
- *Instruction:* Libraries formally teach the means and methods for students to gain information literacy skills.

As can be seen in the completed plan in appendix 1B, these principles separate the sections on the plan and root the assessment work into three distinct categories.

These definitions cover all of the different areas of the library and allowed the librarians to then create performance indicators that fit within these three principles. When first brainstorming, librarians came up with a strong list and tied them to their corresponding principles.

- *Resources:* space (computers and study rooms), hours of operation, staff, format of resources (variety), website
- *Services:* programming, reference help (chat, in person, phone, e-mail), interlibrary loan, technology for checkout
- *Instruction:* library workshops, technology workshops, online classroom instruction, in-person classroom instruction

Once these areas were created for performance indicators, librarians were able to draft wording to define each of them. The next step was creating student learning outcomes. Appendix 1B shows that the definitions of the performance indicators and the student learning outcomes work together to form a full picture of the interaction between library and student. At this point ICC librarians moved from creating the principles, performance indicators, and student learning outcomes to focusing on how to assess all this information.

Returning to the ACRL *Standards*, ICC librarians realized that these can provide more than just the structure of assessment. The *Standards* also provide the benchmark upon which to base the assessment. As mentioned previously, there are nine principles in the ACRL *Standards*. Each of these nine principles has between two and nine performance indicators.[7] The library looked through all of these ACRL performance indicators and assigned one to each of the performance indicators on the ICC assessment plan. In this first draft, librarians tried to hit a majority of the ACRL principles to have better coverage. Of the nine principles, ICC touched on five of them (principles 3, 4, 5, 6, and 8). By starting with one for each performance indicator, ICC library guaranteed a benchmark allowing for a baseline goal for all of the assessment work. Therefore, the library would know what it was striving to achieve when assessing student learning outcomes and performance indicators on its assessment plan.

When ICC Library looked at how to set the various assessment methods, it was important to focus on the variety of ways assessment can be done. Librarians decided to set at least two assessment methods for each student learning outcome. Having met with the chairs of the College-wide Assessment Committee previously, the library had ideas for what the various forms of assessment would take. The goal was to have both direct and indirect forms of assessment. These are well-defined by the National Institute for Learning Outcomes Assessment in Champaign, Illinois. Direct assessment is found within the plan through direct student work and raw data, as seen in appendix 1B: "Direct assessment is when measures of learning are based on student performance or demonstrates the learning itself."[8] The student work represents the "student performance" aspect of the definition, and the data represents the "demonstrates the learning itself" aspect of the definition. Indirect assessment is found in the surveys found in all performance indicators. "Indirect assessments use perceptions, reflections or secondary evidence to make inferences about student learning."[9] The surveys represent the "perceptions, reflections or secondary evidence" of the definition. Both direct and indirect assessment are important because they allow for a complete picture of the process. Direct assessment is needed to show that the students can achieve a goal or perform an action. Indirect assessment is needed to determine why they are acting in this way.

As for the assessment period, ICC librarians decided to make this assessment process continual over a three-semester period. This allows for a rotating schedule of assessment, analysis, and schedule improvement—before repeating the process. Also, the library assesses only one principle at a time. Table 1.3 gives a concrete picture of what this looks like.

Table 1.3
First overall assessment schedule

	Assessment Period	Analysis Period	Improvement Period
Instruction	Spring 2017	Fall 2017	Spring 2018
Services	Fall 2017	Spring 2018	Fall 2018
Resources	Spring 2018	Fall 2018	Spring 2019

When the ICC library first began the full assessment process, librarians chose to focus on the instruction principle first since so much work had been done on this process previously. Therefore, based on the first assessment process shown in table 1.3, the instruction principle was assessed during spring 2017, analyzed the following semester in fall 2017, and improved the following semester in spring 2018. The services principle was added in fall 2017, and the resources principle was added in spring 2018. After that, the cycle repeats in a continuous fashion. Once the library got fully up and running on the assessment plan, librarians were on a separate stage of the process for each principle during every semester.

Once the plan was initially in place, the librarians started to collect data using the direct and indirect measures detailed above. For the direct measures, the library pulled data from DeskTracker and LibInsights, the computer programs that record all of the library interactions with students, along with proxy logs, turnaway reports, and other data from ICC's databases. This allowed the library to directly answer whether students at Illinois Central College were getting what they needed out of our resources, services, and instruction. Librarians continued to collect student work as the second direct measure. These methods of assessment, direct and indirect, created a complete picture of how the students were using the library.

To go along with the raw data pulled from reports and student work, librarians also developed student and faculty surveys. The library deployed these in several different ways: at the reference desk, in a virtual chat, at events, and over e-mail. Smaller surveys covered only what was in one principle (either resources, services, or instruction). The smaller surveys were generally handed out through reference interactions (in person and online) and at events. Also, larger surveys covered multiple principles (more than one of resources, services, or instruction). ICC's Institutional Research Department reviewed these larger surveys before deployment. The goal of these surveys was to find out how and why the students were using the library, to go along with what they were using, as determined from the direct measures.

Combining these means of direct and indirect measures allows the library to analyze what is or is not working in each of the principles based on the student learning outcomes. This was first achieved by writing reports for each principle after its assessment period. Each report features an introduction, a rundown of the assessments and results, and a conclusion with recommendations. After a full cycle, ICC library combined these reports into a comprehensive report. This comprehensive report, titled "Assessment of Library Impact Report," summarizes the individual reports and then provides overall recommendations for the whole library. These recommendations were not used only for improving impact at the student level; they also provided insight on work that needed to be done at the plan level.

When looking at improvements to the overall plan, the library made changes to each principle. Under resources, the library made changes to the availability of study rooms and space. This was especially apparent as the library worked through the opening of a new campus location. Regarding services, librarians focused on how to improve programming and reference services to better provide students what they want and need. For the instruction principle, the biggest changes took place once the library realized that the workshops (on both research and technology) were not sustainable. Also, the library focused its instruction assessment on more specific classes in order to control more of the variables within that project. All of these changes had ripple effects, and the plan seen in appendix 1B soon changed once librarians adapted to the individual changes from each semester.

The latest version of the assessment plan, dated September 10, 2019, shows the changes that the library made since the first draft two years previously (see appendix 1C). These changes represent the decisions made by the library based on the suggested recommendations found in the reports from each semester. As can be seen in this newest draft of the plan in appendix 1C, the plan underwent many changes over the course of those two years. Regarding resources, the library had three main types of changes. First, wording was changed on performance indicator 1.2, and the performance indicator for 1.3 was replaced with one directly from the ACRL *Standards*. Second, more benchmarks were added from the *Standards*. Benchmarks were also added from the ACRL Trends and Statistics and IPEDS, both found in the ACRLMetrics portal.[10] Third, new assessment methods were added based on where the library was missing data from the last run of this principle. For the services principle, the biggest change was that performance indicator 2.2 was moved under the instruction principle. Benchmarks from the ACRL Trends and Statistics and IPEDS were also added. And under instruction, performance indicators 3.1 and 3.2 were removed because they were not sustainable, and 2.2 became the new 3.1 as mentioned above. Also, as with the other two principles, benchmarks were added from the ACRL Trends and Statistics and IPEDS. These changes demonstrate that even once completed, the assessment plan is a living document. It will continue to evolve and change as the ICC library makes new discoveries and adds new ideas.

Due to the work of librarians on this plan, ICC Library's assessment framework became a model for other colleges in Illinois. After we presented at several conferences, colleagues in academic libraries across the state have asked for guidance on their own assessment. Also, within ICC, one of our librarians became co-chair of the College-wide Assessment Committee and now serves as an assessment fellow to the institution. The library is now an established stakeholder in the college's assessment process and in the future of assessment at Illinois libraries.

Throughout the years of building up assessment, Illinois Central College librarians learned many useful lessons through trial and error. This allowed the librarians to draft an assessment plan. This plan is a living document that keeps changing and evolving as the team learns more about assessment at the student and library level each semester. As this process continues, the library plans to further adapt this assessment plan by tying it into the college's three institutional learning outcomes (ILOs): reasoning, communication, and responsibility. By tying into the larger college, the library can show its impact in more ways than only the direct and indirect measures already employed. From early conceptual missteps to complex assessment strategies, Illinois Central College Library constructed an assessment framework that continues to grow and thrive in the library and beyond.

Appendix 1A
Research Keyword Activity, ALLI @ ICC Library

1. Write a sentence that describes your topic.
2. Write the main words from #1 in the top boxes below; then, write at least two synonyms for each of those words in the connected boxes.

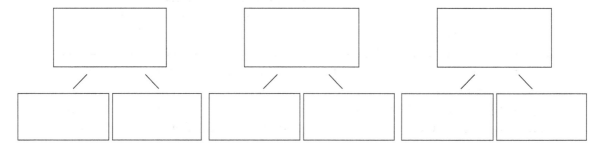

3. Use one combination of keywords from the boxes in #3 to do a search in "Find It @ ICC Library." What search terms did you use? What options from the left side of your results page in "Find It @ ICC Library" did you select to refine your results?

4. Use a second combination of keywords from the boxes in #3 to do a search in "Find It @ ICC Library." What search terms did you use? What options from the left side of your results page in "Find It @ ICC Library" did you select to refine your results?

5. From which search did you find the best articles on your topic? Why do you feel this search was more successful?

6. Write down the following information for at least one of the articles from your search:

   Authors:

   Title of Article:

   Journal Name:

   Publication Date:

   Volume and Issue #:

   Name of Database:

7. Why would the above be a good source for your paper?

Adapted with permission from Kevin Seeber, Colorado State U-Pueblo

Appendix 1B

	Assessment of Library Impact	Benchmarks	Assessment Method	Assessment Period*
	Resources: Libraries curate resources for the college community that assist students with coursework and support overall learning.			
1.1	The library curates a space that fits the student's need for computers, group work, and private study. *Students have the space to meet various learning styles that support their success.*	ACRL Standards 6.6	Student survey Learning styles	Spring 2018
1.2	The library opens physical access to the library on multiple campuses during various hours of operation throughout the week. *Students are able to use the library during hours that meet their research and study needs*	ACRL Standards 6.7	Student survey Course schedules	Spring 2018
1.3	The library hires and trains professional staff who assist students in and outside of the library. *Students receive assistance from library staff which meets their class and educational needs.*	ACRL Standards 8.2	DeskTracker HR/Data on degrees	Spring 2018
1.4	The library creates access to material in various physical and electronic formats which increases accessibility. *Students access library resources in different formats according to their personal or educational needs to further college learning.*	ACRL Standards 5.2	Student survey Database stats Proxy logs Holding/Circ format	Spring 2018
1.5	The library website enables access to the best available electronic resources from anywhere with an internet connection. *Students access information according to their schedule and need to further their ability to complete classwork.*	ACRL Standards 4.2	Student survey Proxy logs Summon Turnaway reports	Spring 2018

	Assessment of Library Impact	Benchmarks	Assessment Method	Assessment Period*
	Services: Libraries provide services to the college community which allow students to prepare for college and lifelong learning.			
2.1	The library provides various programming choices related to the One Book One College yearly book selection. *Students attend programming for One Book One College which engages them in their coursework and the larger college community.*	ACRL Standards 3.1	Quality survey at events LibInsight	Fall2017
2.2	The library offers professional reference assistance in a variety of physical and virtual settings. *Students receive one-on-one instruction which helps them meet their information needs.*	ACRL Standards 4.6	YouTube LibraryH3lp LibInsight Quality survey	Fall2017
2.3	The library requests and receives items from other libraries through the library's Interlibrary Loan program. *Students can request needed material from outside libraries in order to complete research for coursework.*	ACRL Standards 5.1	Survey of needs met Processing of dead requests ILL stats	Fall2017
2.3	The library provides access to technology that can be used in and outside of the library. *Students can access technology that will help them complete coursework in the same way as their peers.*	ACRL Standards 6.3	Survey of outside libraries Student survey Circ stats	Fall 2017
	Instruction: Libraries formally teach the means and methods for students to gain information literacy skills.			
3.1	The library teaches workshops led by librarians throughout the semester on research skills. *Students have opportunities to learn skills from librarians that assist in the research process from beginning to end.*	ACRL Standards 3.4	Narrative DeskTracker Students Survey Faculty Survey	Spring 2017

	Assessment of Library Impact	Benchmarks	Assessment Method	Assessment Period*
3.2	The library develops opportunities to attend workshops on various educational technologies. *Students have the opportunity to learn how to use various computer technologies to improve their coursework and support their success*	ACRL Standards 3.1	Narrative TAP Survey Students Survey Faculty Survey	Spring 2017
3.3	The library instructs students virtually on using the library and its resources to improve their knowledge base. *Students receive formal instruction from librarians in an online setting to further learning opportunities for all classes.*	ACRL Standards 3.3	DeskTracker YouTube Student Survey Faculty Survey	Spring 2017
3.4	The library collaborates with faculty to provide professional instruction on information literacy concepts tied to their course needs. *Students learn information literacy concepts and research skills that assist in their coursework and future success.*	ACRL Standards 3.2	DeskTracker Student Survey Faculty survey Assessment of student work	Spring 2017

Appendix 1C

	Assessment of Library Impact	Benchmarks	Assessment Method	Assessment Period*
	Resources: Libraries curate resources for the college community that assist students with coursework and support overall learning.			
1.1	The library curates a space that fits the student's need for computers, group work, and private study. *Students have the space to meet various learning styles that support their success.*	ACRL Standards- 6.2, 6.6, 6.7	Student survey Learning styles	Spring 2021
1.2	The library provides physical access to the library on multiple campuses during various hours of operation throughout the week. *Students are able to use the library during hours that meet their research and study needs*	ACRL Standards- 6.7 ACRL Trends & Stats- 72	Student survey Course schedules Evening/ Weekend Patron Tally Gatecount	Spring 2021
1.3	The library personnel are sufficient in quantity and quality to meet the diverse teaching and research needs of the college. *Students receive assistance from library staff which meets their class and educational needs.*	ACRL Standards- 8.1, 8.2, 8.5 ACRL Trends & Stats- 01-06	Comparison to Other Colleges FTE Data	Spring 2021
1.4	The library creates access to material in various physical and electronic formats which increases accessibility. *Students access library resources in different formats according to their personal or educational needs to further college learning.*	ACRL Standards- 5.1, 5.2, 5.4 ACRL Trends & Stats- 40-44 IPEDS- Sect. 1	Student survey Database stats & Proxy logs Holding/Circ format Reserves	Spring 2021
1.5	The library website enables access to the best available electronic resources from anywhere with an internet connection. *Students access information according to their schedule and need to further their ability to complete classwork.*	ACRL Standards- 4.2, 5.3, 6.1	Student survey Proxy logs EDS Turnaway reports	Spring 2021
	Services: Libraries provide services to the college community which allow students to prepare for college and lifelong learning.			

	Assessment of Library Impact	Benchmarks	Assessment Method	Assessment Period*
2.1**	The library provides various programming choices related to the One Book One College yearly book selection. *Students attend programming for One Book One College which engages them in their coursework and the larger college community.*	ACRL Standards-3.1	Quality survey at events LibInsight	Fall 2020
2.2	The library requests and receives items from other libraries through the library's Interlibrary Loan program. *Students can request needed material from outside libraries in order to complete research for coursework.*	ACRL Standards-5.1 ACRL Trends & Stats- 80-82d IPEDS- Sect. 1	Survey of needs met Processing of dead requests ILL stats	Fall 2020
2.3	The library provides access to technology that can be used in and outside of the library. *Students can access technology that will help them complete coursework in the same way as their peers.*	ACRL Standards-4.5, 6.3	Survey of outside libraries Student survey Circ stats	Fall 2020
	Instruction: Libraries formally teach the means and methods for students to gain information literacy skills.			
3.1	The library offers professional reference assistance in a variety of physical and virtual settings. *Students receive one-on-one instruction which helps them meet their information needs.*	ACRL Standards-4.6 ACRL Trends & Stats- 64-67	YouTube LibraryH3lp LibInsight Quality survey	Spring 2020
3.2	The library instructs students virtually on using the library and its resources to improve their knowledgebase. *Students receive formal instruction from librarians in an online setting to further learning opportunities for all classes.*	ACRL Standards-3.3, 3.4 ACRL Trends & Stats- 70-71(A-C)	LibInsight YouTube Student Survey Faculty Survey	Spring 2020
3.3**	The library collaborates with faculty to provide professional instruction on information literacy concepts tied to their course needs. *Students learn information literacy concepts and research skills that assist in their coursework and future success.*	ACRL Standards-2.4, 2.6, 3.2, 3.3 ACRL Trends & Stats- 70-71(A-C)	LibInsight Student Survey Faculty survey Assessment of student work	Spring 2020

Notes

1. "Assessment in Action: Academic Libraries and Student Success," American Library Association, last updated October 9, 2012, http://www.ala.org/acrl/AiA.
2. Amy Glass, "Illinois Central College: Project Description," 3 Assessment in Action, Association of College and Research Libraries, accessed April 3, 2020, https://apply.ala.org/aia/docs/project/5346.
3. Kevin Seeber and Jessica Critten, "Building an Instruction Arsenal: Using Standardized Elements to Streamline Class Planning and Ease Student Learning Assessment across the Curriculum" (address, ACRL 2013 Conference, Indianapolis Convention Center, Indianapolis, IN, April 13, 2013).
4. Katherine S. Dabbour, "Oviatt Library Assessment Plan, 2011–2016," Oviatt Library, California State University, accessed September 22, 2020, https://library.csun.edu/sites/default/files/users/kdabbour/documents/5Year_Assessment_Plan_C_OV_9-2011.docx.
5. "CCSF Library and Learning Resources Academic Service Area SSO Plan: 2015–2018," City College of San Francisco Library, accessed September 22, 2020, https://archive.ccsf.edu/dam/Organizational_Assets/Department/library/Assessment/LLRservicesAssessmentPlan.pdf.
6. Association of College and Research Libraries, *Standards for Libraries in Higher Education* (Chicago: Association of College and Research Libraries, 2011, rev. 2018), 6.
7. Association of College and Research Libraries, *Standards for Libraries*, 10–14.
8. "Assessment Glossary," National Institute of Learning Outcomes Assessment, accessed March 30, 2020, https://www.learningoutcomesassessment.org/wp-content/uploads/2019/05/NILOA-Glossary.pdf.
9. "Assessment Glossary."
10. "ACRLMetrics," Association of College and Research Libraries, accessed April 3, 2020, https://www.acrlmetrics.com/.

Bibliography

American Library Association. "Assessment in Action: Academic Libraries and Student Success." Last modified October 9, 2012. Accessed April 3, 2020. https://www.ala.org/acrl/AiA.
Association of College and Research Libraries. "ACRLMetrics." Accessed April 3, 2020. https://www.acrl-metrics.com/.
———. *Standards for Libraries in Higher Education*. Chicago: Association of College and Research Libraries, 2011, rev. 2018.City College of San Francisco Library. "CCSF Library and Learning Resources Academic Service Area SSO Plan: 2015–2018." Accessed September 22, 2020. https://archive.ccsf.edu/dam/Organizational_Assets/Department/library/Assessment/LLRservicesAssessmentPlan.pdf.
Dabbour, Katherine S. "Oviatt Library Assessment Plan, 2011–2016." Oviatt Library, California State University. Accessed September 22, 2020. https://library.csun.edu/sites/default/files/users/kdabbour/documents/5Year_Assessment_Plan_C_OV_9-2011.docx.
Glass, Amy. "Illinois Central College: Project Description." Assessment in Action, Association of College and Research Libraries. Accessed April 3, 2020. https://apply.ala.org/aia/docs/project/5346.
National Institute of Learning Outcomes Assessment. "Assessment Glossary." Accessed March 30, 2020. https://www.learningoutcomesassessment.org/wp-content/uploads/2019/05/NILOA-Glossary.pdf.
Seeber, Kevin, and Jessica Critten. "Building an Instruction Arsenal: Using Standardized Elements to Streamline Class Planning and Ease Student Learning Assessment across the Curriculum." Address, ACRL 2013 Conference, Indianapolis Convention Center, Indianapolis, IN, April 13, 2013.

CHAPTER 2

Creating and Implementing a Comprehensive Academic Library Assessment Plan at Tulsa Community College

Robert Holzmann and Gwetheldene Holzmann

Introduction

Assessment is the research that produces information and analyses about library effectiveness and provides the in-depth detailed evidence required for program review and continual improvement of library programs and services.[1] Achieving meaningful continual improvement is essential for institutions like Tulsa Community College (TCC) not only to survive in today's higher education environment, but also to provide the academic resources necessary for students to academically succeed as they develop the knowledge and skills they will need after college. The library should play an integral role in students' academic achievement through its services, programs, and resources if the library is to remain relevant and have an ongoing contributing role to the mission and goals of the college.

Quality reporting requires a comparative strategy for recording and conveying library statistics, evaluating the data from use of services and programs, and considering their impact on student success. Traditionally, libraries may have a few sentences buried somewhere in a higher education institution's accreditation self-study. As everything in higher education institutions is being more closely examined and analyzed,[2] libraries are no exception. Libraries need to demonstrate academic effectiveness to justify the costs for their facilities, services, programs, and resources. What value do libraries provide for the money allocated to their budgets? Are academic libraries effective in today's digital world?[3] Are academic libraries still the heart of college and university education? These observations point to a growing need for good assessment, relevant reporting, data-informed decisions, meaningful planning, and continual improvement.

Environmental Scan

A review of the current higher education landscape reveals several significant issues. One such issue is that "demographics are beginning to work against traditional colleges and universities. The pool of 18-year-olds is starting to decline."[4] Specifically, the pool of incoming qualified young students, such as those coming out of high school, is shrinking,[5] which increases interinstitutional competition and results in declining enrollments.[6] Students are also becoming viewed more as customers and treated like consumers of higher academic education. Higher education institutions, including community colleges, are in dire trouble if they continue to rely on traditional eighteen-to-twenty-two-year-old students who tend to attend full-time in degree or certificate programs.[7]

There is a national concern about the cost of education skyrocketing relative to almost anything else.[8] Consequently, private and public colleges and universities are being required to tighten budgets, substantiate their academic value, and demonstrate the effectiveness and compliance of their operations. Within the academic institution, internal competition for funding is increasing, and libraries are finding it increasingly essential to justify their costs. Some cases concerning recent significant library cuts are documented and may be due in part to lack of complete meaningful analysis and reporting.[9]

Tulsa Community College and the TCC Library

Tulsa Community College (TCC) is Oklahoma's largest community college, with four full-service campuses located in Tulsa County. Tulsa County is an ethnically and culturally diverse community comprised of both urban and rural areas. The city of Tulsa represents about two-thirds of the county population and is surrounded by thirteen suburban communities. Approximately 16 percent of the county population is below the United States federal poverty line. TCC has a full-time equivalent (FTE) enrollment of approximately 9,000 and an annual enrollment of approximately 22,000 students representing the diversity of the county. Forty-four percent of TCC students self-report as racial and ethnic minorities, almost two-thirds of the students are female, and over two-thirds of the students are under age twenty-four.

Each TCC campus has a full-service library facility including a library director, librarians, and staff. All four campus libraries operate as one library under the leadership of the dean, who reports to the vice president of academic affairs. Each campus library has a complete collection and provides a wide range of services and programs for students and faculty, including computer labs, classrooms, reserves, study rooms, instruction, consultations, and more. The TCC Library also has a strong online presence with a fully developed website, complete online services, and a well-developed electronic collection.

Launching the Assessment Plan Work Group

In May 2017, the TCC Library Management Team (LMT), comprised of TCC Library's four directors and led by the dean of libraries and knowledge management, initiated a library work group tasked with the development of a formal library services evaluation plan examining all library services and programs (excluding assessment of librarians who perform classroom instruction). The work group consisted of a cross section of TCC librarians and library staff who were selected from the various campus locations. A campus library director was appointed to serve as the work group liaison to the LMT. The plan was to be completed by May 2018.

Library management provided no other specific directives or general guidelines for this rather broad project, so the team was able to determine how best to approach, define, and complete the assignment by addressing key questions such as: How does the academic library contribute to the college's strategic plan? and How do library services impact student success?

Project Charter: Assessing Services beyond Instruction Work Group

TCC Library needed a comprehensive plan that consolidated assessment in the library and outlined assessment requirements. The first step for the new work group was to clarify its tasks, outcomes, and scope through a formal project charter. Creating a project charter was a new library management requirement for all project work groups and used a template designed by one of our library directors who had a Project Management Professional (PMP) certification. The project charter was completed in August 2017 and approved by the dean.

The project charter contained key sections including: (1) relevant elements from the TCC strategic plan strategy that were pertinent to library assessment, (2) completion date, (3) project team members with library positions and project roles listed, (4) project scope, (5) risks, and (6) sign-off with the date of approval. This assessment plan project was tied to TCC's strategic plan about performance-based culture, which states, "Develop and implement an institutional effectiveness plan including the assessment of all college operations, programs, and activities."[10] The charter's strategic planning section included details concerning the project's relationship to two library strategies: (1) create a formal library services evaluation/assessment plan, and (2) tie data to activities and programs. Thus, the charter recognized that "in a data-driven organization committed to continuous improvement, an effective evaluation plan for assessing services and programs is essential."[11]

Getting Started

After creating the project charter, the team worked from September 2017 to May 2018 researching and developing the assessment plan. To achieve a performance-based academic culture that is meaningful and enables our students to achieve their goals, we needed to create a formal library services evidence-based assessment plan that would collect and evaluate data concerning the academic relevance of the library's operations, activities, and programs.

In the first team meeting we realized that we had to first understand the meaning and purpose of library assessment and what it encompasses. The team considered questions such as: What comprises library assessment? How can we accomplish it? and Why do we count, measure, and report operational details? We concluded that data reporting and assessment are for both internal and external audiences, including our library, TCC, state and federal agencies, and the academic and library professions. We further determined that assessment is driven by a desire to ultimately improve services, justify library services to the administration, and demonstrate what is being achieved. The points mentioned in the environmental scan would also become factors that needed to be considered in the development of this plan.

The scope and limitations of our work were further refined by reviewing the 2016–2017 Library Data Task Force data decisions, current data collection methods and procedures, and the TCC Library Annual Report. Furthermore, the scope of the plan was focused upon those specific items related to or directly impacting academic purposes. Once those academic library services and programs were identified, we determined which services and programs were already being assessed and which needed to be assessed. Those academic services and programs requiring full development of an assessment component would require most of the team's effort.

Key Questions, Research, and Action

With all the preliminaries now understood and documented in detail, the next action steps involved addressing the key questions, performing research, articulating fundamental insights for our project, setting up a schedule, and delegating responsibilities. What outcomes would be essential for the intended audiences of reports produced as a result of this comprehensive assessment plan? What information would be most valuable to substantiate the value of academic library services or lead to program review and program improvement?

The work group had to determine what measures and data collection methods should be used, what types of analyses and statistics reporting would be most appropriate, and how best to document these details for each plan component. A key question was: How could the team design the plan to go beyond the traditional forms of library statistics and performance measures and include information similar to other forms of evaluation and outcomes used elsewhere in the academic institution for internal and external reporting and compliance? This consideration would make it possible for the library to more easily align library strategies and outcomes with institutional standards and provide comparable results.

Although the original assignment directed the team to evaluate all library services and programs, the project charter noted several exemplary library services, such as circulation, reference, e-resources, interlibrary loan (ILL), and technical services. Furthermore, leaving this exemplary list open-ended allowed room for other academic library services and programs to be included as the plan was being developed or added in the future as necessary. Non-academic library programs and services were excluded from the assessment plan.

Statistics, data, and reporting for academic libraries were also included and revised as needed. The team determined that library effectiveness data and assessment methods would be included if these served a meaningful purpose or provided a balanced mix of qualitative and quantitative data. For example, collection size, number of items circulated per semester, use of full-text e-resources and course reserves, door counts, survey and focus group feedback, the number of students using library services like ILL and e-resources remain valid measures of library use, services, and workloads.

Almost Finished but Not Quite Yet

The work group was reaching a point where we believed we were finished with the background research for all the components identified for the library assessment plan and that we were ready to compose the plan document. We had considered and prepared details about our current, routine, and traditional data collection and reporting; electronic resources use; workload measures for staffing and hours, such as door counts and library surveys; and technical services cataloging and processing. Most of the data we identified for the plan was already being collected. The scope was expanded to include specific statistics in the annual report also needed for external reporting to the Integrated

Postsecondary Education Data System (IPEDS) and Association of College and Research Libraries (ACRL). The work group considered how to organize the plan document to have it completed ahead of schedule.

However, we became aware of some library assessment articles demonstrating library impact on student success. These studies combined a wide range of institutional student data coupled with library services and programs use data and produced reliable statistical analyses. Initially the work group came upon some articles written by authors and researchers from the University of Minnesota that provided insights into these methods of assessment that applied quantifiable library services use data to determine library impact upon student academic success.[12] Similar articles were found further demonstrating that this method of quantitative correlation was important although not yet commonplace.[13] After reviewing the research, the work group decided to include statistical analyses as another vital component in the library's assessment plan.

As the work group developed this additional component of the plan, the library needed to find ways to collect more student use data for our services. Could we reasonably and reliably record all the hard data required for student use of library services and programs and perform a statistical study of impact on students' academic success? The work group met with TCC's institutional research and assessment department (IR&A) and found that this type of study was feasible and received the department's encouragement and commitment to work with us. As we delved further into this type of assessment, brainstorming sessions were held with library leadership and other staff and further developed and implemented some new methods of data collection.

While the assessment plan was being completed and implemented, more information on other plan components or tools came to our attention, such as the development of the ACRL Project Outcome for Academic Libraries. Additionally, the library management team requested that the work group research and include focus groups as part of the plan. The work group also decided that the library's collections were an important service, so a collection development assessment component was developed, which included collection use data plus ILL use considerations. Since other departments' services within the library, such as printing and Wi-Fi, affect perception of library service and quality, these services were mentioned in the plan.

The plan required implementing some procedures for library staff to record or enter data about student use of services, including the student's TCC identification number (TCC-ID). The TCC-ID is a key data field particularly for the assessment of library academic services that impact student success because data from many different automated systems must be matched and statistically analyzed. The team also recognized that some components of the plan required submission of institutional review board (IRB) forms for approval to proceed.

Plan Completion and Approval

It took several months of additional work to fully develop the plan. This work included obtaining approval to implement some changes to the existing annual report and the data collection that was already in place. At the same time, the work group implemented new methods of data collection for some TCC library services. The work group also completed the IRB form in order to get approval to begin collecting and harvesting data and planning with IR&A staff for the analysis of library services impact on student success component of the plan. Our comprehensive library services and programs assessment plan was completed on time, presented to the LMT in May 2018, and subsequently approved. The library assessment plan is currently in place, and our assessment work is ongoing with recording and collecting data and analyzing and reporting statistics.

The TCC library services assessment plan contains the following sections.

A. Executive summary

B. Assessment planning details

C. Seven library services assessment components with details

    1.   Routine and traditional data collection and reporting

    2.   Focus groups

    3.   Surveys

    4.   Electronic resources usage, data, and reporting

    5.   Collection assessment

    6.   Services provided by other TCC departments

    7.   Library services impact upon student success

D. Conclusion and recommendations

E. Bibliography and appendices

Each of the plan's seven library services components will be discussed in detail in the following sections.

One: Routine and Traditional Data Collection and Reporting

Our routine and traditional data collection and the library annual report are related to the previous work of the 2015 Library Data Task Force. This previously completed project had modified some routine data collection practices and streamlined and standardized data collection, which resulted in improving the library annual report. This earlier project provided the starting point for some of the work on the 2018 library assessment plan.

The new assessment plan included details about the data collection and expanded upon data collection and reporting to include: complete door counts for library entrances; study rooms use; instruction provided; e-resources details for searches, views, and downloads; checkouts and renewals; collections counts; reserves use; ILL borrowing and lending; and hits on the library website. Technical services workload and production statistics and logins on computers located in the libraries were added to data collection and reporting. The plan also stipulated that the library annual report would include annual statistics specifically required by external agencies such as IPEDS and ACRL.

In the course of creating this part of the assessment plan, some items were approved and implemented immediately. For example, collection of technical services workload and output for cataloging and processing began, and improvements were made for collecting data about reference services research consultations, library instruction, and print and electronic materials. Data about overall use of computers located in the libraries was acquired, and these statistics were added to the library annual report.

Lastly, it was decided that the library annual report would include college-wide totals only and no longer provide separate statistics for each campus library. This was out of a perspective that, like TCC, which considers itself one college located on several campuses, the library should be similarly viewed as one library. However, we continued to record and report campus-only statistics to the library leadership for purposes of planning and collection review because each campus has different academic programs that its specific campus library supports.

Two: Focus Groups

The team researched and developed the use of focus groups as an assessment method. The research and information written in the assessment plan included best practices for focus groups and detailed steps for developing a successful group interview. Also included was information about combining library surveys with focus groups and a recommendation to couple focus groups with customer service mapping techniques.

After the plan was approved, TCC Library proceeded to develop and implement focus groups for academic year 2018–2019. An IRB form was completed and approved later in 2018. Working with TCC IR&A staff, the library developed and executed a successful focus group on each of the four campuses, which took place in March, April, and May 2019. Each focus group was limited to ten to twelve participants, and prescribed issues were discussed. These focus groups were facilitated by IR&A staff, and no library staff were present.

Three: Surveys

Surveys were researched and developed as another assessment method. The plan included best practices for using surveys and detailed steps for developing effective surveys. Also included was information about creating a template for an internal library survey instrument. The plan recommended that the library surveys should address only library issues and services and not duplicate questions on other TCC surveys. It also recommended that the questions already proposed for the biannual TCC student satisfaction survey be reviewed and revised.

After plan approval, TCC Library proceeded to develop and implement a survey for academic year 2018–2019. The first library survey, also approved through the IRB process and developed with assistance from IR&A, was incorporated into our first focus groups in 2019. In the future, TCC Library's survey efforts may also include ACRL's Project Outcome for Academic Libraries, an evidence-based online tool kit developed for use by all academic libraries in all Carnegie classifications, launched in April 2019. ACRL recognized that traditional library metrics were not going as far as needed. This tool kit also collects consistent outcomes data for academic libraries to benchmark at the national and state levels.

Four: Electronic Resources Usage, Data, and Reporting

TCC Library's electronic resources usage reports have been provided semiannually on a July 1 to June 30 fiscal year basis. Reporting on a fiscal year basis rather than on a semester or academic year basis enables the library usage report to be the foundation for an accurate cost analysis of each e-resource based upon annual spending. The usage and cost-analysis data also enabled the library to analyze, plan, and select appropriate subscription renewals and cancellations for the beginning of each fiscal year on July 1, which aligns library e-resources use and costs with other items found in the college's fiscal year reporting. Furthermore, this consistent approach is important because it aligns the required annual data with data provided to IPEDS and ACRL.

Details in the plan outlined all the data elements being recorded by vendors' systems for the library's subscription e-resources that can be harvested using proprietary data reports, previous COUNTER 4 reports, and the new COUNTER 5 standards for reports. Such data is in the aggregate, and no individual use information is recorded or disclosed because our initial authentication to access a subscription e-resource is internal through TCC's single sign-on, and subsequent data traffic is handled between the source and the user through our EZproxy system.

Five: Collection Assessment

The team considered collection assessment to be an essential component of library service and incorporated this into the plan. The research and information written in the assessment plan included best practices for library collection review and development, and the plan included steps to further develop evaluation of the library collection. Items noted in the plan include obtaining or creating tools and reports for collection evaluation and development, analysis of ILL borrowing, selection of electronic versus hard-copy resources based upon academic trends like online versus on-campus course offerings, and selection of appropriate formats that support access to resources for new academic programs.

In addition to documenting procedures already in use, steps to implement collection assessment included providing the following items:

- a report for staff to use in reconsidering items tagged for withdrawal
- a report of missing items and lost titles for replacement consideration
- a spreadsheet with cost analysis of e-resources format versus print format
- a report to evaluate circulation and holds for strengthening the collection's weak areas

- a report of ILL requests for borrowing analysis to determine collection needs
- an analysis reviewing overlap of print journals versus journal titles in databases, which also becomes a consideration of acquisition versus access

The plan's collection component also included developing and revising procedures for patrons to request databases and titles in specific formats and noted the incorporation of online open education resources (OER) and eCore into new academic programs.[14]

Six: Services Provided by Other TCC Departments

The assessment work group recognized that certain services, such as printing, computers for student use, and Wi-Fi connectivity, are not provided by the library directly but impact students' use and perception of the library. For example, access to printers is one of several important services that is provided in the library. Therefore, difficulties with printing could negatively affect students' perception of the library. Similarly, problems using campus Wi-Fi in the libraries could cause a negative perception of library services. Examples of other departments' services within the library include lighting, computers, electrical outlets and charging stations, heat and air, carpeting, and cleanliness. Library assessment of these services may be considered in the future but was not included in the current plan.

Seven: Library Services Impact upon Student Success

This component of the assessment plan focused on the impact of library services on student success. Consequently, the team embarked on a journey into this unusual but vital area of library assessment territory that few other academic libraries and no community colleges to our knowledge, have explored. This renewed focus regarding library impact on student success, as noted above, grew out of specific published studies and articles and became an integral component of the overall plan.

Historically, quantitative assessment of a library's impact upon student academic success has been difficult, if not impossible.[15] A statistical impact study is a very new and groundbreaking approach for providing valid and meaningful assessment of TCC Library services. Because TCC is developing a data-informed culture through evidence-based analysis and decisions, the library is driven to show its effectiveness and provide reliable evidence that correlates students' use of library services and programs to retention, academic achievement, and graduation or transfer.[16] The plan recommendation included long-term longitudinal correlation studies as well as future predictive statistical impact reports based upon significant historical data.

To implement this type of assessment, methods of recording data had to be reviewed. Where data collection was nonexistent, plans had to be developed and implemented.

As we developed this component of our plan, we needed to find ways to collect additional student use data for services such as study rooms, research assistance, use of library computers, reference help, and general use of electronic resources. To accomplish this, we worked with TCC information technology and some of our vendors, such as OCLC and Springshare. Several computer systems enhancements were also requested to assist the implementation. An IRB form was completed for this portion of the plan, and approval from the institutional review board allowed the project to proceed immediately. Each semester, the library harvests and provides specific library services data to IR&A for use in their analyses about the impact of TCC library services and programs upon student success (see chapter 5 in this book).

Conclusion

The results of creating and implementing a comprehensive library assessment plan have been numerous. We have improved reporting through streamlining statistics and including new data as needed. Interdepartmental cooperation, essential for the implementation of our plan, has been successful between library staff, administration, other TCC departments, and vendors. As a data-informed institution, we use a blend of qualitative and quantitative data from multiple assessment instruments to make evidence-based evaluations that lead to program improvements.[17]

Because assessment enables ongoing improvement of a library's collection, spaces, and services,[18] the library can demonstrate its contribution to the success of the institution, fulfilling TCC's new mission and strategic goals. This is accomplished through a revitalized and informed focus on the library's impact upon student success and learning outcomes. Ultimately, "students who are academically successful at TCC and who subsequently move into the workplace or continue with additional higher education contribute to a vibrant community, successful businesses, and the economic stability and growth of the city and the region."[19]

Notes

1. Association of College and Research Libraries, *Academic Library Impact*, prepared by Lynn Silipigni Connaway, William Harvey, Vanessa Kitzie, and Stephanie Mikitish of OCLC Research (Chicago: Association of College and Research Libraries, 2017), 10–12, 74.
2. Goldie Blumenstyk, *American Higher Education in Crisis?* (Oxford: Oxford University Press, 2015), 109–15; Patricia L. Thibodeau and Steven J. Melamut, "Proving and Improving the Value of the Academic Library: The Role of the Academic Library in Academic Accreditation," in *Reviewing the Academic Library: A Guide to Self-Study and External Review*, ed. Eleanor Mitchell and Peggy Seiden (Chicago: Association of College and Research Libraries, 2015), 62.
3. Crystal A. Baird and Ellie A. Fogarty, "An Introduction to the Higher Education Accreditation Process," in *Reviewing the Academic Library: A Guide to Self-Study and External Review*, ed. Eleanor Mitchell and Peggy Seiden (Chicago: Association of College and Research Libraries, 2015), 17–19; Melissa Bowles-Terry, "Proving and Improving the Value of the Academic Library," in *Reviewing the Academic Library: A Guide to Self-Study and External Review*, ed. Eleanor Mitchell and Peggy Seiden (Chicago: Association of College and Research Libraries, 2015), 292–93.

4. James Hodgkin, "The Library in a Big Bad World: Opening Keynote" (keynote speech, OCLC World-Share Management Services Global Community and User Group Meeting, Columbus, OH, October 16, 2019).
5. Michael B. Horn, "Will Half of All Colleges Really Close in the Next Decade?" Editors' Pick, *Forbes,* December 13, 2018, https://www.forbes.com/sites/michaelhorn/2018/12/13/will-half-of-all-colleges-really-close-in-the-next-decade/#3ddc9f8852e5.
6. Hodgkin, "Library in a Big Bad World".
7. Robert P. Hogan, *Global Demand for Borderless Online Degrees* (Hershey, PA: IGI Global, Information Science Reference, 2020), 30.
8. Blumenstyk, *American Higher Education,* 1, 56–57; Hodgkin, "Library in a Big Bad World."
9. Lisa Peet, "Tenured Library Faculty Laid Off at St. Cloud State U," *Library Journal* 144, no. 10 (November 2019): 9–11; Tulsa Community College, *2016–2020 Strategic Plan* (Tulsa, OK: Tulsa Community College, 2016), 12, https://www.tulsacc.edu/sites/default/files/TCC%202016-2020%20Strategic%20Plan_FINAL.pdf.
10. Robert Holzmann, *Project Charter* (Tulsa, OK: Tulsa Community College Library, 2017), 1.
11. Holzmann, *Project Charter,* 1.
12. Krista M. Soria, Jan Fransen, and Shane Nackerud, "Library Use and Undergraduate Student Outcomes: New Evidence for Students' Retention and Academic Success," *portal: Libraries and the Academy* 13, no. 2 (April 2013): 147–64; Krista M. Soria, Jan Fransen, and Shane Nackerud, "Stacks, Serials, Search Engines, and Students' Success: First-Year Undergraduate Students' Library Use, Academic Achievement, and Retention," *Journal of Academic Librarianship* 40, no. 1 (January 2014): 84–91.
13. Gaby Haddow and Jayanthi Joseph, "Loans, Logins, and Lasting the Course: Academic Library Use and Student Retention," *Australian Academic and Research Libraries* 41, no. 4 (December 2010): 233–44; Mark Emmons and Frances C. Wilkinson, "The Academic Library Impact on Student Persistence," *College and Research Libraries* 72, no. 2 (March 2011): 128–49, https://doi.org/10.5860/crl-74r1.
14. eCore is a collection of TCC's high-enrollment general education courses that can be taken from a distance via online learning. eCore allows a student to complete all general education courses at a distance.
15. Bowles-Terry, "Proving and Improving," 291–92.
16. Megan Oakleaf, *Library Integration in Institutional Learning Analytics,* research report (Syracuse, NY: Syracuse University, November 15, 2018), 10–12, 20.
17. Sara Goek, "Project Outcome for Academic Success: An Introductory Workshop" (presentation, OLA 2020: Virtual Oklahoma Library Association Annual Conference, July 29, 2020).
18. Association of College and Research Libraries, *Academic Library Impact,* 10.
19. Tulsa Community College Library, *Library Services and Programs Assessment Plan* (Tulsa, OK: Tulsa Community College Library, August 2018), 15.

Bibliography and Additional Resources

Association of College and Research Libraries. *Academic Library Impact: Improving Practice and Essential Areas to Research.* Prepared by Lynn Silipigni Connaway, William Harvey, Vanessa Kitzie, and Stephanie Mikitish of OCLC Research. Chicago: Association of College and Research Libraries, 2017.

Baird, Crystal A., and Ellie A. Fogarty. "An Introduction to the Higher Education Accreditation Process." In *Reviewing the Academic Library: A Guide to Self-Study and External Review.* Edited by Eleanor Mitchell and Peggy Seiden, 3–27. Chicago: Association of College and Research Libraries, 2015.

Blumenstyk, Goldie. *American Higher Education in Crisis? What Everyone Needs to Know.* Oxford: Oxford University Press, 2015.

Bowles-Terry, Melissa. "Proving and Improving the Value of the Academic Library." In *Reviewing the Academic Library: A Guide to Self-Study and External Review.* Edited by Eleanor Mitchell and Peggy Seiden, 291–313. Chicago: Association of College and Research Libraries, 2015.

Emmons, Mark, and Frances C. Wilkinson. "The Academic Library Impact on Student Persistence." *College and Research Libraries* 72, no. 2 (March 2011): 128–49. https://doi.org/10.5860/crl-74r1.

Goek, Sara. "Project Outcome for Academic Libraries: Interactive Workshop." Presentation, New Mexico Library Association/Mountain Plains Library Association Annual Conference, Albuquerque, NM, October 30, 2019.

———. "Project Outcome for Academic Libraries: An Introductory Workshop." Presentation, OLA 2020: Virtual Oklahoma Library Association Annual Conference, July 29, 2020.Haddow, Gaby, and Jayanthi Joseph. "Loans, Logins, and Lasting the Course: Academic Library Use and Student Retention." *Australian Academic and Research Libraries* 41, no. 4 (December 2010): 233–44.

Hodgkin, James. "The Library in a Big Bad World: Opening Keynote." Keynote speech, OCLC WorldShare Management Services Global Community and User Group Meeting, Columbus, OH, October 16, 2019.

Hogan, Robert P. *Global Demand for Borderless Online Degrees.* Hershey, PA: IGI Global, Information Science Reference, 2020.

Holzmann, Robert. *Project Charter: Assessing Services beyond Instruction Work Group.* Tulsa, OK: Tulsa Community College Library, 2017.

———. "Strategic Planning and Assessment: Academic Library Assessment Planning." *Arkansas Libraries* 77, no. 1–2 (Spring/Summer 2020): 39–42.

Horn, Michael B. "Will Half of All Colleges Really Close in the Next Decade?" Editors' Pick, *Forbes,* December 13, 2018. https://www.forbes.com/sites/michaelhorn/2018/12/13/will-half-of-all-colleges-really-close-in-the-next-decade/#3ddc9f8852e5.

Luo, Lili. "Evidence Based Practice—Ideas for Academic Librarians." Keynote address, Oklahoma Association of Research Libraries Annual Conference, Edmond, OK, November 9, 2018.

Matthews, Joseph R. "Assessing Library Contributions to University Outcomes: The Need for Individual Student Level Data." *Library Management* 33, no. 6/7 (2012): 389–402.

Mikitish, Steph. "Inching Along: Making Measured Progress over Common Assessment Obstacles." Keynote address, Oklahoma Association of Research Libraries Annual Conference, Edmond, OK, November 9, 2018.

Nackerud, Shane, Jan Fransen, Kate Peterson, and Kristen Mastel. "Analyzing Demographics: Assessing Library Use across the Institution." *portal: Libraries and the Academy* 13, no. 2 (2013): 131–45.

Oakleaf, Megan. *Library Integration in Institutional Learning Analytics.* Research report. Syracuse, NY: Syracuse University, November 15, 2018.

———. *The Value of Academic Libraries: A Comprehensive Research Review and Report.* Chicago: Association of College and Research Libraries, 2010.

Oakleaf, Megan, Scott Walter, Malcolm Brown, Dean Hendrix, and Joe Lucia. "What Could We Do, If Only We Knew? Libraries, Learning Analytics, and Student Success." Presentation, Library Assessment Conference, Houston, TX, December 7, 2018.

Peet, Lisa. "Tenured Library Faculty Laid Off at St. Cloud State U." *Library Journal* 144, no. 10 (November 2019): 9–11.

Platt, R. Eric, Steven R. Chesnut, Melandie McGee, and Xiaonan Song. "Changing Names, Merging Colleges: Investigating the History of Higher Education Adaptation." *American Educational History Journal* 44, no. 1 (2017): 49–67.

Soria, Krista M. "Factors Predicting the Importance of Libraries and Research Activities for Undergraduates." *Journal of Academic Librarianship* 39, no. 6 (November 2013): 464–70.

Soria, Krista M., Jan Fransen, and Shane Nackerud. "Library Use and Undergraduate Student Outcomes: New Evidence for Students' Retention and Academic Success." *portal: Libraries and the Academy* 13, no. 2 (April 2013): 147–64.

———. "Stacks, Serials, Search Engines, and Students' Success: First-Year Undergraduate Students' Library Use, Academic Achievement, and Retention." *Journal of Academic Librarianship* 40, no. 1 (January 2014): 84–91.

Thibodeau, Patricia L., and Steven J. Melamut. "Proving and Improving the Value of the Academic Library: The Role of the Academic Library in Academic Accreditation." In *Reviewing the Academic Library:*

A Guide to Self-Study and External Review. Edited by Eleanor Mitchell and Peggy Seiden, 61–84. Chicago: Association of College and Research Libraries, 2015.

Tulsa Community College. *2016–2020 Strategic Plan: We All Impact Student Success.* Tulsa, OK: Tulsa Community College, 2016. https://www.tulsacc.edu/sites/default/files/TCC%202016-2020%20Strategic%20Plan_FINAL.pdf.

Tulsa Community College Library. *Library Services and Programs Assessment Plan.* Tulsa, OK: Tulsa Community College Library, August 2018.

CHAPTER 3

A Library-Friendly Assessment Framework

Administrative, Educational, Student Support Services (AES) Unit Assessment at the Community College of Philadelphia

Michael J. Krasulski, Elizabeth Gordon, and Courtney Raeford

Much has been written about the assessment of the academic library. Today it is nearly impossible to avoid the topic at our conferences, professional meetings, or various electronic mailing lists.[1] Fred Heath has even suggested that assessment activities have occupied the minds of library practitioners for at least a century.[2] Library assessment activities today have higher stakes since these activities are mandated by our institutions to remain in compliance with regional accreditation bodies; however, institutional assessment activities frequently focus on the assessment of student learning within the subject disciplines. Traditionally, student learning outcomes assessment is a part of a course or program, where student progress over time can be measured relatively linearly. As such, these frameworks do not adequately capture the diverse ways libraries support students and, by extension, the institution outside of information literacy instruction. Assessing traditionally formulated student learning outcomes in the library for non-classroom-related library functions is like attempting to put the proverbial square peg in a round hole. It is frustrating and rarely produces actionable data. This creates a culture of resentment toward assessment, which can come to be seen as administrative busywork. There must be a better way.

As is typical in many institutions, assessment activities at the Community College of Philadelphia (CCP) have traditionally focused on the nine-month teaching departments. Student learning outcomes have been developed for each course and aligned with program and general education outcomes as appropriate. Until recently, the administrative, educational support, and student support (AES) units, broadly, have lacked a systematic and formalized assessment process, and assessment activities in these units were sporadic at best. In 2017, with the support of CCP's Institutional Effectiveness Committee, the director of institutional research (IR) and the library's department head created an assessment framework to capture the unique contributions of administrative, educational support, and student support units in supporting student success and providing high-quality educational experiences to students and the broader Philadelphia community. Within its first year of implementation, over 90 percent of AES units created five-year assessment plans and successfully completed their first assessment reporting cycles. This success can be attributed to the framework's simplicity—by encouraging AES units to build upon work already happening.

This chapter will discuss the development and implementation of the administrative, educational, and student support services assessment framework at CCP and the experiences and involvement of the college's library therein. This chapter will illustrate how the library department head and the director of institutional research worked collaboratively to develop a framework that was nimble enough to meet the needs of the library as well as all the non-teaching areas of the college. Finally, this chapter will report on lessons learned: namely, how libraries are uniquely positioned to be leaders of assessment on campus, and why librarians should become active partners with their IR and assessment offices and officers.

The Community College of Philadelphia is a large urban community college with the main campus located near Center City, Philadelphia. The college enrolls, on average, about 4,900 full-time and 11,700 part-time students annually, with 65 percent of students identifying as female and 45 percent identifying as Black or African American.[3] Additionally, 70 percent of first-time, full-time students receive the Pell Grant.[4] CCP offers fifty-six academic degree programs, forty-seven certificate programs, and over ninety non-credit personal and professional development programs with the support of over 500 faculty, administrators, and staff. The CCP Library is an academic department within the Division of Educational Support Services. Its nine full-time librarians have faculty rank and status, and eight of its faculty have earned tenure; the ninth will earn tenure in 2021. There are also twelve adjunct faculty in the department. Although the faculty librarians provide information literacy instruction, institutional assessment of information literacy general education requirements is conducted through courses in the English department.

Why Start a New Assessment Framework Now?

CCP is accredited by the Middle States Commission on Higher Education (MSCHE). The college submitted its most recent self-study to MSCHE in 2014, in accordance with the 2006 *Characteristics of Excellence in Higher Education*.[5] MSCHE's response at that time indicated that CCP had not met Standard 14, which addressed assessment of student learning, which placed the institution in jeopardy of losing its accreditation and necessitated a multi-year monitoring report response from CCP. MSCHE ultimately requested that two monitoring reports be submitted, documenting evidence "that the College '[had] achieved and [could] sustain compliance with Standard 14 (Assessment of Student Learning),'"[6] and this request was punctuated by a second on-site visit from a team of reviewers. As has been the experience at many institutions, the threat of losing accreditation renewed the College's commitment to creating and fostering a culture of assessment at the Community College of Philadelphia.

To ensure a sustainable and ongoing commitment to assessment from across all segments of the College, a structural response was required. In fall 2015, CCP College President Dr. Donald Generals, created a new Institutional Effectiveness Committee (IEC), for the broad purpose of "[ensuring] that the College community is aware of and follows best practices in planning, assessment and resource allocation."[7] The committee was to be chaired by the director of institutional research, and its membership initially comprised administrators at the vice president, dean, and director levels, along with five faculty representatives. After the IEC's first year, most administrators at the vice president and director levels were rotated off, along with some of the deans, to be replaced with administrators from lower levels of the organizational chart while remaining committed to representing as broad a cross-section of the campus as possible. At this time, the department head-elect of the library and learning resources department was invited to serve on IEC as a faculty representative, at the behest of the dean of the educational support services division.[8]

This asymmetrical membership rotation strategy was employed to imbue the IEC with both authority and authenticity. Initially composing the committee of college leaders would lend the community buy-in and authority needed to enact serious changes. It was believed, though, that the ongoing presence of high-ranking administrators could stifle open and honest conversations about institutional performance. Among the several tasks entrusted to the IEC by its charge were to "provide recommendations for alignment of budget, planning, and assessment"; to "establish an annual assessment calendar and a cycle for planning"; and to "ensure assessment of planning processes."[9]

Administrative, Educational Support, and Student Support Assessment

At the spring 2016 IEC meeting, the director of institutional research and chair of the IEC asked for volunteers to help develop an assessment framework for the administrative, educational support, and student support unit of the college. There was only one volunteer, the incoming department head of the library. As a committee of two, they reviewed the literature, and they spent that summer designing this process.[10] The overarching principles were to make the process as simple and painless as possible. It was taken as a given that units would approach this new framework with a broad range of preexisting assessment knowledge and experiences. As a result, in the interest of approaching all units equitably, it was decided to treat each unit as if it had never practiced formal assessment before. Each unit would be asked to start at the beginning. A workbook was created to guide those new to assessment through the theory and process of formal institutional assessment. Units would have the option to develop their assessment plans independently or with the consultation of one of the two AES assessment designers. The two AES committee members divided the thirty-five AES units to follow up with and offer advice as needed.

The Assessment Design Process, Step by Step

First, each unit was asked to create a new mission statement or affirm its existing mission statement. Unit leaders and staff were asked to consider three questions:

1. What do you do?
2. Who do you serve?
3. How do you make a difference to the college community?

Using these questions as a prompt, unit leaders and staff were able to identify and articulate their core mission while considering the primary constituents and beneficiaries of their services and the unit's unique contributions in support of the college's mission. As an option for units, to guide them through the mission statement development process, a survey was developed and administered by IR prior to the units' discussions of their mission statement. Using a word cloud to present survey results, units could easily discern how they see themselves, who it is they serve, and what it is they do. A mission statement template was provided to take the guesswork out of the mission statement language. Throughout the process the AES committee only advised units on their mission statements; unit staff and leadership were ultimately responsible for the final statement. Units were encouraged to share their proposed mission statements with their deans or vice presidents for feedback and approval.

Second, units were asked to develop three goals that derived from the mission statement that were aspirational in nature and intentionally not focused on concrete measurability. Units were advised that goals should make plain how the unit intended to accomplish its mission. Because goals of this nature are meant to be more abstract and visionary than traditional operations planning may include, writing them can be challenging for some administrators. To smooth the learning curve, units were asked to consider two questions when writing their goals:

1. What does the unit hope to accomplish?

2. What is the unit's vision of itself?

Several unit staff expressed concern that writing aspirational goals would lead to penalization if the goal was not accomplished. Unit leaders, staff, and supervisors alike were encouraged to view goals as a long hoped-for future, one that can be seen but is just out of reach. As the AES assessment cycle spans a five-year period, units needed goals broad enough to remain relevant throughout the entire AES cycle.

Each unit was advised to develop no more than three support outcomes in support of each of its three goals. A decision was made early to encourage units to focus on activities they would already be doing rather than proposing entirely new projects or initiatives, to pre-empt their creating extra work for themselves. To that end, units were asked to focus on the efficiency, effectiveness, timeliness, and accuracy of delivering services, processes, activities, or functions to students, faculty, or staff. In creating their goals and outcomes, units were asked to consider the following questions:

1. What services does your unit provide?

2. How will the unit accomplish providing these services, and how long will it take?

3. What value is being added by these services?

4. What does success look like in providing these services?

Most units had never practiced formal assessment prior to the beginning of this period. Units that were new to assessment cycle documentation were encouraged to create service benchmarks for the first year of this new framework and then write goals for subsequent years after collecting one cycle's worth of data. Units with prior formal assessment experience were asked to consider what new services or processes they planned to implement over the next five years and to develop goals that tracked these implementations over the five-year AES process. For example, one unit planned to implement a new applicant tracking system. A year-one support outcome for this goal could be successfully initiating the actual implementation of the system. A support outcome in subsequent years could measure the success or effectiveness of implementing this new process or service. Because units were susceptible to falling into traditional business operations reporting habits, they were advised to avoid establishing goals and objectives that were easily assessed but were of little value in improving the quality of programs and services. AES assessment was intended and designed to be more meaningful than standard practices of activity reporting.

Articulating a coherent set of goals and support outcomes in a single document, especially for unit leaders who had not previously engaged with formal assessment practices, can be extraordinarily challenging. The Shults Dorime-Williams (SDW) Support Outcomes Taxonomy was employed by the AES committee to assist units in visualizing the assessment process. Developed at the Borough of Manhattan Community College (BMCC), the SDW Taxonomy "is a resource for the development of support outcomes in the same way that Bloom's taxonomy functions for the development of student learning outcomes."[11] The taxonomy includes an action verb wheel that provides appropriate and relevant terms that ensure measurability. These visuals proved popular with many units since they reassured new and experienced assessment practitioners alike that their outcomes would remain relevant and measurable at the end of the assessment cycle.

After units created support outcomes, they developed assessment measures, which were defined for them as any qualitative or quantitative measures of achievement of departmental objectives. Assessment measures could include both evaluations already in use and others the department would like to put into place. Assessment measures were linked to support objectives one to one; for each support objective, units were asked to identify one specific measure of effectiveness. Measuring effectiveness could be accomplished by reporting changes in usage, surveying users to see if services improved, or convening a focus group to determine if training or support materials helped users understand the new process or service. Concrete quantitative assessment measures were preferred; however, if a unit preferred to use a qualitative measure, these units were not discouraged from doing so.

Once units had created mission statements, goals, support outcomes, and measures, they then aligned their goals and support outcomes to the various campus master plans, including the college's master plan and the division of academic and student success's academic plan. This step was essential, as it made clear to both units and administration how each unit contributed to the successful completion of the institutional mission. Additionally, frontline staff could see how their efforts contribute to the broader success of the college. The AES assessment cycle timeline was intentionally aligned to the college's budget cycle so that goals and outcomes that required additional funding would be a part of that year's budget planning process.

The AES framework is informed by the college's academic program review (APR) process. It affirms that unit goals are linked to the institutional mission and strategic plan and that they conform to the expectations of the *Middle States Commission on Higher Education Standards for Accreditation.*[12] By engaging in this process, units can determine how effectively they are achieving their unit goals and, by extension, their unit mission.

Self-Study and Review Process

CCP's AES assessment framework is both annual and cumulative within a five-year cycle. Annually, units assess planning goals and support outcomes. Each planning goal is assessed at least once within the five-year cycle with the intention of using the results to improve the planning, processes, operations, and outcomes of the unit. In the fifth year of the cycle, units undergo a comprehensive self-study process to reflect on the previous four years and to develop their next five-year plan. AES units were strategically assigned to self-study cohorts based on the current status and maturity of their assessment activities; the first cohort is currently undertaking its self-study process after only two cycles of formalized assessment.

AES Assessment and the Library

While the AES assessment framework would naturally have been designed to meet the needs of administrative, educational support, and student support units at CCP, there was added benefit to the library's being represented during its creation. The specific assessment intricacies of the library could be adequately addressed. Because institutional assessment of information literacy is coordinated through the English department, the creation of student learning outcomes for other library functions would have ranged from difficult to nonsensical. Using student support outcomes, the library was better able to demonstrate its contributions to student success, the academic master plan, and the college's strategic plan.

The AES assessment framework was designed to be nimble. Although the intention was for units to maintain one consistent set of goals during the five-year period, outcomes could change over time, and units planned to assess a different subset of their outcomes each year. For example, a disruption in spring 2020 caused the Community College of Philadelphia to move the provision of all services to online modes within two weeks. The relevant library AES assessment support outcomes were changed to assess user satisfaction of the move to online-only library services. This flexibility in the assessment framework allows areas to continue their efforts, even in the face of unexpected challenges.

The development of the library's AES assessment plan was delegated to a group of faculty and library support staff called the Library Assessment Working Group (LAWG). This was the first time in recent memory that library support staff were directly involved in both the creation and implementation of a formal assessment plan. The AES *workbook* and other materials supported full participation in the creation of goals and outcomes from both new and experienced assessment practitioners. Both library faculty and support staff were able to see that writing and implementing an assessment plan could be neither difficult nor onerous. Many of the outcomes developed for the initial five-year plan were things the library would have likely done anyway. The AES assessment process gave the library a formalized way to document and report on progress, rather than the ad hoc and informal reporting that had been done before. After the five-year plan was developed, it was shared with the entire library department for comment and feedback. Changes were made based upon this feedback, and the final draft was presented at the fall 2016 library-wide meeting for a vote. The involvement of library support staff lent both a practical perspective to the development of the assessment plan and important unit-wide buy-in to its implementation.

The plan passed unanimously and was subsequently implemented. Although the process was transparent and had significant buy-in from the beginning, it was not without its controversies. There was concern among some library faculty and support staff that if an outcome was not assessed in a particular year, it would not be regarded as important to the functioning and mission of the library. Viewed through another lens, there was some fear that the work those particular faculty and support staff performed would be devalued if it was not assessed. This legitimate apprehension was resolved after the first cycle of the AES process. Since the first cycle involved establishing initial benchmarks, staff in particular were able to see they had a significant role to play in meeting the AES assessment outcomes.

Being both cocreators and users of the AES assessment, the director of IR and the library department head were able to help other units create and implement their AES assessment plans. They were able to share how they had engaged staff to get their plans finished. Often with the AES assessment *workbook* in hand, they marched across campus to help colleagues. The AES committee was able to meet and consult with all of the AES units in one summer. As the library is often seen as a neutral or third space on campus, several units were more comfortable working with the library department head than they were with the director of IR. Because of the position of the Office of Institutional Research in the organizational hierarchy, the department head of the library would work with units that might be particularly sensitive to their presentation in the eyes of upper administration. As the library department head did not have any administrative power over these units, unit leaders and staff were able to speak more freely about their concerns or fears in engaging with a new assessment process without fear of their comments reaching upper administration.

Conclusion

Serendipitously, the library department head was uniquely placed to shape CCP's administrative and educational support services assessment framework. Since the library lives in both the academic and support sides of the institution, the library department head was able to communicate fluently about both modes of the assessment process. Additionally, because the library required that an assessment framework be flexible enough to document and assess its unique contributions to student success and retention, the library department head's input during the design phase resulted in a framework that is inclusive of both academic and administrative service approaches. This bilateral approach strengthens the assessment framework for all AES units at the college. The new assessment process is designed to encourage staff from all levels of each unit to participate in assessment activities, which means that both library faculty and library staff can now clearly see how their work contributes to the institution's success. Community college librarians would be well served to partner with their institution's assessment and institutional research offices in all phases of new assessment initiatives. It is not only an important way to be of service to the institution, but it also ensures that assessment activities developed at their institution will be relevant and responsive to the unique assessment needs of today's libraries.

Notes

1. Robert Detmering, Samantha McClellan, and Amber Willenborg, "A Seat at the Table: Information Literacy Assessment and Processional Legitimacy," *College and Research Libraries* 80, no. 5 (2019): 720.
2. Fred Heath, "Library Assessment: The Way We Have Grown," *Library Quarterly* 81, no. 1 (2011): 8.
3. Community College of Philadelphia, "Credit Enrollment Dashboard," July 22, 2020, https://public.tableau.com/profile/communitycollegeofphiladelphia#!/vizhome/CreditEnrollmentAgeRaceGenderDashboard/CreditEnrollmentbyAgeRaceandGender.
4. National Center for Education Statistics, "Community College of Philadelphia," College Navigator, Institute of Education Sciences, US Department of Education, accessed September 1, 2020, https://nces.ed.gov/collegenavigator/?id=215239.
5. Don Generals and Judith Gay, "Monitoring Report to the Middle States Commission on Higher Education from Community College of Philadelphia," Community College of Philadelphia, November 25, 2015, https://www.myccp.online/sites/default/files/documents/InstitutionalAssessment/MSCHE/FinalCCPMonitoringReport12012015.pdf.
6. Generals and Gay, "Monitoring Report," 1.
7. Don Generals, "Monitoring Report to the Middle States Commission on Higher Education from Community College of Philadelphia," Community College of Philadelphia, October 31, 2017, https://www.myccp.online/sites/default/files/documents/InstitutionalAssessment/community_college_of_philadelphia_10-31-17-1submitted.pdf.
8. The Community College of Philadelphia Library does not have a library director. Rather the activities of the library are administered by the department head. The head of the library and learning resources department is elected six months prior to start of term by the department's faculty and retains faculty rank and status while on administrative leave.
9. Elizabeth Gordon, personal interview with Judith Gay, Philadelphia, June 25, 2020.
10. Linda Sukie, *Assessing Student Learning* (San Francisco: Jossey-Bass, 2018), 189–204.
11. Marjorie L. Dorimé-Williams and Christopher Shults, "Conducting Comprehensive Assessment within Community Colleges: Administrative, Educational, and Student Support (AES) Assessment with the Shults Dorimé-Williams Taxonomy," *New Directions for Community Colleges* 2019, no. 186 (Summer 2019): 65–66.
12. Middle States Commission on Higher Education, *Standards for Accreditation and Requirements of Affiliation* (Philadelphia: Middle States Commission on Higher Education, 2015), 14.

Bibliography

Community College of Philadelphia. "Credit Enrollment Dashboard." July 22, 2020. https://public.tableau.com/profile/communitycollegeofphiladelphia#!/vizhome/CreditEnrollmentAgeRaceGenderDashboard/CreditEnrollmentbyAgeRaceandGender.

Detmering, Robert, Samantha McClellan, and Amber Willenborg. "A Seat at the Table: Information Literacy Assessment and Processional Legitimacy." *College and Research Libraries* 80, no. 5 (2019): 720–36.

Dorimé-Williams, Marjorie L., and Christopher Shults. "Conducting Comprehensive Assessment within Community Colleges: Administrative, Educational, and Student Support (AES) Assessment with the Shults Dorimé-Williams Taxonomy." *New Directions for Community Colleges* 2019, no. 186 (Summer 2019): 61–69.

Gordon, Elizabeth. Personal interview with Judith Gay. Philadelphia, June 25, 2020.

Generals, Don. "Monitoring Report to the Middle States Commission on Higher Education from Community College of Philadelphia." Community College of Philadelphia, October 31, 2017. https://www.myccp.online/sites/default/files/documents/InstitutionalAssessment/community_college_of_philadelphia_10-31-17-1submitted.pdf.

Generals, Don, and Judith Gay. "Monitoring Report to the Middle States Commission on Higher Education from Community College of Philadelphia." Community College of Philadelphia, November 25,

2015. https://www.myccp.online/sites/default/files/documents/InstitutionalAssessment/MSCHE/FinalCCPMonitoringReport12012015.pdf.

Heath, Fred. "Library Assessment: The Way We Have Grown." *Library Quarterly* 81, no. 1 (2011): 7–25.

Middle States Commission on Higher Education. *Standards for Accreditation and Requirements of Affiliation*. Philadelphia: Middle States Commission on Higher Education, 2015.

National Center for Education Statistics. "Community College of Philadelphia." College Navigator, Institute of Education Sciences, US Department of Education. Accessed September 1, 2020. https://nces.ed.gov/collegenavigator/?id=215239.

Suskie, Linda. *Assessing Student Learning: A Common Sense Guide*. San Francisco: Jossey-Bass, 2018.

CHAPTER 4

Academic Libraries

Seeing the Full Picture through Program Review

Melinda (Mindy) Wilmot

Purpose

Program review is an important component of self-assessment and continuous improvement of any instructional institution. The Academic Senate for California Community Colleges, in its missive *Program Review: Setting a Standard*, states that "program review is essential to the integrity of the college community and its educational programs."[1] Of additional importance, program review is a vital part of ongoing self-evaluation mandated by institutional accrediting bodies. More often than not, however, the program review form that each program area is asked to complete for its institution is written either from the perspective of an instructional entity or from that of a non-instructional entity. What does one do if the represented program area is both instructional *and* non-instructional? Most academic libraries fall into this category of offering both instructional and non-instructional services. In order to provide a more vibrant and accurate assessment of library services and to demonstrate subsequent needs, academic libraries must be able to present data and information from both points of view. The Program Review Committee at Bakersfield College has recognized the necessity of a combined instructional/non-instructional program review process in order to capture the full scope of data from departments that fall into this category—including library services—and has developed a hybrid program review form to satisfy this need.

Program Review Overview

Bakersfield College is one of three community colleges in the Kern Community College District and is part of the massive 116-campus California Community College system. Its accrediting body, Accrediting Commission for Community and Junior Colleges (once a part of Western Association of Schools and Colleges and now a separate entity), identifies four standards that "work together to define and promote student success, academic quality, institutional integrity, and excellence."[2] It is desirable that these standards be addressed in each instructional self-evaluation report (ISER) completed by each institution prior to a visit of an accreditation team. The standards to be addressed are outlined below.

- Standard I: Mission, Academic Quality, and Institutional Effectiveness, and Integrity—The mission of the institution needs to demonstrate the institution's adherence to student learning and student achievement. The institution should conduct continuous and thorough evaluation of all student programs and services.[3]
- Standard II: Student Learning Programs and Support Services—All programs and services offered by the institution that directly or indirectly affect student learning should be aligned with the mission of the institution.[4]
- Standard III: Resources—The institution should use its myriad resources (human, technological, financial) to advance student success in alliance with the institution's mission.[5]
- Standard IV: Leadership and Governance—The institution should recognize and support shared governance on its campus.[6]

While the accreditation process is held on an instructional campus every six years (at a maximum), it is strongly recommended that colleges in California have their institutional programs conduct ongoing and continuous evaluation that leads to improvement of goals and objectives, student achievement, and planning. The Accrediting Commission for Community and Junior Colleges requires institutions to "provide evidence that program review was conducted and that plans to improve education were developed and implemented"[7] on a constant basis. This continuous evaluation by the institution is accomplished through the annual program review process.

The Program Review Process at Bakersfield College

Bakersfield College is committed to the annual program review process to ensure student learning, program efficacy, and adherence to the college's mission and to the college's institutional learning outcomes. To this end, every institutional program at Bakersfield College—be it an academic program, an administrative unit, academic service, or student support service—completes an annual program review form and submits it to the Program Review Committee during the middle of each fall semester.

The Program Review Committee is one with shared governance representation and is therefore comprised of members from each instructional program on campus, as well as a liaison from both the Curriculum and Assessment Committees and representatives from classified, management, and student constituencies. With the library being an instructional program, a library faculty member has served as a participant of this committee for many years. Once the program review forms are submitted, members of the Program Review Committee are partnered in groups of two to read, review, and provide detailed feedback on every program review form. For the sake of transparency, all submitted program review forms and feedback reports are posted on the Program Review Committee's web page of Bakersfield College's website.

The Academic Senate for California Community Colleges, which supports and assists faculty members of the California Community College system, encourages a continuous and transparent linkage between the planning and budget of each academic institution.[8] It is in these program reviews that "each program puts forward resource requests needed to accomplish program goals intended to support student success, the college mission, and long-term strategic planning goals."[9] Requests for facilities, staffing (both faculty and classified), technology, specialized equipment, or professional development, depending on the type of program, are submitted as part of the annual program review at Bakersfield College. The individual requests are then disseminated to the appropriate committees across campus, such as Budget, Information Services, Instructional Technology, Professional Development, and Facilities and Sustainability. It is the annual program review that provides the analytical evidence and justification for these requests and assists the institution's shared governance committees in the prioritization of every request. Scoring rubrics are completed for each request, with results published on the respective web page of each committee on Bakersfield College's website.

The program review process at Bakersfield College, therefore, is vital in showing how the institution closes the loop on its budgeting process, as shown in Figure 4.1. Beginning with the completion of the program review form, resources for the program are requested and defended, budgets are considered and prioritized, and previously received resources are assessed.[10]

Figure 4.1
Bakersfield College "Closing the Loop" on budgeting process diagram

To assist in the completion of annual program reviews, the Program Review Committee at Bakersfield College developed a process that can be easily completed by institutional staff and faculty. Two versions of annual program review forms have been made available for programs to complete: one for instructional programs and another for non-instructional programs. On each version of the form, members of individual programs are asked to respond to the following prompts:

- Describe how the program supports the institutional mission.
- List the program's current goals and any new goals, being certain to include any resources needed to attain the new goals (which assists in justifying the need of additional resources).
- Reflect on previous goals and, if applicable, the application of received resources that assisted in attainment of the previous goals.
- Analyze and assess the program.[11]

It is this final prompt where the two reports deviate considerably. Faculty of instructional programs analyze and assess the attainment of the student learning outcomes associated with affiliated courses. Other meaningful student information is delineated, such as the number of student enrollments and completions, percentage of attainment of student learning outcomes, program recognition of equity and diversity gaps, and so on. It should be noted that assessment data is forwarded to the college's Assessment Committee for further evaluation. Meanwhile, faculty, staff, or both from the non-instructional programs, such as those identified as student support services, administrative units, and learning support services, do not disaggregate student completion data, since there is none. Instead, they assess their programs using administrative unit outcomes, which are meant to describe the overall services provided by the department or program and are aligned to the college's institutional learning outcomes.[12] An example would be the number of students using a particular service on campus, such as the library and its myriad resources.

The Conundrum

The full-time reference librarians employed in the Grace Van Dyke Bird Library at Bakersfield College are tenure-track faculty and are teachers of record for several courses taught on campus: one for-credit research skills class, and eight non-credit research skills workshops. Each of these courses has student learning outcomes attached. In this regard, the library is considered an instructional program and is required to complete assessment data for each course taught, including completion numbers and attainment rates of student learning outcomes. Additionally, the library is an academic student support service, which would be defined as a non-instructional program. The library offers support to students and faculty by providing, among other things, physical and electronic access to academic resources and offers reference guidance. For this reason, the library has administrative unit outcomes that must be assessed.

Herein lies the problem. When the instructional program review form was completed by the library faculty, there was no place to reflect on the important elements the administrative unit outcomes addressed. Conversely, when the non-instructional program review form was completed, there was no place to reflect on the assessment data for the courses taught. Figure 4.2 (taken partly from the Course Outline of Record for the for-credit library course) shows the significant differences between the student learning outcomes (SLOs) and the administrative unit outcomes (AUOs) for the library

INSTRUCTIONAL	NON-INSTRUCTIONAL
LIBR Bl SLOs	**LIBR AUOs**
Upon successful completion of the course, the student will be able to:	Provide materials that support academic programs and the research interest of students and faculty.
Differentiate between ethical uses of information and plagiarism and apply correct use of documentation.	Provide an environment that supports learning, faculty teaching, and research.
Locate relevant information using keywords and controlled vocabulary, Boolean operators, truncation, and other advanced methods.	
Evaluate the credibility and quality of information using established criteria.	
Find a range of sources appropriate for research, including reference materials, books and eBooks, periodical articles, and internet sources.	

Figure 4.2
Comparison of Bakersfield College Library course SLOs and AUOs.

The data used to support these administrative unit outcomes includes, but is not limited to, library holdings, the number of circulations, database use, and reference inter-actions during the academic year. While this data is imperative for demonstrating how integral library services are to student success and achievement, there was no method of including this data, as well as specific anecdotal evidence, on the instructional program review form in its previous state. Without sharing this important information, the library was unable to adequately demonstrate its value to the campus, its staff, and its students. This omission limited the library's ability to effectively articulate the need for additional resources and advocate for funding through the program review process.

While the library at Bakersfield College, as an entity on campus, is asked to complete an annual program review, the problem is this: Which program review form is to be completed? Does the library complete the instructional version or the non-instructional version? Should the library focus on instruction of the courses taught, or should it focus on the provision of services to the college's faculty, staff, and students? When *all* resource requests and prioritization for those funds are based on what is written in the annual program review, it is important to paint as accurate a picture as possible. This is nearly impossible when only one version of the form was made available for completion.

With the annual program review process being the primary tool for budgetary consideration and prioritization, the library needed a program review form that could address *both* the instructional and non-instructional aspects of the department. Being able to present information submitted in *both* versions of the program review forms would most accurately show the library's use and subsequent need of faculty, technology, and resources—ultimately demonstrating its reach into multiple disciplines and proving the depth of its value on campus. It is from this need for a more comprehensive analysis that the hybrid form was born.

The Hybrid Form

In prior years, library faculty, during Program Review Committee meetings and throughout the annual program review process, conveyed their concern about an inaccurate representation of library services and needs expressed in the program review forms provided by the committee. Once the committee was educated on the uniqueness of the services provided by the library and the ineffectiveness of the program review forms in regard to delineating those services, it was mutually understood that a new hybrid form should be developed in order to adequately showcase both the instructional and non-instructional aspects of the library department. The chairpersons of the Program Review Committee at Bakersfield College, with the insistence and assistance of library faculty, including the library department chair and the library faculty member of the Program Review Committee, developed a hybrid form. This new form was piloted in academic year 2019–2020 and was fully implemented in fall 2020. In order to showcase both the instructional and non-instructional aspects, the new hybrid form (appendix) addresses the administrative unit outcomes of the department while simultaneously assessing student learning outcomes for the courses taught by faculty of the department.

The new hybrid form allows the library to present vital data such as circulation statistics, number of holdings, database usage, reference interactions (including face-to-face and live chat), engagement with both students and faculty, and one-shot instruction (what Bakersfield College librarians term "orientations"). In addition, the library can also articulate enrollment numbers, completion rates, and student learning outcomes data for the multitude of for-credit and non-credit courses taught by library faculty. With this new annual program review form, the library at Bakersfield College can now effectively share the breadth of its instructional reach while adequately showing the need for additional resources. The annual program review process for the library will no longer be one-sided, and a more accurate portrait of services and needs will be represented.

The Future

At the end of each academic year, members of the Program Review Committee at Bakersfield College meet and discuss the prior program review cycle. Questions and answers on the program review forms are scrutinized. Contributors are also asked to provide positive and negative feedback on the current program review process. From these discussions, the Program Review Committee updates the forms for the next cycle to elicit brevity and clarity. For each of the last fifteen years, the forms used in program review have been modified and improved upon. What was once a long and arduous process has become more precise and concise each year. Beginning with the 2018–2019 cycle, the program review process was recreated in eLumen (a curriculum and assessment management system). At the moment, two departments at Bakersfield College, the library and student success/ counseling, are eligible to use the hybrid form. Both departments are making use of the hybrid form for the latest cycle of program reviews. It is anticipated that both departments will evaluate their experience using the hybrid form in order to provide meaningful feedback to the Program Review Committee and continue to improve the process each year.

Acknowledgment

Special thanks to Bakersfield College Program Review Committee co-chairs Kristin Rabe and Kimberly Nickell for sharing their expertise.

Appendix
Bakersfield College Program Review—Hybrid Form

PROGRAM INFORMATION

Program Mission Statement:

Describe how your program supports the College Mission:

PROGRAM GOALS 2020-21

List the program's current goals. For each goal (minimum of 2 goals), discuss progress and changes. If the program is addressing more than two (2) goals, please duplicate this section. Please provide an action plan for each goal that gives the steps to completing the goal and the timeline.

Program Goal	ILO(s) Supported	Status	Action Plan/Timeline/ Resource Needs

ADMINISTRATIVE UNIT OUTCOMES 2020-21

Assess your program using the following:

AUO #1: Use effective budgeting and categorical funding practices.

AUO #2: Organize positive communications between the community, administration, faculty, staff, and students.

AUO #3: Engage administrators, faculty, and staff in professional development.

AUO #4: Develop internal and external partnerships that benefit the College.

Use this space to create/discuss additional area-specific AUOs.

ASSESSMENT REPORT (PART 1 ASSESSMENT TABLE) 2020-21

Courses	% Students Exceeds	% Students Meets	% Students Does Not Meet

Assessment Report (Part 2 Responses) 2020-21

PLAN: Describe the process, timing, and tools used to access the courses for the program.

REFLECT: Based on the SLO performance data listed in the table, describe both the strengths and weaknesses of the program.

REFINE: Summarize the changes that discipline faculty plan to implement based on the program's strengths and weaknesses listed above.

DIALOGUE: Explain the frequency and content of assessment planning for the program (e.g., department meetings, advisory boards, etc.).

Program Reflection Hybrid 2020-21

1. Describe any changes or activities your program or service area has made that are not addressed in your goals; identify the factors that triggered the changes and indicate the expected or anticipated outcomes.
2. Please describe any recent achievements in your program by faculty and staff who have won awards or distinctions, new projects or initiatives your program has implemented or contributed to, committee work, professional development work, conference presentations, community engagement, or recently published work.

Student Success and Equity Hybrid 2020-21

Examine the success and retention data disaggregated by gender, age, and ethnicity. For any groups that have success rates in your program at lower or higher than college-wide success rates, what factors do you think cause those patterns?

Provide examples of any changes you made to improve student success/retention, especially for groups that have equity gaps.

Describe specific examples of departmental or individual efforts, including instructional and/or special projects, aimed at encouraging students to become actively engaged in the learning process in their classes.

Current & Future Trends, Program Planning, Conclusion, and Recommendation 2020-21

Present any conclusions and findings about the program. This is an opportunity to provide a brief abstract or synopsis of your program's current circumstances and needs. Consider this a snapshot of your program if someone were to only read this portion of your annual program review.

The original form was uploaded to eLumen. This form has been modified slightly for printing.

Notes

1.   Academic Senate for California Community and Junior Colleges, *Program Review: Setting a Standard* (Sacramento: Academic Senate for California Community and Junior Colleges, Educational Policies Committee, Spring 2009), 2, https://www.asccc.org/sites/default/files/publications/Program-review-spring09_0.pdf.
2.   Accrediting Commission for Community and Junior Colleges, Western Association of Schools and Colleges, *Accreditation Standards* (Novato, CA: Accrediting Commission for Community and Junior Colleges, Western Association of Schools and Colleges, June 2014), 1, https://accjc.org/wp-content/uploads/Accreditation-Standards_-Adopted-June-2014.pdf.
3.   Accrediting Commission for Community and Junior Colleges, *Accreditation Standards*, 1.
4.   Accrediting Commission for Community and Junior Colleges, *Accreditation Standards*, 5.
5.   Accrediting Commission for Community and Junior Colleges, *Accreditation Standards*, 9.
6.   Accrediting Commission for Community and Junior Colleges, *Accreditation Standards*, 14.
7.   Accrediting Commission for Community and Junior Colleges, Western Association of Schools and Colleges, *Guide to Institutional Self-Evaluation, Improvement, and Peer Review* (Novato, CA: Accrediting Commission for Community and Junior Colleges, Western Association of Schools and Colleges, January 2020), 7, https://www.merritt.edu/accreditation/wp-content/uploads/sites/3/2020/02/Guide-to-Institutional-Self-Evaluation-Improvement-Peer-Review_Jan2020.pdf.
8.   Academic Senate for California Community and Junior Colleges, *Program Review: Developing a Faculty Driven Process* (Sacramento: Academic Senate for California Community and Junior Colleges, Educational Policies Committee, Spring 1996), 8, https://www.asccc.org/sites/default/files/publications/ProgReview_0.pdf.
9.   Bakersfield College Program Review Committee, "Program Review and the Budget Connection," https://committees.kccd.edu/sites/committees.kccd.edu/files/4%20Program%20Review%20and%20the%20Budget%20Connection2.pdf.
10. Bakersfield College Program Review Committee, "Program Review and the Budget Connection."
11. Bakersfield College Program Review Committee, *Program Review Handbook* (Bakersfield, CA: Bakersfield College, May 10, 2017), https://do-prod-webteam-drupalfiles.s3-us-west-2.amazonaws.com/bcedu/s3fs-public/IA_PRC_2017Handbook_doc.pdf.
12. Bakersfield College Program Review Committee, "Program Review and the Budget Connection."

Bibliography and Additional Resources

Academic Senate for California Community Colleges. *Program Review: Developing a Faculty Driven Process*. Sacramento: Academic Senate for California Community Colleges, Educational Policies Committee, Spring 1996. https://www.asccc.org/sites/default/files/publications/ProgReview_0.pdf.

Academic Senate for California Community and Junior Colleges. *Program Review: Setting a Standard*. Sacramento: Academic Senate for California Community Colleges, Educational Policies Committee, Spring 2009. https://www.asccc.org/sites/default/files/publications/Program-review-spring09_0.pdf.

Accrediting Commission for Community and Junior Colleges, Western Association of Schools and Colleges. *Accreditation Standards*. Novato, CA: Accrediting Commission for Community and Junior Colleges, Western Association of Schools and Colleges, June 2014. https://accjc.org/wp-content/uploads/Accreditation-Standards_-Adopted-June-2014.pdf.

———. *Guide to Institutional Self-Evaluation, Improvement, and Peer Review*. Novato, CA: Accrediting Commission for Community and Junior Colleges, Western Association of Schools and Colleges, January 2020. https://www.merritt.edu/accreditation/wp-content/uploads/sites/3/2020/02/Guide-to-Institutional-Self-Evaluation-Improvement-Peer-Review_Jan2020.pdf.

Bakersfield College Program Review Committee. "Program Review and the Budget Connection." Accessed July 17, 2020. https://committees.kccd.edu/sites/committees.kccd.edu/files/4%20Program%20Review%20and%20the%20Budget%20Connection2.pdf.

———. *Program Review Handbook*. Bakersfield, CA: Bakersfield College, May 10, 2017. https://do-prod-webteam-drupalfiles.s3-us-west-2.amazonaws.com/bcedu/s3fs-public/IA_PRC_2017Handbook_doc.pdf.

CHAPTER 5

Assessing Impact on Student Success Using Statistical Analyses in a Data-Informed Community College

Robert Holzmann, Gwetheldene Holzmann, and Joseph Harris

Introduction

Historically, quantitative assessment of a library's impact upon student academic success has been nearly impossible to provide based solely on library data such as the number of visits to the library, the number of holdings in the collection, or the number of items checked out. A statistical impact study is a new and groundbreaking approach for demonstrating meaningful assessment of library services.[1] This chapter provides practical information about collecting library services data and coupling this library data with student academic and demographic data to provide reliable statistical analyses that demonstrate the impact libraries have upon student success.

This quantitative approach is one of several components developed in Tulsa Community College's (TCC) comprehensive library assessment plan in 2018 (see chapter 2 in this book). Academic libraries need to demonstrate academic effectiveness to justify the budgets for their services, programs, and resources.[2] This requires good assessment data that informs decisions, promotes meaningful planning, and contributes to continual improvement as higher education becomes more competitive. Therefore, it is essential that librarians, faculty, and administrators understand the impact that libraries have on student success.

Assessing Library Impact on Student Success

Generally, typical library analysis of services and programs related to academic achievement is more anecdotal or inferred. Evaluation is often based upon mostly qualitative data such as feedback and opinion and some quantitative data having no correlation to student success. Such library assessment methods may be informative but do not demonstrate the direct impact of library services upon student success. These conventional approaches to library evaluation are based on use, volume, and self-reporting instruments that often result in misinterpretation.[3] This type of reported information may simply indicate a coincidence, reveal periods of high-volume workload, or imply that academically successful students use the library.

While researching and creating the assessment plan for the TCC Library, the team discovered articles describing the application of statistical analyses using a wide range of institutional data coupled with library services and programs data. Studies authored by Soria, Fransen, and Nackerud demonstrated through statistical analyses the impact library services have on student academic success criteria.[4] Recognizing that TCC is an evidence-based data-informed organization, this approach seemed timely and well suited for our work.

Therefore, the library's comprehensive assessment plan included Library Services Impact upon Student Success as a major component. The team embarked on a journey into this exciting new assessment territory that few other libraries, and no community college libraries to our knowledge, had explored up to that point. This information will enable the TCC Library to measure its academic effectiveness and develop actionable and empirically supported assessment results.[5]

Hard Data and Soft Data

Hard data is the foundation of quantitative statistics and analyses. *Hard data* is defined "as data in the form of numbers or graphs, as opposed to qualitative information."[6] Some traditional library examples include door counts, how many items were checked out, the number of books in the collection, or how many patrons were registered. Hard data also includes quantifiable data generated from applications and machines such as computers, sensors, and other devices, which can be measured, validated, and used for predictions and analysis.[7] TCC Library's aim is to collect hard data from computer systems including complete details about interlibrary loan (ILL) transactions, items that students check out, computers that students use, and e-resources use that can be connected to student demographics and academic outcomes for analysis.

On the other hand, "qualitative information that is susceptible to interpretation or opinion is known as soft data,"[8] which libraries often obtain through focus groups, surveys, and feedback. Data should demonstrate an outcome that is a "specific benefit from a library program [or] service that can be qualitative or quantitative" and answers the questions "how have learners changed as a result of library services [and] what good did we do?"[9] While TCC Library's assessment plan incorporated a combination of essential qualitative and quantitative data to provide a complete and balanced assessment,[10] this chapter focuses upon the one component using quantitative analyses and hard data.

The Research Question

Developing the research question is a pivotal step in the research process. We designed our research question to match the attributes of a well-structured research question that sets the foundation for the whole study,[11] including the methods, data set variables or fields, the analyses, the results, and the accuracy of the reporting. We determined that our study is about relationship questions that "aim at examining the correlation between two or more variables."[12] The research question should state precisely what we want to study, the subject or topic being addressed, and clearly articulate the specific research problem or objective being considered. A good research question will pass a "So what?" test, is well grounded in existing research, unambiguous, operationally definable, empirically answerable, and feasible when considering constraints.[13] The following research question meets these requirements and is the statement that drives and frames the study for the Library Services Impact upon Student Success component of the library's assessment plan: "What impact do library services have upon student success including persistence, academic achievement, and completion?"[14]

Additionally, we expressed a hypothesis for this study asserting that "Academic library services and programs have a positive impact upon student academic success."[15] Our hypothesis, which is related to the research question and influenced the creation of the research question, is "a predictive statement about the expected outcome of the research."[16] Whether or not the hypothesis is true will depend upon the results of the study and the answers to the research question. Academic libraries have asserted for centuries that their position as an institutional centerpiece where knowledge was gathered, shared, and used is essential, and thus we would hope this is true. However, the hypothesis is an assertion, and it may not be fully supported by the analyses for services and programs included in the study.

Institutional Review Board: Correlating Library Use to Student Academic Success

Because we were going to use data from various sources regarding students, an institutional review board (IRB) form was necessary. The process of getting approval from the IRB by carefully completing and submitting the IRB form is important for several reasons. The IRB process is necessary when doing a human study to ensure that the persons in the study will not be harmed, and it provides a written document to that effect.

The process of completing the IRB form also caused those persons involved in planning the study to thoroughly consider every aspect and carefully articulate all of the details about the study or project, including the research question, prior to IRB review and approval. This process was both informational and educational for those on the team unfamiliar with this level of institutional academic research.

The IRB process required us to better organize our plan and document items such as a specific description about how the study would be conducted, details about which library services would be included, and specifics about what data would be required. Seeking IRB approval required specific information about the scope of the project, the type of study, the data collection processes, the data analyses, the data reporting and confidentiality, and the potential risk factors. The work of preparing a comprehensive IRB application helped define the research and continues to serve as a useful reference and guide for our work.

The IRB form stipulates that this study is archival using hard data collected from our systems and gathered at the points of service (POS). This study is long-term, meaning it will last at least five to seven years. The results of the project will be reported in the form of cumulative anonymous aggregate impact reports correlating library use to student academic outcomes. The IRB form was also drafted in such a way that it provided reasonable latitude to further develop or expand elements of the study that may fall within the scope and purpose of the study in the future.

Collaboration

Collaboration among those individuals, groups, and organizations involved in the project is essential and required for the project to be successful and sustained.[17] TCC administration and other departments support the library's assessment efforts. Especially noteworthy is successful collaboration and cooperation with information technology (IT) and institution research and assessment (IR&A) because so much is continually required of these two college departments in relation to this project. The following is a list of specific collaborative partners that have contributed to and that are involved in the study:

- TCC library staff and leadership
- TCC administration
- TCC Institutional Research and Assessment

- TCC Information Technology
- TCC academic departments
- providers of library systems and applications
- vendors of library services and resources

Without the involvement and cooperation of all those listed above, this comprehensive project would not be possible.

Parameters

The team decided to include in the study only library services that relate specifically to coursework and academic achievement.[18] TCC Library also decided not to collect detailed data for certain services. For example, we excluded in-person reference desk questions from the study, although this was listed on the IRB form. In a brainstorming session, our staff made the valid observation that when a student is asking for help at the reference desk, (1) it usually is in context of using another library service already being measured; (2) data collection would require too much time at a busy desk; and (3) data collection most likely would be overly intrusive and time-consuming. TCC Library has other services where one cannot acquire the data or the data cannot be measured, including which individuals enter the library, read the journals, or use open spaces. Therefore, services such as these, as well as data about non-academic services and programs, are not part of the study.

Nine categories of specific services are included in this study regarding library impact upon student success:

- Circulation: only checkout of library collection items (not renewal or check-in)
- Course reserves: only checkout, which also includes items owned by professors
- Interlibrary loan (ILL): initial borrowing requests only (whether or not fulfilled)
- E-resources: only the connection to a provider's e-resources domain or website
- Computers: located in the campus libraries and provided by IT
- Virtual reference: chat and e-mail only
- Study rooms: also includes other group work spaces in the library
- Research consultations: for in-depth individual student research assistance
- Library instruction: requests for in-library, in-classroom, or virtual instruction

Seven of the TCC Library services and programs listed on the TCC IRB form provide data collected via automated systems, and three other library services require manually recorded data about use and individual information.[19] No individual private information, such as the TCC Identification Number (TCC-ID) and Family Educational Rights and Privacy Act (FERPA) protected data, will be revealed in any of the reports produced for the library. All individual confidential and private data used for the study is internal to TCC systems and will remain protected.

The primary and universal data elements collected for the library services categories include which specific service or program was used; the TCC-ID; and the date or date range, which includes year, month, and day, and if available the hour. Other data elements may be essential and recorded for other specialized library services and programs, such as TCC course and section number, whether the access occurred on a TCC campus or off campus, library computer name or IP address, a transaction number, the specific room used, and the type or format of materials.

Another consideration in a comparative study such as this is how to determine or select a control group. We cannot create a control group by informing selected students that they cannot use library services. In this case we determined that, simply stated, the control group consists of those students who do not use the library.

TCC Systems Data, Standards, and Data Definitions

This plan identified library users as full-time students enrolled in a degree or certificate program. The study uses academic and demographic data from other TCC systems including data elements such as class registration, grades, completion, and demographics consistent with those used in other TCC institutional assessment. In addition to grade point average (GPA), the student success criteria measured also included persistence and completion.[20] At TCC, persistence is enrollment in successive fall and spring semesters, and completion is defined as graduation or transfer.

For our study, we use TCC's academic year, defined as August through July, which consists of the three semesters beginning with the fall semester (August through December), followed by the spring semester (January through May), and ending with the summer semester (June and July). Academic and demographic data included in the research are for those students who are full-time, enrolled in a degree or certificate program, and as noted above are persistent in attending every fall and spring until completion. A cohort of incoming students begins with those entering freshmen in the fall semester of each academic year. Completion is categorized as 100 percent, 150 percent, and 200 percent, which are defined as two years, three years, and four years of enrollment, respectively.

Data Collection

With the parameters and population defined, the next step was to determine how to collect the data. The library had some data collection methods already in place. For example, methods that are in place for automated recording of the essential data elements include checkout, e-resources use, and use of computers. The systems that record and store this data at TCC Library include:

- OCLC WorldShare (WMS) for circulation checkout and course reserves
- OCLC Tipasa for ILL borrowing requests
- OCLC EZproxy log files of connections to vendor domains after authentication
- TCC IT archives of computer authentication log files
- Springshare modules for research consultations, library instruction, chat, and e-mail

Methods of manual data entry to record essential data elements were necessary for some library services, and the library proceeded to implement data collection procedures for staff to record student use of specific library services on existing systems. The most error-prone procedure is manual entry of data. Manual data entry is configured and recorded in Springshare for these services at TCC Library:

- Virtual reference added information specifically for chat and e-mail only
- Study rooms use also includes student use of library classrooms and think tanks
- Individual research consultations for scheduled and non-scheduled sessions
- Library instruction scheduling details including TCC course and section

For manual data entry, certain modules and features of the Springshare LibApps product were used to design a quick and easy method to collect data. Staff enter data about the study room used and the TCC-ID numbers of all the students working in the study room as a group via a simple online LibWizard survey form created for each campus library. Chat and e-mail are recorded in LibAnswers and reported as tickets or transcripts, but the student TCC-ID number must be entered manually by the student when initiating service. LibInsight has separate forms with all the data fields preset for research consultations and library instruction where the student TCC-ID is a required field. However, using SMS for texting and Facebook does not allow libraries to configure an ID field at this time.

Some of our systems automatically store additional data elements as part of the transaction recorded for specific services. These additional data elements are not currently being used but could have potential for future use. Examples of these additional data elements include the time a service was provided, the campus library where the service occurred, and even the subject classification of library materials used. Recently, we have implemented changes that would accommodate collecting data for asynchronous library instruction that includes the use of librarian-created streaming videos and web pages or librarians teaching via recorded instruction with links imbedded in the courses.

Data Harvesting

After the data is collected, harvesting the data is the step that should be performed in a timely manner and then checked for accuracy and completeness. If any problems are observed, then the specific data files in question may be reviewed and checked and perhaps harvested again with potentially better results. As noted in table 5.1, TCC Library harvests the data from several different sources after the end of each semester with two exceptions: ILL borrowing transactions are harvested twice each semester, and the EZproxy logs are harvested at the end of each month.

Table 5.1

Data harvesting

Library Service	Location of Data and Other Details	Key Data Field
Circulation	WMS Analytics Custom Report; complete transaction details for checkouts, patrons, and items	Includes TCC-ID
Course Reserves	WMS Analytics Custom Report; complete transaction details for checkouts, patrons, and items	Includes TCC-ID

Table 5.1

Data harvesting

Library Service	Location of Data and Other Details	Key Data Field
Interlibrary Loan	Tipasa home page requests list; complete details of borrowing transactions (exported twice per semester)	Includes TCC-ID
Electronic Resources	EZproxy customized Starting Point URLs (SPU) file; (exported monthly)	Includes TCC-ID
Computers	Computer logins archive provided by TCC Information Technology	Includes TCC-ID
Virtual Reference	Springshare LibAnswers reports; transaction details for chat and e-mail only	Includes TCC-ID or TCC e-mail address
Study Rooms	Springshare LibWizard survey report	TCC-IDs of all in the group using a room
Research Consultations	Springshare LibInsight form report; includes scheduled and non-scheduled	Includes TCC-ID
Library Instruction	Springshare LibInsight form report; instruction requested by professor	Includes course and section for retrieving TCC-IDs

All the files of data shown in table 5.1 are either exported as a Microsoft Excel file or converted to Excel after downloading.

Harvesting data is not always easy. Some important data fields are not available in generic reports bundled with a system and can be retrieved only by creating a customized report. TCC Library created customized reports that may require future revisions as systems are updated. Other data must be collected and provided through a request to other departments such as IT or be manually downloaded from system-level files such as those generated through library customized EZproxy usage logging. Lastly, acquiring data that is required to record some library services usage may require a system enhancement by the system provider. For example, TCC Library submitted an enhancement request to allow entry of the TCC-ID for virtual reference via texting.

Data Cleaning

The next step following harvesting data is data cleaning, also referred to as data cleansing or data preparation. The objective of data cleaning is to put the data in a consistent and usable format while maintaining its integrity.

> Data cleansing or cleaning is the process of detecting and correcting (or removing) corrupt or inaccurate records from a record set, table, or database and refers to identifying incomplete, incorrect,

inaccurate or irrelevant parts of the data and then replacing, modifying, or deleting the dirty or coarse data.[21]

The tool most used at TCC Library for data cleaning is Microsoft Excel. The original
raw data files must remain untouched and unchanged just as they were harvested. Copies
of the original data files are then cleaned and used as the input for analyses.

Concerning the data, the assessment plan team considered the accuracy of the data:
Is the data perfect? If not, then how perfect is perfect enough? Most data collected is not
100 percent perfect, especially with large quantities of data covering a wide range of data
types, some of which is manually recorded. Our assumption is that some data errors are
reasonable and acceptable since some data fields may not be completely recorded, may
have typos, or may be subject to momentary technology glitches.[22]

Data cleaning ensures that the data is accurate, complete, and uniform to make the
results as reliable as possible. In many reports or files there are data elements or fields of
data records that are not needed or that are redundant, and these may be removed. All
data records must include the key data element: the TCC-ID number, which conforms to
a standard format starting with "T1" or "T2" followed by seven digits. If this key element
is missing or entered so incorrectly that recovery through making a correction is not
possible, that record is unusable and may be removed from the data set. For example,
omitting the letter T as the first character in a TCC-ID number could be corrected, but
a TCC-ID not having the correct eight digits following the T would render the record
unusable unless that record also contained another unique identifying field such as the
TCC student e-mail address.

Once the data has been cleaned, it may be normalized across systems to make the data
format consistent. Normalizing is a process to standardize one element of the data within
a data file and among two or more data files that will be combined in a statistical analysis.

> Data normalization is a process of making your data less redun-
> dant by grouping similar values into one common value…. Data
> must always be usable…. Normalizing data ensures that you have
> actionable segments. You can derive reliable analytics based on the
> segment…. [23]

There may be similar data types that are represented in different forms. For example,
date, time, the name for a service, or a computer host name are data elements that may
need normalizing. Other exemplary data problems requiring normalization may include
inconsistencies such as interchangeably using or omitting dashes, dots, hyphens, spaces,
or leading zeros.

The examples and information noted above are typical for our data cleaning and data
normalization. At this stage, after cleaning, a data set and its elements will have consistency and uniformity with other data sets used in the study. Some of the data cleaning is
performed at the time that files are harvested by the library, and additional data cleaning,
including data normalization, is performed by the analysts in IR&A, who will be including other institutional data in their work with the library data.[24] For example, the study is

looking at student data, so if there are library data records representing faculty and staff, these may be removed. If any data that was cleaned out may be needed again for future use, it may be retrieved from the original raw files that have remained untouched.

Lastly, the data files must be organized and stored in secure systems and archives. Data that is used in the process of statistical analysis should be kept entirely separate from the original files of raw data. Access should always be secure and restricted following institutional standards, and the study's data must be backed up following institutional best practices. As stipulated in the IRB form, the library may collect operational use data including some related confidential personal data so that the library may combine its data with other TCC data and research projects. Furthermore, the library will adhere to protection of private confidential data based upon professional as well as legal standards.[25]

Analysis

Using a copy of the cleaned and normalized data, there may be further work involved such as standardizing the names of files and fields of data elements to match the systems and tools that the analyst and researchers use. Such requirements may necessitate the renaming of file or data elements for consistency and conformity with other systems and database requirements. Having a table that maps the differences between how the library labels a file or data element and how the analyst needs to label that item is very helpful for all involved in the project.

Once the data is ready to be analyzed, potential statistical analyses include:[26]

- Correlation analysis: Determines the strength and nature of a relationship between two quantifiable variables, quantified by the correlation coefficient, but does not imply cause and effect.[27]
- Regression analysis: A simple linear regression model describes the relationship between one independent and one dependent variable such that the value of the dependent variable can be predicted, to a given level of confidence, from the value of the independent variable.[28]
  - Analysis of variance (ANOVA): Method "used to evaluate the mean differences between two or more treatments (or populations)."[29] This procedure reveals levels of variability leading to comparisons between treatments.[30]
- Multiple regression analysis: Also referred to as multiple linear regression, a form of simple linear regression analysis using more than one explanatory predictor or independent variables.[31]
  - Multicollinearity: A test within a multiple regression that "occurs when there are high correlations between two or more predictor variables. In other words, one predictor variable can be used to predict the other. This creates redundant information, skewing the results in a regression model."[32]
- Stepwise regression: Another type of regression analysis that identifies a set of useful predictor variables. A form of regression where it is possible to build a regression model in steps, either adding or removing variables and recomputing the regression

coefficients. It is especially useful for dealing with a large number of potential independent variables in fine-tuning a model.[33]

The initial analyses are not meant to establish definitive cause and effect but to provide a baseline and establish a relationship. Statistical analyses early in the study may provide an indication of impact. For example, a correlation analysis can establish whether two variables of interest are related in some way. This can be followed up with a simple regression analysis to test whether one variable changes in tandem with the other, such as testing whether average student GPA varies consistently as a function of how much they use a particular library service.

Over time, as researchers ask more complicated questions, they will begin to conduct more complicated analyses, which may require the collection of additional data. For example, if the researchers become interested in the long-term implications of library services for students, they may follow the academic progress of student cohorts for a number of years in a longitudinal study. Predictive studies may be conducted that require five to seven years or more to gather and analyze data.

Conclusion

Once the data is analyzed the results can be used in a variety of ways. The results will demonstrate how library programs and services directly contribute to students' academic success. In a data-informed organization such as TCC, the results provide an evaluation of programs and services that can lead to program improvement.[34] They will allow library leadership to make informed decisions based on identified strengths and weaknesses so that meaningful planning for expansion or improvements can be initiated along with providing the requisite budget justifications.

As an essential component of the comprehensive library assessment plan, the study's results can be combined with other quantitative and qualitative results to document the library's integral role, value, and impact.[35] While providing specific self-evaluation statements for accreditation purposes,[36] the results will also strengthen the library's academic position within the college and document it for the strategic plan.[37] The assessment plan, details about the study, methods, and results will also add to the body of knowledge for the library profession and hopefully inspire others to engage in this type of practical scholarly activity.

Notes

1. Melissa Bowles-Terry, "Proving and Improving the Value of the Academic Library," in *Reviewing the Academic Library: A Guide to Self-Study and External Review*, ed. Eleanor Mitchell and Peggy Seiden (Chicago: Association of College and Research Libraries, 2015), 292, 299.
2. Megan Oakleaf, *The Value of Academic Libraries* (Chicago: Association of College and Research Libraries, 2010), 17, 39–41, 179; Association of College and Research Libraries, *Academic Library Impact*, prepared by Lynn Silipigni Connaway, William Harvey, Vanessa Kitzie, and Stephanie Mikitish of OCLC Research (Chicago: Association of College and Research Libraries, 2017), 2, 6, 72.
3. Oakleaf, *Value of Academic Libraries*, 29–31; Megan Oakleaf, *Library Integration in Institutional Learning Analytics*, research report (Syracuse, NY: Syracuse University, November 15, 2018), 11–14.

4. Krista M. Soria, Jan Fransen, and Shane Nackerud, "The Impact of Academic Library Resources on Undergraduates' Degree Completion," *College and Research Libraries* 78, no. 6 (September 2017): 817–21.

5. Tulsa Community College Library, *Library Services and Programs Assessment Plan* (Tulsa, OK: Tulsa Community College Library, August 2018), 1, 5.

6. *McGraw-Hill Dictionary of Scientific and Technical Terms,* 6th ed., s.v. "hard data" (New York: McGraw Hill, 2003).

7. Objectivity, "Hard Data vs. Soft Data," June 3, 2015, https://www.objectivity.com/hard-data-vs-soft-data/.

8. Objectivity, "Hard Data."

9. Sara Goek, "Project Outcome for Academic Libraries: Interactive Workshop" (presentation, New Mexico Library Association/Mountain Plains Library Association Annual Conference, Albuquerque, NM, October 30, 2019).

10. Association of College and Research Libraries, *Academic Library Impact,* 53.

11. Lund Research, Ltd., "How to Structure Quantitative Research Questions," *Laerd Dissertation* (online textbook), http://dissertation.laerd.com/how-to-structure-quantitative-research-questions-p2.php.

12. Lili Luo, Kristine R. Brancolini, and Marie R. Kennedy, *Enhancing Library and Information Research Skills* (Santa Barbara, CA: Libraries Unlimited, 2017), 46; Lili Luo, "Evidence Based Practice—Ideas for Academic Librarians" (keynote address, Oklahoma Association of Research Libraries Annual Conference, Edmond, OK, November 9, 2018).

13. Goek, "Project Outcome: Interactive Workshop"; Luo, Brancolini, and Kennedy, *Library and Information Research,* 43–44; Luo, "Evidence Based Practice."

14. Library Services and Programs Assessment Plan Workgroup, *Application for IRB Review for Unfunded Research Tulsa Community College Institutional Review Board* (Tulsa, OK: Tulsa Community College, 2017), 2.

15. Robert Holzmann, "Library Services Assessment: Electronic Resources Impact on Student Success by Configuring, Harvesting, and Preparing Hard Data from Proxy Logs as Input for Statistical Analysis" (presentation, Electronic Resources and Libraries: 2020 Conference, Austin, TX, March 9, 2020).

16. Luo, Brancolini, and Kennedy, *Library and Information Research,* 43–44; Luo, "Evidence Based Practice."

17. Karen Brown and Kara J. Malenfant, *Academic Library Impact on Student Learning Success (Chicago: Association of College and Research Libraries, 2017),* 3, 23–25.

18. Shane Nackerud et al., "Analyzing Demographics: Assessing Library Use across the Institution." *portal: Libraries and the Academy* 13, no. 2 (2013): 132–33.

19. Lisa Massengale, Pattie Piotrowski, and Devin Savage, "Identifying and Articulating Library Connections to Student Success," *College and Research Libraries* 77, no. 2 (March 2016): 230; Oakleaf, *Value of Academic Libraries,* 13.

20. Mark Emmons and Frances C. Wilkinson, "The Academic Library Impact on Student Persistence," *College and Research Libraries* 72, no. 2 (March 2011): 128–31; Nackerud et al., "Analyzing Demographics," 132–33; Bowles-Terry, "Proving and Improving," 291.

21. Simone Maase and Robert van den Hoed, "EV Charging Data Management: Five Issues to Solve" (presentation, International Electric Vehicle Symposium 32, Lyon, France, May 2019), 6.

22. Fakhitah Ridzuan and Wan Mohd Nazmee Wan Zainon, "Review on Data Cleansing Methods for Big Data," in "The Fifth Information Systems International Conference, 23–24 July 2019, Surabaya, Indonesia," ed. Arjumand Younus, special issue, *Procedia Computer Science* 161 (2019): 732–34, https://doi.org/10.1016/j.procs.2019.11.177.

23. Strategic DB Corporation, "What Is Data Normalization?" *Strategic DB Blog, July 3, 2016, https://strategicdb.com/2016/07/03/what-is-data-normalization/.*

24. Soria, Fransen, and Nackerud, "Undergraduates' Degree Completion," 813–15; Ula Gaha, Suzanne Hinnefeld, and Catherine Pellegrino, "The Academic Library's Contribution to Student Success: Library Instruction and GPA," *College and Research Libraries* 79, no. 6 (September 2018): 740–41.

25. Association of College and Research Libraries, *Academic Library Impact,* 31, 54; Library Services and Programs Assessment Plan Workgroup, *Application for IRB,* 2.

26. Dr. Mary Lou Miller (professor, Oral Roberts University), in discussions with authors, November 7, 2018, and October 26, 2020.

27. Lorraine R. Gay, Geoffrey E. Mills, and Peter W. Airasian, *Educational Research Competencies for Analysis and Application*, 10th ed. (Boston: Pearson Education, 2012), 10, 29, 213–14, 226; Yale University Department of Statistics and Data Science, "Correlation," in Statistical Topics (website), Yale University, 1997, http://www.stat.yale.edu/Courses/1997-98/101/correl.htm.
28. Frederick J. Gravetter and Larry B. Wallnau, *Statistics for the Behavioral Sciences*, 9th ed. (Belmont, CA: Thompson Wadsworth, 2013), 557–69; David M. Levine and David F. Stephan, *Even You Can Learn Statistics* (Upper Saddle River, NJ: Pearson Education, 2005), 182–87.
29. Gravetter and Wallnau, *Statistics for the Behavioral Sciences*, 387.
30. Yale University Department of Statistics and Data Science, "ANOVA for Regression," in Statistical Topics (website), Yale University, 1997, http://www.stat.yale.edu/Courses/1997-98/101/anovareg.htm; Graham Upton and Ian Cook, "ANOVA (Analysis of Variance)," in *A Dictionary of Statistics* (Oxford: Oxford University Press, 2014), Oxford Reference.
31. Graham Upton and Ian Cook, "Multiple Regression Model," in *A Dictionary of Statistics* (Oxford: Oxford University Press, 2014), Oxford Reference; Yale University Department of Statistics and Data Science, "Multiple Linear Regression," in Statistical Topics (website), Yale University, 1997, http://www.stat.yale.edu/Courses/1997-98/101/linmult.htm.
32. Stephanie Glen, "Multicollinearity: Definition, Causes, Examples," Statistics How To: Statistics for the Rest of Us! (website), last updated September 22, 2015, https://www.statisticshowto.com/multicollinearity/.
33. Gary Smith, "Step away from Stepwise," *Journal of Big Data* 5, no. 32 (2018): 32, https://doi.org/10.1186/s40537-018-0143-6; Stephanie Glen, "Stepwise Regression," Statistics How To: Statistics for the Rest of Us! (website), last updated September 24, 2015, https://www.statisticshowto.com/stepwise-regression/; Alisdair Rogers, Noel Castree, and Rob Kitchin, "Stepwise Regression," in *A Dictionary of Human Geography* (Oxford: Oxford University Press, 2013), Oxford Reference.
34. Karen Brown, "Evidence of Academic Library Impact on Student Learning and Success," in *Shaping the Campus Conversation on Student Learning and Experience: Activating the Results of Assessment in Action*, ed. Karen Brown, Deborah Gilchrist, Sarah Goek, Lisa Janicke, Kara Malenfant, Chase Ollis, and Allison Payne (Chicago: Association of College and Research Libraries, 2018), 18; Robert Holzmann, "Strategic Planning and Assessment: Academic Library Assessment Planning," *Arkansas Libraries* 77, no. 1–2 (Spring/Summer 2020): 39; Eric Ackermann, Sara Goek, and Emily Plagman, "Outcome Measurement in Academic Libraries: Adapting the Project Outcome Model" (presentation. Library Assessment Conference, Houston, TX, December 5, 2018), 3, 11.
35. Association of College and Research Libraries, *Academic Library Impact*, 53; Goek, "Project Outcome Interactive Workshop"; Holzmann, "Strategic Planning," 39; Sara Goek and Emily Plagman, *Outcome Measurement in Libraries* (Urbana, IL: University of Illinois and Indiana University, National Institute for Learning Outcomes Assessment, June 2020), 2, 4.
36. Patricia L. Thibodeau and Steven J. Melamut, "The Role of the Academic Library in Academic Accreditation," in *Reviewing the Academic Library: A Guide to Self-Study and External Review*, ed. Eleanor Mitchell and Peggy Seiden (Chicago: Association of College and Research Libraries, 2015), 68–78; Bowles-Terry, "Proving and Improving," 296. See also chapter 2 in this book.
37. Ackermann, Goek, and Plagman, "Adapting the Project Outcome," 3, 11; Holzmann, "Strategic Planning," 39; Goek and Plagman, *Outcome Measurement*, 2, 4.

Bibliography and Additional Resources

Ackermann, Eric, Sara Goek, and Emily Plagman. "Outcome Measurement in Academic Libraries: Adapting the Project Outcome Model." Presentation, Library Assessment Conference, Houston, TX, December 5, 2018.

Association of College and Research Libraries. *Academic Library Impact: Improving Practice and Essential Areas to Research.* Prepared by Lynn Silipigni Connaway, William Harvey, Vanessa Kitzie, and Stephanie Mikitish of OCLC Research. Chicago: Association of College and Research Libraries, 2017.

Bowles-Terry, Melissa. "Proving and Improving the Value of the Academic Library." In *Reviewing the Academic Library: A Guide to Self-Study and External Review*. Edited by Eleanor Mitchell and Peggy Seiden, 291–313. Chicago: Association of College and Research Libraries, 2015.

Brown, Karen. "Evidence of Academic Library Impact on Student Learning and Success." In *Shaping the Campus Conversation on Student Learning and Experience: Activating the Results of Assessment in Action*. Edited by Karen Brown, Deborah Gilchrist, Sarah Goek, Lisa Janicke, Kara Malenfant, Chase Ollis, and Allison Payne, 9–21. Chicago: Association of College and Research Libraries, 2018.

Brown, Karen, and Kara J. Malenfant. *Academic Library Impact on Student Learning Success: Findings from Assessment in Action Team Projects*. Chicago: Association of College and Research Libraries, 2017.

Emmons, Mark, and Frances C. Wilkinson. "The Academic Library Impact on Student Persistence." *College and Research Libraries* 72, no. 2 (March 2011): 128–49.

Gaha, Ula, Suzanne Hinnefeld, and Catherine Pellegrino. "The Academic Library's Contribution to Student Success: Library Instruction and GPA." *College and Research Libraries* 79, no. 6 (September 2018): 737–46.

Gay, Lorraine R., Geoffrey E. Mills, and Peter W. Airasian. *Educational Research Competencies for Analysis and Application*, 10th ed. Boston: Pearson Education, 2012.

Glen, Stephanie. "Multicollinearity: Definition, Causes, Examples." Statistics How To: Statistics for the Rest of Us! (website). Last updated September 22, 2015. https://www.statisticshowto.com/multicollinearity/.

———. "Probability and Statistics Topic Index." In Statistics How To: Statistics for the Rest of Us! (website), 2020. https://www.statisticshowto.com/probability-and-statistics/.

———. "Stepwise Regression." Statistics How To: Statistics for the Rest of Us! (website). Last updated September 24, 2015. https://www.statisticshowto.com/stepwise-regression/.

Goek, Sara. "Project Outcome for Academic Libraries: Interactive Workshop." Presentation, New Mexico Library Association/Mountain Plains Library Association Annual Conference, Albuquerque, NM, October 30, 2019.

———. "Project Outcome for Academic Libraries: An Introductory Workshop." Presentation, OLA 2020: Virtual Oklahoma Library Association Annual Conference, July 29, 2020.

Goek, Sara, and Emily Plagman. *Outcome Measurement in Libraries: The Project Outcome Model*. Urbana, IL: University of Illinois and Indiana University, National Institute for Learning Outcomes Assessment, June 2020.

Gravetter, Frederick J., and Larry B. Wallnau. *Statistics for the Behavioral Sciences*, 9th ed. Belmont, CA: Thompson Wadsworth, 2013.

Hodgkin, James. "The Library in a Big Bad World: Opening Keynote." Keynote address, OCLC WorldShare Management Services Global Community and User Group Meeting, Columbus, OH, October 16, 2019.

Holzmann, Robert. "Library Services Assessment: Electronic Resources Impact on Student Success by Configuring, Harvesting, and Preparing Hard Data from Proxy Logs as Input for Statistical Analysis." Presentation, Electronic Resources and Libraries: 2020 Conference, Austin, TX, March 9, 2020.

———. "Strategic Planning and Assessment: Academic Library Assessment Planning." *Arkansas Libraries* 77, no. 1–2 (Spring/Summer 2020): 39–42.

Levine, David M., and David F. Stephan. *Even You Can Learn Statistics*. Upper Saddle River, NJ: Pearson Education, 2005.

Library Services and Programs Assessment Plan Workgroup. *Application for IRB Review for Unfunded Research Tulsa Community College Institutional Review Board*. Tulsa, OK: Tulsa Community College, 2017.

Lund Research Ltd. "How to Structure Quantitative Research Questions." *Laerd Dissertation* (online textbook), 2012. https://dissertation.laerd.com/how-to-structure-quantitative-research-questions-p2.php.

Luo, Lili. "Evidence Based Practice—Ideas for Academic Librarians." Keynote address, Oklahoma Association of Research Libraries Annual Conference, Edmond, OK, November 9, 2018.

———. "Experiencing Evidence-Based Library and Information Practice (EBLIP): Academic Librarians' Perspective." *College and Research Libraries* 79, no. 4 (May 2018): 554–67.

Luo, Lili, Kristine R. Brancolini, and Marie R. Kennedy. *Enhancing Library and Information Research Skills: A Guide for Academic Librarians*. Santa Barbara, CA: Libraries Unlimited, 2017.

Maase, Simone, and Robert van den Hoed. "EV Charging Data Management: Five Issues to Solve." Presentation, International Electric Vehicle Symposium 32, Lyon, France, May 2019.

Massengale, Lisa, Pattie Piotrowski, and Devin Savage. "Identifying and Articulating Library Connections to Student Success." *College and Research Libraries* 77, no. 2 (March 2016): 227–35.

Matthews, Joseph R. "Assessing Library Contributions to University Outcomes: The Need for Individual Student Level Data." *Library Management* 33, no. 6/7 (2012): 389–402.

McGraw-Hill Dictionary of Scientific and Technical Terms, 6th ed. New York: McGraw Hill, 2003.

Mikitish, Steph. "Inching Along: Making Measured Progress over Common Assessment Obstacles." Keynote address, Oklahoma Association of Research Libraries Annual Conference, Edmond, OK, November 9, 2018.

Nackerud, Shane, Jan Fransen, Kate Peterson, and Kristen Mastel. "Analyzing Demographics: Assessing Library Use across the Institution." *portal: Libraries and the Academy* 13, no. 2 (2013): 131–45.

Oakleaf, Megan. *Library Integration in Institutional Learning Analytics*. Research report. Syracuse, NY: Syracuse University, November 15, 2018.

———. *The Value of Academic Libraries: A Comprehensive Research Review and Report*. Chicago: Association of College and Research Libraries, 2010.

Oakleaf, Megan, Scott Walter, Malcolm Brown, Dean Hendrix, and Joe Lucia. "What Could We Do, If Only We Knew? Libraries, Learning Analytics, and Student Success." Presentation, Library Assessment Conference, Houston, TX, December 7, 2018.

Objectivity. "Hard Data vs. Soft Data." June 3, 2015. https://www.objectivity.com/hard-data-vs-soft-data/.

Ridzuan, Fakhitah, and Wan Mohd Nazmee Wan Zainon. "A Review on Data Cleansing Methods for Big Data." In "The Fifth Information Systems International Conference, 23–24 July 2019, Surabaya, Indonesia," edited by Arjumand Younus, special issue, *Procedia Computer Science* 161 (2019): 731–38. https://doi.org/10.1016/j.procs.2019.11.177.

Rogers, Alisdair, Noel Castree, and Rob Kitchin. "Stepwise Regression." In *A Dictionary of Human Geography*. Oxford: Oxford University Press, 2013. Oxford Reference.

Smith, Gary. "Step away from Stepwise." *Journal of Big Data* 5, no. 32 (2018). https://doi.org/10.1186/s40537-018-0143-6.

Soria, Krista M. "Factors Predicting the Importance of Libraries and Research Activities for Undergraduates." *Journal of Academic Librarianship* 39, no. 6 (November 2013): 464–70.

Soria, Krista M., Jan Fransen, and Shane Nackerud. "Beyond Books: The Extended Academic Benefits of Library Use for First-Year College Students." *College and Research Libraries* 78, no. 1 (January 2017): 8–22.

———. "The Impact of Academic Library Resources on Undergraduates' Degree Completion." *College and Research Libraries* 78, no. 6 (September 2017): 812–23.

———. "Library Use and Undergraduate Student Outcomes: New Evidence for Students' Retention and Academic Success." *portal: Libraries and the Academy* 13, no. 2 (April 2013): 147–64.

———. "Stacks, Serials, Search Engines, and Students' Success: First-Year Undergraduate Students' Library Use, Academic Achievement, and Retention." *Journal of Academic Librarianship* 40, no. 1 (January 2014): 84–91.

Soria, Krista M., Shane Nackerud, and Kate Peterson. "Socioeconomic Indicators Associated with First-Year College Students' Use of Academic Libraries." *Journal of Academic Librarianship* 41, no. 5 (September 2015): 636–43.

Soria, Krista M., Kate Peterson, Jan Fransen, and Shane Nackerud. "The Impact of Academic Library Resources on First-Year Students' Learning Outcomes." *Research Library Issues*, no. 290 (January 2017): 5–20. https://doi.org/10.29242/rli.290.2.

Strategic DB Corporation. "What Is Data Cleaning?" *Strategic DB Blog*, October 30, 2020. https://strategicdb.com/2020/10/30/what-is-data-cleaning-2/.

———. "What Is Data Normalization?" *Strategic DB Blog*, July 3, 2016. https://strategicdb.com/2016/07/03/what-is-data-normalization/.

Thibodeau, Patricia L., and Steven J. Melamut. "The Role of the Academic Library in Academic Accreditation." In *Reviewing the Academic Library: A Guide to Self-Study and External Review*. Edited by Eleanor Mitchell and Peggy Seiden, 61–84. Chicago: Association of College and Research Libraries, 2015.

Tulsa Community College Library. *Library Services and Programs Assessment Plan*. Tulsa, OK: Tulsa Community College Library, August 2018.

Upton, Graham, and Ian Cook. "ANOVA (Analysis of Variance)." In *A Dictionary of Statistics*. Oxford: Oxford University Press, 2014. Oxford Reference.

———. "Multiple Regression Model." In *A Dictionary of Statistics*. Oxford: Oxford University Press, 2014. Oxford Reference.

Weaver, Kayleigh. "What Is Impact and How Do We Measure It?" Clear Impact, 2016. https://clearimpact.com/how-to-define-impact.

Yale University Department of Statistics and Data Science. "ANOVA for Regression." In Statistical Topics (website), Yale University, 1997. http://www.stat.yale.edu/Courses/1997-98/101/anovareg.htm.

———. "Correlation." In Statistical Topics (website), Yale University, 1997. http://www.stat.yale.edu/Courses/1997-98/101/correl.htm.

———. "Multiple Linear Regression." In Statistical Topics (website), Yale University, 1997. http://www.stat.yale.edu/Courses/1997-98/101/linmult.htm.

———. Statistical Topics (website), Yale University, 2017. http://www.stat.yale.edu/Courses/1997-98/101/toplist.htm.

CHAPTER 6

Investigating and Communicating Library Instruction's Relationship to Student Retention

A Study of Two Community Colleges

Angela L. Creel, Wendy Hoag, and Kendra Perry

Introduction

Student retention is critical to all institutions of higher education including community colleges. Not only does it affect success from a humanitarian viewpoint, but it can also affect state funding and accreditation. The library has long been known as the hub or heart of the campus; however, due to increasingly tight budgets, cost reduction efforts across the country, and misconceptions regarding the abundance and cost of online resources, the intrinsic value of the library is called into question. Linking student success and retention rates, at least in part, to library instruction (LI) demonstrates relevance and importance of the library and encourages administrative and faculty support.

Previous research using ACRL/IPEDS survey data and student tracking technology has suggested a relationship between LI and student retention at community colleges.[1] Building on O'Kelly's methodology for collaborating with institutional research offices to investigate this relationship based on course enrollment, both Arizona Western College and Hagerstown Community College conducted retrospective cohort studies that showed higher semester-to-semester and year-to-year retention rates for students enrolled in sections of classes that included classroom LI.[2] Because all students in a specific section of the course are required to attend the instruction session, this methodology excludes the "motivation factor" that O'Kelly spoke of in her 2016 presentation for the Carterette Series Webinar. The "motivation factor" suggests that more highly motivated students seek out library resources and are also more motivated to persist in school.[3]

The authors present suggestions for using such assessment data in library strategic planning as well as communicating the value of the library to administrators and other members of the campus community.

Literature Review

A review of the literature shows that a variety of studies have investigated relationships between student persistence and library services in an attempt to demonstrate the relevance of the library and library staff. While the results of such studies show a correlation between student persistence and the budget for library staffing and collections, they often have difficulty demonstrating a significant linkage between LI and student retention. As scholarly communication continues to explore this issue over time, the narrative moves closer to that goal.

In a 2007 study of retention rates and library data, Mezick demonstrated a relationship between student retention and library budgets and found results suggesting that the number of professional library staff also played a role in retention.[4] Emmons and Wilkinson, using data from IPEDS and ARL, demonstrated that correlation in 2011 and went on to find a positive relationship between professional library staff and graduation rates.[5] LI, however, was found to have a slight but not significant association.[6] While the findings were positive, the authors were unable to answer what action librarians took that led to student success.[7] Vance, Kirk, and Gardner's 2012 study of Middle Tennessee State University freshmen and instruction similarly found that LI had little relationship to retention but found that it did have a significant correlation with student GPAs.[8] In a study of Southern Regional Education Board colleges, Teske, DiCarlo, and Cahoy's findings agreed with those of Emmons and Wilkinson in regard to the correlation of LI on retention, finding no statistically significant relation between the two.[9]

First-year, first-time students at the University of Minnesota were the focus of Soria, Fransen, and Nackerud's study to see if students who used the library had higher retention rates and GPAs than students who did not.[10] Those who used library resources showed higher GPAs and retention rates than those students who did not.[11] In regard to LI, there were higher retention rates and GPAs for students who attended an Intro to Library Research Part 2 workshop.[12]

Crawford's study of retention and graduation rates using 2010 college and university data from IPEDS and the Academic Libraries Survey from the National Center for Education Statistics found that the variable "library use per FTE" did have a positive relationship with retention and graduation rates, although not as much as expected.[13] The variable "library expenses per FTE" in comparison, had a greater relationship with those rates, with those institutions investing more money in the library showing higher retention rates.[14] The value of library acquisitions for student success is illustrated in a study by Catalano and Phillips that did not find a significant correlation between LI and student success, but did find that there was a positive relationship correlating student use of books and other library resources with retention and graduation.[15]

Eng and Stadler built upon Mezick's 2007 methodology to see if they would obtain similar results, while expanding the research to look at associate-level institutions and also looking into the role that instruction might have on retention.[16] The positive results regarding retention and library expenditures at bachelor institutions, using more recent data from 2010 and 2011, was similar to the 2007 study, while the results from graduate institutions showed a weak relationship on retention, and doctoral institutions had a negative relationship.[17] In contrast, however, Eng and Stadler found that there was no relationship between total library expenditures and retention at associate-level institutions, though professional salaries and staff FTEs did have a slightly positive relationship with retention.[18] They also found that LI had a slight positive relationship with student retention, with the number of presentation participants showing a slightly higher positive relationship.[19]

In conference proceedings from 2017, Mary O'Kelly reported on a multi-year study conducted at Grand Valley State University (GVSU) that began in 2012 and found that LI did have a significantly positive correlation with retention.[20] Factoring out the student motivation in seeking out library services, the study gathered course-level information from faculty-requested, librarian-led instruction sessions.[21] While the results from the analysis were significant, O'Kelly was unable to demonstrate the causation.[22] Exploring this relationship further, O'Kelly found that faculty who invited LI into at least one course showed significantly higher student retention rates than those faculty who did not invite LI.[23] Students in that more highly retained group may or may not have received LI; however, O'Kelly hypothesized that faculty who had incorporated LI may also promote library resources in classes where they did not invite LI.[24] O'Kelly posits the importance of the relationships between the library, faculty, and other student support services in student success.[25]

In another multi-year study, Hargis, Rowe, and Leuzinger analyzed four years of data from freshman English courses and found relationships between LI and student success.[26] The study found positive relationships between LI and pass/fail rates, GPAs, and retention.[27] Also, first-generation students who attended LI were found to have higher GPAs than those who did not.[28]

Dennis Krieb found a significant positive relationship between reference, LI, and student retention in his study at Lewis and Clark Community College.[29] Students who visited the reference desk or an instruction session were tracked, with permission, by their student identification number.[30] Krieb found that retention rates for both reference and instruction were significant, with reference showing a greater significance, which he attributed to one-on-one interactions between students and librarians.[31]

Drawing on inspiration from the existing literature and O'Kelly's research, Arizona Western College and Hagerstown Community College began their process to obtain data to explore the possibility of a positive correlation between student retention and LI. Similarities exist between these two institutions, such as serving areas with similar population sizes, areas that have high poverty rates, and higher-than-average veteran populations. Students of both institutions have high rates of students under twenty-five who attend college part time.

Institutional Background
Hagerstown Community College (HCC)

Founded in 1946, Hagerstown Community College (HCC) was Maryland's first community college. More than 100 programs of study are currently available for university transfer, career preparation, or personal development, as well as non-credit continuing education courses, customized training programs, and the county's adult education program.

HCC is located in Washington County in western Maryland, between the nearby borders of West Virginia and Pennsylvania, and serves students from all three states. Although there are only about 40,000 residents in Hagerstown proper, the Hagerstown, Maryland–Martinsburg, West Virginia metropolitan statistical area (MSA) contains a population of over 265,000.[32] It is the fifth-largest of six MSAs in Maryland. The primary industries in this area are retail, health care and social assistance, and manufacturing.[33] At 11.5 percent, the poverty rate in this MSA is high compared to the rest of Maryland (9 percent), though a bit lower than the national average of 13.1 percent. The veteran population is higher than the rest of Maryland and the national average, but the rate of foreign-born residents is considerably lower. Although 88.2 percent of the population has a high school diploma, only 21.4 percent has a bachelor's degree or higher.

HCC serves more than 5,000 credit students and 7,000 non-credit students each year. More than 800 area high school students are enrolled in the ESSENCE Early College Program and STEMM Technical Middle College.[34] The majority of HCC students are age twenty-five or younger and attend part time. Females represent 62 percent of the students. Minority students represent approximately 25 percent of the students. The majority of HCC students are Washington County residents, but approximately 21 percent live in Pennsylvania or West Virginia.

Arizona Western College (AWC)

Arizona Western College (AWC) is a public community college that was established in 1963 in Yuma, Arizona. The college offers "over 100 degrees and certificates in a wide range of academic and career technical programs, as well as non-credit courses in professional development, customized training, and personal enrichment areas."[35] The college serves a two-county area, Yuma and La Paz counties, over 10,000 square miles of territory. While the majority of students are located on the Yuma campus, the college has twelve campus locations positioned around the two-county area. AWC hosts all three state universities on the Yuma campus, where they provide face-to-face instruction on campus, an arrangement that lends itself to easy transfer from the community college to the university level for continued study. The college offers associate degrees, including courses that qualify for transfer to universities, occupational certificates, workforce development training, and personal development courses.

Yuma is located in the southwestern corner of Arizona and is considered to be the smallest of three MSAs in Arizona, with an estimated population of 213,787 as of 2019.[36] The primary industries are agriculture, military installations, and tourism, which leads to a transitory population. Also contributing to that factor is the population increase in the winter months due to the extensive winter visitor population. Yuma also has a large veteran population. Yuma is located twenty miles from the Mexican border state of Sonora and is a hub for several smaller towns in the area. Parker, located in La Paz County, has the largest AWC facility and is the epicenter of AWC students in that county. Seventy-two percent of the population have a high school diploma, but only 14.8 percent have a bachelor's degree or higher.[37] Furthermore, in 2018, the median income rate was $44, 058 with a poverty rate of 19.5 percent.[38]

AWC is classified as a Hispanic-Serving Institution (HSI) and serves both traditional and non-traditional students. Most students are female, between the ages of eighteen and twenty-five, attend college part-time, are degree-seeking, and are classified as first-generation college students. AWC also offers a successful dual-enrollment program for area high schoolers that has realized an increase of 274 percent in enrollment by students eighteen and under in the past four years.[39] Official data reports that the total enrollment is 7,434 students, equaling 4,143 as the FTSE (full-time student equivalent) for fall 2018.[40]

Methods

Our statistical assessment methodologies from this point on are based on a study model called retrospective cohort studies. In a retrospective cohort study, a group is evaluated based on past events of "exposure and outcome."[41] This methodology is used in epidemiology, where exposure to a disease and the outcome are examined. Both cohorts are identical except for the exposure. We chose to use this way of calculating the relationships of students who did and did not receive LI and their rate of retention because our study is observational rather than experimental; in other words, we observed what happened after students were exposed to the two different conditions (LI vs. non-LI) rather than randomly assigning them to one of the treatments.[42]

We did not assess risk factors for students in our retrospective cohort study. Future studies might include identifying possible risk factors to refine our current results. However, all groups were identical in their designation as students at a particular institution and were presumably a representative sample of students enrolled in classes that sometimes receive LI. Our study looks at their encounter with and participation in (or exposure to) LI. The measured outcome is the retention status as of the following semester and then the following year.

The primary biases that can occur in medical or epidemiological retrospective cohort studies are selection bias, information bias, and confusion bias.[43] We do not believe that our study includes any selection or information biases, but confounding variables could lead to confusion bias as we have not controlled for different characteristics of instructors or students. Again, further data gathered about the types of students studied, with variables accounted for, may lead to more definitive answers and more useful reflection on current practices.

Our journey with this project began in September 2016, when AWC librarians attended a Carterette Series Webinar, "Getting Started with Assessing Student Retention," presented by Mary O'Kelly, currently the associate dean for education and user services in the University Libraries at Western Michigan University.[44] This webinar spurred a conversation about demonstrating library value through assessment of LI and its correlation with student retention.

In early 2017, the AWC Academic Library submitted a research request to the college's Institutional Effectiveness, Research, and Grant department (IERG) to analyze retention data from fall 2014 to spring 2017. The research request asked to measure the impact that LI had on student retention by comparing the percentage of students who participated in LI and were retained the following semester and the following academic year with the percentage of students who did not participate in LI.

The AWC library provided the IERG with LI data for the academic years of 2014–2015, 2015–2016, 2016–2017, 2017–2018, and 2018–2019. Data included name of class, professor name, section number, and date of instruction. AWC data analyzed in this chapter includes all years of the study from fall 2014 to spring 2019.

IERG provided retention data on the students who were enrolled in at least one course section with LI, then compared and analyzed that data with students who were enrolled in at least one course but received no LI. They reported students who were enrolled in any course section in the subsequent spring term (term-to-term data) as retained, and students who enrolled in any course section in subsequent fall term (year-to-year data) as retained. Retention was defined as the student enrolling in any course for either of the two different time frames. The number of students was unduplicated within each term but may have been duplicated across terms and years, and students enrolled in more than one course were counted only once in a given term.

AWC librarian Christina Sibley subsequently answered a query via a library e-mail discussion list regarding LI and its relationship to retention and shared AWC's findings with Kendra Perry, librarian at Hagerstown Community College. The partnership between AWC and HCC began as we discussed findings from our data collection and analysis.

For HCC's initial analysis, the library provided the Planning and Institutional Effectiveness (PIE) office with LI data for the years of 2016–2017 and 2017–2018. Data included instructor name; course and section number; and date, time, and location of LI.

PIE provided and analyzed enrollment data for the given terms to be assessed. Students who were enrolled in at least one course section that received in-class LI were included in the Library Instruction group. Retention was measured from both semester to semester and year to year; however, summer semester was excluded in both cases. Students who enrolled in any course section in the subsequent indicated term were considered retained. For additional comparison, students enrolled in at least one similar course to those that attended a LI session but did *not* participate in LI (non-LI) were included in the Similar Course group. For example, students in sections of English 101 that did not include LI were compared to students in sections of English 101 that did include it. For other courses with lower enrollment or where all sections received LI, similar courses in the same discipline were compared: for example, Sociology 101 (Introduction to Sociology) might be compared to Sociology 102 (Sociology of Social Problems). Courses typically receiving no LI were excluded from the study altogether. The number of students was unduplicated within the given term but might be duplicated across terms.

For the first study, all students were analyzed; however, this did not adequately take into account students who might not return due to graduation or transfer to another institution. As a result, a second study was completed to refine the definition of retention. First, students who successfully completed a certificate or associate's degree between the first and subsequent measured terms were excluded. Second, students who transferred to another institution between the two terms were also excluded. The remaining students, defined as Eligible Students, were analyzed for retention following the same procedures as the first study. As before, the number of eligible students was unduplicated within the given term but might be duplicated across terms.

During our initial conversations between the two institutions, we found that HCC's PIE office had removed the graduates and transfer students from the retention data whereas AWC's data analysis had counted these students as retained. Although either methodology could be followed, it seemed best to follow the same approach for this project at both institutions in the interest of consistency and accurate comparisons. AWC's IERG department was able to replicate HCC's data analysis while also providing raw data for two additional years.

In addition, IERG added analysis of similar courses and removed course data from those that do not typically utilize LI. For our final results, presented in this chapter, both HCC and AWC used the same definition for Similar Courses and for Eligible Students. Based on that data, information was provided that addressed the retention rates of those courses.

Our initial analyses at both institutions simply compared the percentage of students receiving course-based LI to students in similar courses who did not receive LI. In an effort to determine whether or not the differences we noted in percentages were statistically significant, we went on to perform a chi-square test of independence on the data from each institution as well as our combined data. The chi-square test of independence tests the relationship between two variables to determine whether or not a relationship actually exists between them.[45] In this case, we wanted to know whether retention rates are significantly different for students who receive library instruction compared to those who do not. Our null hypothesis (H_0) was that LI and retention are independent or unrelated. Our research hypothesis (H_1) was that there *is* a relationship between LI and retention at the conventional significance level of .05 or less.

Because there is only one row and one column in our data summary table, the degrees of freedom equal 1, and the positive critical value at .05 significance is 3.841.[46] In other words, if the chi-square test result is greater than 3.84, the null hypothesis is rejected, showing an association between the two variables. The higher the number, the stronger the relationship.

As an additional measure to ascertain the effect of LI, we conducted an odds ratio test on the data. This test assumes a relationship between the two variables and provides information on how strong that relationship is.[47] Commonly used in medical studies, this test examines the odds of one outcome over another when a specific treatment is provided. In our case, the treatment is LI, and the outcome is being retained in the following semester or year. The research question can be stated as: What are the odds of students being retained with LI as opposed to without it? An odds ratio of 1 would indicate that the odds are equal for students to be retained regardless of their exposure to LI. A number higher than 1 indicates that the odds of being retained are higher with LI. A number lower than 1 would suggest that LI reduces the odds of being retained. As with the chi-square test, we looked for a significance level of .05 or less.

The odds ratio must also be interpreted in light of the confidence interval (CI). We selected the 95 percent CI for our study.

> [A] 95% confidence interval means that if the same population were sampled on numerous occasions and confidence interval estimates were made on each occasion, the resulting intervals would contain the true population parameter in approximately 95% of the cases, assuming that there were no biases or confounding. However, people generally apply this probability to a single study. Consequently, an odds ratio of 5.2 with a confidence interval of 3.2 to 7.2 suggests that there is a 95% probability that the true odds ratio would be likely to lie in the range 3.2–7.2 **assuming there is no bias or confounding** [emphasis in original].[48]

Finally, we conducted a relative probability test (also known as the risk ratio or relative risk) to ascertain the comparative probability that students would be retained when their class included in-class LI as opposed to not including it. While the odds ratio tells us whether the probability of a given outcome is higher or lower, it cannot tell us by how much. The relative probability helps to quantify how large the difference is.[49] Commonly referred to in medical studies as the risk ratio, the relative probability examines the probability of a given outcome based on exposure to something.[50] For example, the risk (or probability) of an outcome of developing lung cancer is higher among those who are exposed to secondhand smoke. In most medical studies, the outcome under investigation is negative, such as development of a disease, and so the ratio is commonly referred to as the risk ratio. Since the outcome in our study is positive (retention in the following term or year), we are referring to this as the relative probability, but it may be important for the reader to be aware that this term is synonymous with risk ratio or relative risk.

In our study, the exposure is LI, and the outcome is being retained in the following semester or year. The research question can be stated as: What is the probability of students being retained with LI as opposed to without it? A relative probability of 1 would indicate that it is equally probable for students to be retained, regardless of their exposure to LI. A number higher than 1 indicates that the probability of being retained increases by a specific amount with exposure to LI (for example, a relative probability of 1.2 indicates that a given outcome is 20 percent more probable). A number lower than 1 indicates that the probability of being retained is decreased by a specific amount (for example, a relative probability of 0.8 would indicate a decreased probability of 20 percent). Again, we looked for a significance level of .05 or less and a CI of 95 percent.

Both institutions analyzed their data independently. AWC's data included a longer time span than HCC's as well as a larger number of overall students due to institution size. In addition, we completed a combined analysis for all semesters in which we both had data.

Statistical analysis was performed in R version 4.02, "Taking Off Again," using RStudio version 1.3.1093, "Apricot Nasturtium" for Windows, as well as the package fmsb (Functions for Medical Statistics Book with some Demographic Data) version 0.7.0.[51]

Results

Hagerstown Community College (HCC)

The second HCC study, presented here, excluded graduates and transfer students from the calculation altogether and examined only students in similar courses. In similar courses during the same term, retention rates of students who did receive LI tend to be slightly higher the subsequent term (fall-to-spring and spring-to-fall) than those students who did not, with a difference in percentage points ranging from 4.9 to 15.1. That trend appears to diminish slightly as retention rates are calculated a full year later (fall to fall and spring to spring); three semesters demonstrate a difference of 3.3 to 14.3 percentage points. In fall 2016, the year-to-year retention rate for those with and without LI was roughly equivalent with a very slightly higher rate of retention among those who did *not* receive LI. Other than this semester, there is some evidence of a slightly higher retention rate for LI students (see table 6.1).

Table 6.1

Hagerstown Community College retention of students with library instruction versus students without library instruction

Term	Group	Eligible Students	Retained Subsequent Term[a]			Eligible Students	Retained Subsequent Year		
			#	%	*DIFF LI vs. No LI*		#	%	*DIFF LI vs. No LI*
Fall 2016	Library Instruction	488	408	83.6%	*8.7%*	366	239	65.3%	*−0.2%*
	No Library Instruction[b]	*744*	*557*	*74.9%*		*589*	*386*	*65.5%*	
Spring 2017	Library Instruction	247	191	77.3%	*4.9%*	220	150	68.2%	*4.1%*
	No Library Instruction[b]	*563*	*408*	*72.5%*		*524*	*336*	*64.1%*	
Fall 2017	Library Instruction	387	342	88.4%	*11.0%*	287	202	70.4%	*3.3%*
	No Library Instruction[b]	*790*	*611*	*77.3%*		*647*	*434*	*67.1%*	
Spring 2018	Library Instruction	267	227	85.0%	*15.1%*	219	167	76.3%	*14.3%*
	No Library Instruction[b]	*644*	*450*	*69.9%*		*620*	*384*	*61.9%*	
a.	Summer semester excluded								
b.	Only similar courses included								

An average of the included semesters reveals an overall percent difference of 9.92 percentage points for similar classes from semester to semester with higher retention among the LI group (see figure 6.1).

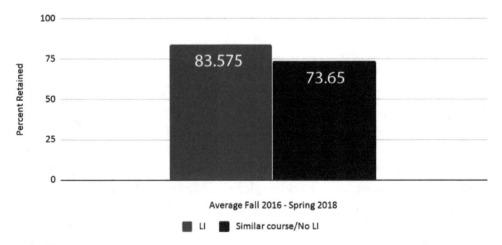

Figure 6.1

Semester-to-semester average retention—graduates and transfers excluded, Hagerstown Community College

The year-to-year average comparison, on the other hand, reveals a difference of only 5.4 percentage points between the LI and non-LI groups in similar courses (see figure 6.2).

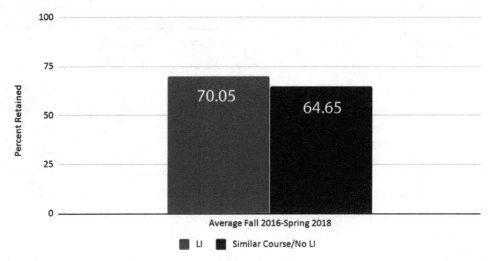

Figure 6.2

Year-to-year retention—graduates and transfers excluded, Hagerstown Community College

A chi-square test of independence of term-to-term retention for each semester produced a result higher than the critical value with a significance (p-value) of less than .001 for all semesters except spring 2017. The chi-square value for spring 2017 did not reach the critical value of 3.84, nor did the p-value for significance fall within the predetermined range of less than .05. This excludes the null hypothesis for most semesters and indicates that, in general, a relationship exists between LI and term-to-term retention (see table 6.2).

Table 6.2

Hagerstown Community College semester-to-semester retention chi-square analysis

Retained Following Term[a]	Received Library Instruction				
	LI Yes	*LI No*	*chi-square*	*degrees of freedom*	*p-value*
Fall 2016					
Ret Yes	408	557	12.754	1	< .001
Ret No	80	187			
Total (*N=*)	1,232				
Spring 2017					
Ret Yes	191	408	1.860	1	0.173
Ret No	56	155			
Total (*N=*)	810				

Table 6.2

Hagerstown Community College semester-to-semester retention chi-square analysis

Retained Following Term[a]	Received Library Instruction				
	LI Yes	*LI No*	*chi-square*	*degrees of freedom*	*p-value*
Fall 2017					
Ret Yes	342	611	19.800	1	< .001
Ret No	45	179			
Total (*N=*)	1,177				
Spring 2018					
Ret Yes	227	450	21.888	1	< .001
Ret No	40	194			
Total (*N=*)	911				
a. Summers excluded					

A chi-square test of independence for all 4,130 students across the studied semesters produced a result of 53.87 with a significance of less than .001, again rejecting the null hypothesis and suggesting that there is a relationship between LI and term-to-term retention at HCC (see table 6.3).

Table 6.3

Hagerstown Community College composite semester-to-semester retention chi-square analysis

Retained Following Term[a]	Received Library Instruction				
	LI Yes	*LI No*	*chi-square*	*degrees of freedom*	*p-value*
Fall 2016 to Spring 2018					
Ret Yes	1,168	221	53.87	1	< .001
Ret No	2,026	715			
Total (*N=*)	4,130				
a. Summers excluded					

A chi-square analysis of year-to-year retention at HCC revealed only one semester with a statistically significant difference: spring 2018. This semester produced a chi-square result of 14.093 with a significance (p-value) of less than .001 (see table 6.4). Since only one semester was found to have a statistically significant result, we did not do a composite calculation. This result fails to exclude the null hypothesis in most cases and therefore suggests that there is no relationship between LI and year-to-year retention for these semesters at HCC; however, it would be interesting to evaluate whether this result would be different if graduates and successful transfer students were counted as retained instead of excluded from the study.

Table 6.4
Hagerstown Community College year-to-year retention chi-square analysis

Retained Following Year	Received Library Instruction				
	LI Yes	*LI No*	*chi-square*	*degrees of freedom*	*p-value*
Fall 2016					
Ret Yes	239	386	0.000	1	1.000
Ret No	127	203			
Total (*N=*)	955				
Spring 2017					
Ret Yes	150	336	0.955	1	0.330
Ret No	70	188			
Total (*N=*)	744				
Fall 2017					
Ret Yes	202	434	0.853	1	0.360
Ret No	85	213			
Total (*N=*)	934				
Spring 2018					
Ret Yes	167	384	14.093	1	< .001
Ret No	52	236			
Total (*N=*)	839				

An odds ratio test on the semester-to-semester data with statistically significant chi-square results revealed odds ratios ranging from 1.71 to 2.45 and 95 percent CIs ranging from 1.27 to 3.56 (see table 6.5). All of these ratios had a significance level (p-value) of less than .001. This indicates that the odds of being retained were, in fact, higher for students in the LI sections during these semesters at HCC.

Table 6.5
Hagerstown Community College semester-to-semester retention odds ratio test

Retained Following Term[a]	Received Library Instruction		(95% CI)			
	LI Yes	*LI No*	*Odds Ratio*	*Low*	*High*	*p-value*
Fall 2016						
Ret Yes	408	557	1.712208	1.279481	2.291	< .001
Ret No	80	187				
Total (*N=*)	1,232					

Table 6.5

Hagerstown Community College semester-to-semester retention odds ratio test

	Received Library Instruction		(95% CI)			
Retained Following Term[a]	LI Yes	LI No	Odds Ratio	Low	High	p-value
Fall 2017						
Ret Yes	342	611	2.227	1.564881	3.168	< .001
Ret No	45	179				
Total (N=)	1,177					
Spring 2018						
Ret Yes	227	450	2.446556	1.679987	3.563	< .001
Ret No	40	194				
Total (N=)	911					
a. Summers excluded						

A composite odds ratio for these three semesters resulted in an overall odds ratio of 2.05, with the 95 percent CI ranging from 1.69 to 2.48 and a p-value (significance) of less than .001 (see table 6.6). This again supports the analysis that the odds of being retained at HCC in the following term are higher for students in course sections receiving LI.

Table 6.6

Hagerstown Community College Composite semester-to-semester retention odds ratio test

	Received Library Instruction		(95% CI)			
Retained Following Term[a]	LI Yes	LI No	Odds Ratio	Low	High	p-value
Fall 2016, Fall 2017, Spring 2018						
Ret Yes	977	1,618	2.05	1.693199	2.480	< .001
Ret No	165	560				
Total (N=)	3,320					
a. Summers excluded						

We also performed an odds ratio test on spring 2018, the single semester with statistically significant chi-square results in year-to-year retention. This resulted in an odds ratio of 1.97, with 95 percent CIs ranging from 1.39 to 2.80 and a statistical significance (p-value of less than .001; see table 6.7). Thus, in this semester, the odds of being retained in the following semester were higher for students who received LI; however, since only one semester demonstrated a statistically significant chi-square result, this result is less likely to be generalizable.

Table 6.7
Hagerstown Community College year-to-year retention odds ratio test

	Received Library Instruction		(95% CI)			
Retained Following Year	LI Yes	LI No	Odds Ratio	Low	High	p-value
Spring 2018						
Ret Yes	167	384	1.973758	1.389578	2.804	< .001
Ret No	52	236				
Total (N=)	839					

Finally, in order to determine the effect size, we calculated the relative probability of semester-to-semester retention with and without LI for those semesters with statistically significant chi-square results: fall 2016, fall 2017, and spring 2018. The relative probability ratios varied from 1.12 to 1.22, and the 95 percent CIs ranged from 1.05 to 1.31. All results had a statistical significance (p-value) of less than .001 (see table 6.8). This indicates that, in most semesters analyzed, students who received LI were anywhere from 5 percent to 31 percent more likely to be retained the following semester than students in similar courses who did not receive LI.

Table 6.8
Hagerstown Community College semester-to-semester relative probability test

	Received Library Instruction		(95% CI)			
Retained Following Term[a]	LI Yes	LI No	Relative Probability	Low	High	p-value
Fall 2016						
Ret Yes	408	557	1.116755	1.054623	1.183	< .001
Ret No	80	187				
Total (N=)	1,232					
Fall 2017						
Ret Yes	342	611	1.143	1.084443	1.204	< .001
Ret No	45	179				
Total (N=)	1,177					

Table 6.8

Hagerstown Community College semester-to-semester relative probability test

Retained Following Term[a]	Received Library Instruction		(95% CI)			
	LI Yes	LI No	Relative Probability	Low	High	p-value
Spring 2018						
Ret Yes	227	450	1.216712	1.132798	1.307	< .001
Ret No	40	194				
Total (N=)	911					
a. Summers excluded						

A composite relative probability test for these semesters resulted in a relative probability ratio of 1.15 overall, with the 95 percent CI ranging from 1.11 to 1.19, suggesting improved retention rates of 11 percent to 19 percent overall (see table 6.9).

Table 6.9

Hagerstown Community College composite semester-to-semester retention relative probability test

Retained Following Term[a]	Received Library Instruction		(95% CI)			
	LI Yes	LI No	Relative Probability	Low	High	p-value
Fall 2016, Fall 2017, Spring 2018						
Ret Yes	977	1,618	1.151616	1.112752	1.192	< .001
Ret No	165	560				
Total (N=)	3,320					
a. Summers excluded						

The relative probability for year-to-year retention was calculated for spring 2018, the one semester with a statistically significant chi-square result. The relative probability ratio was 1.23, with the 95 percent confidence interval ranging from 1.12 to 1.36 (see table 6.10). These results suggest that, for this semester, students who received LI were 12 percent to 36 percent more likely to be retained at HCC than those in similar courses who did not. Again, due to the limited number of semesters that had statistical significance, this result may not be generalizable.

Table 6.10

Hagerstown Community College year-to-year retention relative probability test

	Received Library Instruction		(95% CI)			
Retained Following Year	*LI Yes*	*LI No*	*Relative Probability Ratio*	*Low*	*High*	*p-value*
Spring 2018						
Ret Yes	167	384	1.231212	1.118199	1.356	< .001
Ret No	52	236				
Total (*N=*)	839					

Arizona Western College (AWC)

AWC's initial analysis saw increased retention rates for the students who received LI when compared to students in similar courses who did not receive LI. While HCC data results showed higher LI-associated retention rates between terms, AWC's year-to-year retention rate is higher than semester-to-semester.

For each individual semester between fall 2014 and spring 2019, students in sections that received in-class LI were retained the following semester at higher rates than those in sections not including LI. The difference in retention ranged from 5.1 to 13.4 percentage points. Year-to-year retention rates for classes receiving LI ranged from 5.6 to 14.3 percentage points higher than those in similar courses who did not receive LI (see table 6.11).

Table 6.11

Arizona Western College, retention of students with library instruction versus students without library instruction, fall 2014–spring 2019; graduates and transfers excluded

Term	Group	Eligible Students	Retained Subsequent Semester[a]			Eligible Students	Retained Subsequent Year		
			#	%	*DIFF Library vs. No-Library*		#	%	*DIFF Library vs. No Library*
Fall 2014	Library Instruction	553	455	82.3%	*8.0%*	470	294	62.6%	*9.3%*
	No Library Instruction[b]	3,917	2,909	74.3%		3,657	1,947	53.2%	
Spring 2015	Library Instruction	877	621	70.8%	*9.1%*	779	502	64.4%	*8.4%*
	No Library Instruction[b]	2,617	1,614	61.7%		2,327	1,303	56.0%	

Table 6.11

Arizona Western College, retention of students with library instruction versus students without library instruction, fall 2014–spring 2019; graduates and transfers excluded

Term	Group	Eligible Students	Retained Subsequent Semester[a]			Eligible Students	Retained Subsequent Year		
			#	%	*DIFF Library vs. No-Library*		#	%	*DIFF Library vs. No Library*
Fall 2015	Library Instruction	826	660	79.9%	*5.1%*	755	478	63.3%	*5.6%*
	No Library Instruction[b]	3,247	2,429	74.8%		3,004	1,734	57.7%	
Spring 2016	Library Instruction	1,017	753	74.0%	*7.9%*	918	610	66.4%	*7.5%*
	No Library Instruction[b]	2,554	1,690	66.2%		2,289	1,349	58.9%	
Fall 2016	Library Instruction	1,177	934	79.4%	*6.3%*	1,045	648	62.0%	*8.3%*
	No Library Instruction[b]	3,312	2,420	73.1%		3,060	1,644	53.7%	
Spring 2017	Library Instruction	730	547	74.9%	*13.4%*	655	448	68.4%	*14.3%*
	No Library Instruction[b]	2,662	1,638	61.5%		2,379	1,286	54.1%	
Fall 2017	Library Instruction	928	741	79.8%	*7.4%*	837	511	61.1%	*7.0%*
	No Library Instruction[b]	2,740	1,984	72.4%		2,504	1,353	54.0%	
Spring 2018	Library Instruction	457	332	72.6%	*9.4%*	399	260	65.2%	*10.5%*
	No Library Instruction[b]	2,320	1,467	63.2%		2,065	1,129	54.7%	
Fall 2018	Library Instruction	748	603	80.6%	*11.8%*	657	434	66.1%	*11.5%*
	No Library Instruction[b]	3,109	2,141	68.9%		2,867	1,563	54.5%	
Spring 2019	Library Instruction	539	399	74.0%	*10.3%*	488	334	68.4%	*11.4%*
	No Library Instruction[b]	2,620	1,670	63.7%		2,339	1,334	57.0%	

a. Summer semester excluded
b. Only similar courses included

An average of the included semesters reveals an overall percent difference of 8.82 percentage points for similar classes from semester to semester with higher retention among the LI group (see figure 6.3).

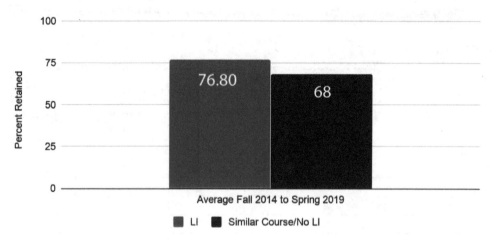

Figure 6.3

Semester-to-semester average retention—graduates and transfers excluded, Arizona Western College

The year-to-year average comparison, on the other hand, reveals a difference of 9.4 percentage points between the LI and non-LI groups in similar courses, higher than the term-to-term retention (see figure 6.4).

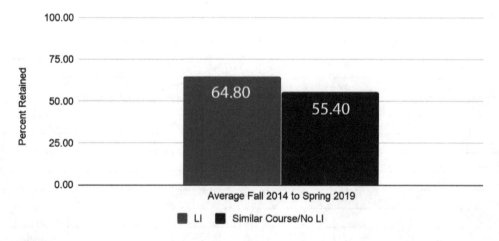

Figure 6.4

Year-to-year average retention—graduates and transfers excluded, Arizona Western College

A chi-square test of independence on each semester's retention figures resulted in chi-square results ranging from 9.06 to 44.3, all greater than the critical value and within the established bounds of statistical significance at .05. In fact, all except one semester had a statistical significance (p-value) of less than .001. A chi-square test of independence on the aggregated semester data produced a result of 208.12 with a significance level of less than .001 (see table 6.12). These results reject the null hypothesis and indicate that a relationship does exist between LI and semester-to-semester retention.

Table 6.12
Arizona Western College semester-to-semester retention chi-square analysis

Retained Following Term[a]	Received Library Instruction				
	LI Yes	*LI No*	*chi-square*	*degrees of freedom*	*p-value*
Fall 2014					
Ret Yes	455	2,909	16.28	1	< .001
Ret No	98	1,008			
Total (N=)	4,470				
Spring 2015					
Ret Yes	621	1,614	23.392	1	< .001
Ret No	256	1,003			
Total (N=)	3,494				
Fall 2015					
Ret Yes	660	2,429	9.0556	1	0.003
Ret No	166	818			
Total (N=)	4,073				
Spring 2016					
Ret Yes	753	1,690	20.488	1	< .001
Ret No	264	864			
Total (N=)	3,571				
Fall 2016					
Ret Yes	934	2,420	17.836	1	< .001
Ret No	243	892			
Total (N=)	4,489				
Spring 2017					
Ret Yes	547	1,638	44.288	1	< .001
Ret No	183	1,024			
Total (N=)	3,392				
Fall 2017					
Ret Yes	741	1,984	19.705	1	< .001
Ret No	187	756			
Total (N=)	3,668				
Spring 2018					
Ret Yes	332	1,467	14.424	1	< .001
Ret No	125	853			
Total (N=)	2,777				

Table 6.12
Arizona Western College semester-to-semester retention chi-square analysis

Retained Following Term[a]	LI Yes	LI No	chi-square	degrees of freedom	p-value
Fall 2018					
Ret Yes	603	2,141	39.98	1	< .001
Ret No	145	968			
Total (N=)	3,857				
Spring 2019					
Ret Yes	399	1,670	20.474	1	< .001
Ret No	140	950			
Total (N=)	3,159				
Grand Total	36,950		208.12	1	<.001
a. Summers excluded					

A chi-square test of independence for year-to-year retention rates of each semester studied ranged from 7.55 to 42.55, all higher than the critical value. The significance level for each semester also fell within the established bounds for statistical significance, and again all semesters except one had a p-value of less than .001. The chi-square analysis of aggregated semester data produced a chi-square result of 193.54 and significance level of less than .001 (see table 6.13). These results reject the null hypothesis and indicate that there is, in fact, a relationship between LI and year-to-year retention of students.

Table 6.13
Arizona Western College year-to-year retention chi-square analysis

Retained Following Year	LI Yes	LI No	chi-square	degrees of freedom	p-value
Fall 2014					
Ret Yes	294	1,947	14.183	1	< .001
Ret No	176	1,710			
Total (N=)	4,127				
Spring 2015					
Ret Yes	502	1,303	16.761	1	< .001
Ret No	277	1,024			
Total (N=)	3,106				
Fall 2015					
Ret Yes	478	1,734	7.5512	1	0.006
Ret No	277	1,270			
Total (N=)	3,759				

Table 6.13

Arizona Western College year-to-year retention chi-square analysis

Retained Following Year		Received Library Instruction				
		LI Yes	LI No	chi-square	degrees of freedom	p-value
Spring 2016						
Ret Yes		610	1,349	15.251	1	< .001
Ret No		308	940			
	Total (N=)	3,207				
Fall 2016						
Ret Yes		648	1,644	21.344	1	< .001
Ret No		397	1,416			
	Total (N=)	4,105				
Spring 2017						
Ret Yes		448	1,286	42.548	1	< .001
Ret No		207	1,093			
	Total (N=)	3,034				
Fall 2017						
Ret Yes		511	1,353	12.243	1	< .001
Ret No		326	1,151			
	Total (N=)	3,341				
Spring 2018						
Ret Yes		260	1,129	14.537	1	< .001
Ret No		139	936			
	Total (N=)	2,464				
Fall 2018						
Ret Yes		434	1,563	28.525	1	< .001
Ret No		223	1,304			
	Total (N=)	3,524				
Spring 2019						
Ret Yes		334	1,334	21.26	1	< .001
Ret No		154	1,005			
	Total (N=)	2,827				
Grand Total		33,494		193.54	1	<.001

Since differences were found to be statistically significant for all semesters, we computed odds ratios for each semester as well. These ranged from 1.34 to 1.87 with 95 percent CIs ranging from 1.11 to 2.25. All semesters except one had a p-value of less than .001, and the remaining semester's significance still fell under .05, making all the results statistically significant and indicating that the odds of being retained in the following semester were indeed higher for students in classes that received LI than those in similar classes who did not.

The overall odds ratio for semester-to-semester retention at AWC was 1.53, again with a statistical significance of less than .001. The 95 percent confidence interval ranged from 1.44 to 1.62, indicating that the odds of being retained are higher for AWC students who receive LI (see table 6.14).

Table 6.14
Arizona Western College semester-to-semester retention odds ratio test

Retained Following Term[a]	Received Library Instruction (95% CI)					
	LI Yes	*LI No*	*Odds Ratio*	*Low*	*High*	*p-value*
Fall 2014						
Ret Yes	455	2,909	1.6088	1.27860	2.024	< .001
Ret No	98	1,008				
Total (*N=*)	4,470					
Spring 2015						
Ret Yes	621	1,614	1.507471	1.27749	1.779	< .001
Ret No	256	1,003				
Total (*N=*)	3,494					
Fall 2015						
Ret Yes	660	2,429	1.338942	1.10978	1.615	0.002255
Ret No	166	818				
Total (*N=*)	4,073					
Spring 2016						
Ret Yes	753	1,690	1.458203	1.23963	1.715	< .001
Ret No	264	864				
Total (*N=*)	3,571					
Fall 2016						
Ret Yes	934	2,420	1.41674	1.20646	1.664	< .001
Ret No	243	892				
Total (*N=*)	4,489					
Spring 2017						
Ret Yes	547	1,638	1.868626	1.55350	2.248	< .001
Ret No	183	1,024				
Total (*N=*)	3,392					
Fall 2017						
Ret Yes	741	1,984	1.50993	1.26000	1.809	< .001
Ret No	187	756				
Total (*N=*)	3,668					

Table 6.14

Arizona Western College semester-to-semester retention odds ratio test

Retained Following Term[a]	Received Library Instruction (95% CI)					
	LI Yes	*LI No*	*Odds Ratio*	*Low*	*High*	*p-value*
Spring 2018						
Ret Yes	332	1,467	1.544354	1.23651	1.929	< .001
Ret No	125	853				
Total (*N*=)	2.777					
Fall 2018						
Ret Yes	603	2,141	1.880217	1.54474	2.289	< .001
Ret No	145	968				
Total (*N*=)	3,857					
Spring 2019						
Ret Yes	399	1,670	1.621257	1.31633	1.997	< .001
Ret No	140	950				
Total (*N*=)	3,159					
Grand Total	36,950		1.53	1.44000	1.620	<.001
a. Summers excluded						

An odds ratio analysis of year-to-year retention for the same semesters at AWC resulted in odds ratios ranging from 1.26 to 1.84 with 95 percent CIs ranging from 1.07 to 2.21. All semesters were significant at the .05 level, with most again falling below .001. This indicates that the odds are higher for students receiving in-class LI to be retained in the following year as compared to those in similar classes who do not receive LI. An odds analysis on the composite figures for all semester resulted in a ratio of 1.47 with a statistical significance level of less than .001 and 95 percent CIs ranging from 1.39 to 1.55, suggesting that odds of year-to-year retention are increased for classes that include LI (see table 6.15).

Table 6.15

Arizona Western College year-to-year retention odds ratio test

Retained Following Year	Received Library Instruction (95% CI)					
	LI Yes	*LI No*	*Odds Ratio*	*Low*	*High*	*p-value*
Fall 2014						
Ret Yes	294	1,947	1.4671	1.20386	1.788	< .001
Ret No	176	1,710				
Total (*N*=)	4,127					

Table 6.15
Arizona Western College year-to-year retention odds ratio test

Retained Following Year	Received Library Instruction (95% CI)					
	LI Yes	*LI No*	*Odds Ratio*	*Low*	*High*	*p-value*
Spring 2015						
Ret Yes	502	1,303	1.424228	1.20399	1.685	< .001
Ret No	277	1,024				
Total (*N*=)	3,106					
Fall 2015						
Ret Yes	478	1,734	1.263871	1.07189	1.490	0.005288
Ret No	277	1,270				
Total (*N*=)	3,759					
Spring 2016						
Ret Yes	610	1,349	1.380051	1.17562	1.620	< .001
Ret No	308	940				
Total (*N*=)	3,207					
Fall 2016						
Ret Yes	648	1,644	1.405873	1.21768	1.623	< .001
Ret No	397	1,416				
Total (*N*=)	4,105					
Spring 2017						
Ret Yes	448	1,286	1.839445	1.53123	2.210	< .001
Ret No	207	1,093				
Total (*N*=)	3,034					
Fall 2017						
Ret Yes	511	1,353	1.333463	1.13674	1.564	< .001
Ret No	326	1,151				
Total (*N*=)	3,341					
Spring 2018						
Ret Yes	260	1,129	1.550745	1.24025	1.939	< .001
Ret No	139	936				
Total (*N*=)	2,464					
Fall 2018						
Ret Yes	434	1,563	1.623691	1.35971	1.939	< .001
Ret No	223	1,304				
Total (*N*=)	3,524					

Table 6.15

Arizona Western College year-to-year retention odds ratio test

Retained Following Year	LI Yes	LI No	Odds Ratio	Low	High	p-value
Spring 2019						
Ret Yes	334	1,334	1.63394	1.32747	2.011	< .001
Ret No	154	1,005				
Total (*N*=)	2,827					
Grand Total	33,494		1.47	1.39000	1.550	<.001

Term-to-term relative probability was also calculated for all semesters studied at AWC. The relative probability ratio for each semester ranged from 1.07 to 1.22. The 95 percent CIs ranged from 1.03 to 1.28, indicating that it is 3 percent to 28 percent more probable that students in classes including LI will be retained for the following semester than those in similar courses that do not include LI. The relative probability for all semesters aggregated was 1.41 with 95 percent CI ranging from 1.34 to 1.48. This indicates that, overall, the students who received LI are 34 to 48 percent more likely to be retained (see table 6.16).

Table 6.16

Arizona Western College semester-to-semester retention relative probability ratio test

Retained Following Term[a]	LI Yes	LI No	Relative Probability	Low	High	p-value
Fall 2014						
Ret Yes	455	2,909	1.107889	1.06142	1.156	< .001
Ret No	98	1,008				
Total (*N*=)	4,470					
Spring 2015						
Ret Yes	621	1,614	1.148133	1.08981	1.210	< .001
Ret No	256	1,003				
Total (*N*=)	3,494					
Fall 2015						
Ret Yes	660	2,429	1.068117	1.02665	1.111	< .001
Ret No	166	818				
Total (*N*=)	4,073					
Spring 2016						
Ret Yes	753	1,690	1.118944	1.06890	1.171	< .001
Ret No	264	864				
Total (*N*=)	3,571					

Table 6.16

Arizona Western College semester-to-semester retention relative probability ratio test

Retained Following Term[a]	LI Yes	LI No	Received Library Instruction (95% CI)			
			Relative Probability	Low	High	p-value
Fall 2016						
Ret Yes	934	2,420	1.086039	1.04792	1.126	< .001
Ret No	243	892				
Total (N=)	4,489					
Spring 2017						
Ret Yes	547	1,638	1.217751	1.15651	1.282	< .001
Ret No	183	1,024				
Total (N=)	3,392					
Fall 2017						
Ret Yes	741	1,984	1.102755	1.05980	1.147	< .001
Ret No	187	756				
Total (N=)	3,668					
Spring 2018						
Ret Yes	332	1,467	1.148893	1.07740	1.225	< .001
Ret No	125	853				
Total (N=)	2,777					
Fall 2018						
Ret Yes	603	2,141	1.17063	1.12209	1.221	< .001
Ret No	145	968				
Total (N=)	3,857					
Spring 2019						
Ret Yes	399	1,670	1.161366	1.09620	1.230	< .001
Ret No	140	950				
Total (N=)	3,159					
Grand Total	36,950		1.407616	1.34223	1.476	<.001
a. Summers excluded						

The year-to-year relative probability ratios for each semester ranged from 1.09 to 1.27 with 95 percent CIs spanning the range of 1.03 to 1.35. Thus, students receiving LI in a given semester were anywhere from 3 percent to 35 percent more likely to be retained in the following year than their peers who did not receive LI. The overall relative probability ratio was 1.36 with 95 percent CI ranging from 1.30 to 1.42, suggesting that students who received LI were 30 percent to 42 percent more likely to be retained in the following year (see table 6.17).

Table 6.17

Arizona Western College year-to-year retention relative probability ratio test

Retained Following Year		Received Library Instruction (95% CI)				
	LI Yes	LI No	Relative Probability	Low	High	p-value
Fall 2014						
Ret Yes	294	1,947	1.17492	1.08865	1.268	< .001
Ret No	176	1,710				
Total (N=)	4,127					
Spring 2015						
Ret Yes	502	1,303	1.150849	1.08016	1.226	< .001
Ret No	277	1,024				
Total (N=)	3,106					
Fall 2015						
Ret Yes	478	1,734	1.096811	1.03053	1.167	0.005288
Ret No	277	1,270				
Total (N=)	3,759					
Spring 2016						
Ret Yes	610	1,349	1.127512	1.06473	1.194	< .001
Ret No	308	940				
Total (N=)	3,207					
Fall 2016						
Ret Yes	648	1644	1.154193	1.08944	1.223	< .001
Ret No	397	1,416				
Total (N=)	4,105					
Spring 2017						
Ret Yes	448	1,286	1.26529	1.18698	1.349	< .001
Ret No	207	1,093				
Total (N=)	3,034					
Fall 2017						
Ret Yes	511	1,353	1.129879	1.05871	1.206	< .001
Ret No	326	1,151				
Total (N=)	3,341					
Spring 2018						
Ret Yes	260	1,129	1.191864	1.09826	1.293	< .001
Ret No	139	936				
Total (N=)	2,464					
Fall 2018						
Ret Yes	434	1,563	1.211694	1.13634	1.292	< .001
Ret No	223	1,304				
Total (N=)	3,524					
Spring 2019						
Ret Yes	334	1,334	1.200055	1.11919	1.287	< .001
Ret No	154	1,005				
Total (N=)	2,827					
Grand Total	33,494		1.360848	1.30239	1.422	< .001

Combined Data

We also analyzed our combined data for semesters in which both institutions had it. Combined, both institutions saw higher rates of semester-to-semester as well as year-to-year retention each semester for students receiving LI when compared to those in similar classes who did not. The differences in semester-to-semester retention ranged from 7.2 to 12.5 percentage points, while year-to-year differences varied between 6.7 and 12.7 percentage points (see table 6.18).

Table 6.18

Both institutions, retention of students with library instruction versus students without library instruction, fall 2016–spring 2018—graduates and transfers excluded

Term	Group	Eligible Students	Retained Subsequent Semester[a]			Eligible Students	Retained Subsequent Year		
			#	%	*DIFF*		#	%	*DIFF*
Fall 2016	Library Instruction	1,665	1,342	80.6%	*7.2%*	1,411	887	62.9%	*7.2%*
	No Library Instruction[b]	4,056	2,977	73.4%		3,649	2,030	55.6%	
Spring 2017	Library Instruction	977	738	75.5%	*12.1%*	875	598	68.3%	*12.5%*
	No Library Instruction[b]	3,225	2,046	63.4%		2,903	1,622	55.9%	
Fall 2017	Library Instruction	1,315	1,083	82.4%	*8.8%*	1,124	713	63.4%	*6.7%*
	No Library Instruction[b]	3,530	2,595	73.5%		3,151	1,787	56.7%	
Spring 2018	Library Instruction	724	559	77.2%	*12.5%*	618	427	69.1%	*12.7%*
	No Library Instruction[b]	2,964	1,917	64.7%		2,685	1,513	56.4%	

a. Summer semester excluded
b. Only similar courses included

An aggregate average revealed an overall difference of 10.3 percentage points between semester-to-semester retention of students in sections receiving LI and those who did not. For year-to-year retention, the aggregate was a difference of 9 percentage points (see table 6.19, figures 6.5 and 6.6).

Table 6.19
Both institutions, retention of students with library instruction versus students without library instruction, fall 2016—spring 2018—graduates and transfers excluded

	Retained Subsequent Semester[a]		Retained Subsequent Year	
	%	*DIFF*	*%*	*DIFF*
AVG Library Instruction	79.5%	10.3%	65.2%	9.0%
AVG No Library Instruction[b]	69.2%		56.1%	
a. Summers excluded				
b. Similar classes only				

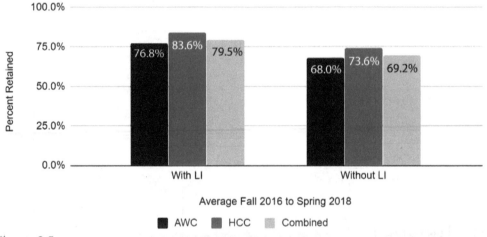

Figure 6.5

Semester-to-semester average retention, graduates and transfers excluded, both institutions

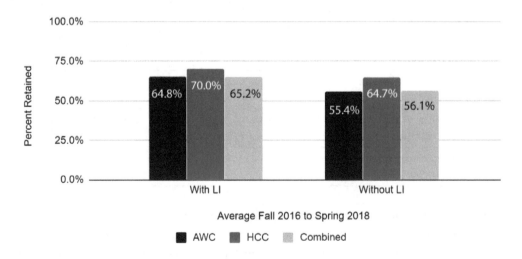

Figure 6.6

Year-to-year average retention, graduates and transfers excluded, both institutions

For the semesters fall 2016 to spring 2018, a chi-square test of independence for semester-to-semester retention revealed values of 32.7 to 48.5, well above the critical value. Each semester was statistically significant with a p-value of less than .001. This excludes the null hypothesis and suggests a relationship between LI and retention in the following semester.

The combined analysis across all semesters and both institutions included retention data for a total of 18,456 eligible students who participated in course-based LI or in similar classes that did not receive LI. The chi-square test of independence for this data produced a result of 182.43 with a significance level of less than .001, strongly suggesting a relationship between LI and retention (see table 6.20).

Table 6.20
Combined semester-to-semester retention chi-square analysis

	Received Library Instruction				
Retained Following Term[a]	*LI Yes*	*LI No*	*chi-square*	*degrees of freedom*	*p-value*
Fall 2016					
Ret Yes	1,342	2,977	32.717	1	< .001
Ret No	323	1,079			
Total (*N=*)	5,721				
Spring 2017					
Ret Yes	738	2,046	48.527	1	< .001
Ret No	239	1,179			
Total (*N=*)	4,202				
Fall 2017					
Ret Yes	1,083	2,595	40.507	1	< .001
Ret No	232	935			
Total (*N=*)	4,845				
Spring 2018					
Ret Yes	559	1,917	40.865	1	< .001
Ret No	165	1,047			
Total (*N=*)	3,688				
Grand Total	18,456		182.43	1	<.001
a. Summers excluded					

The chi-square test of independence for combined year-to-year retention also yielded significant results (p < .001) for each semester analyzed. The chi-square values ranged from 15.1 to 42.6, again well above the critical value. The number of students included in both institutions' year-to-year analysis totaled 16,416. The chi-square result for the aggregate analysis of all semesters across both institutions was 102.06 with a significance level of less than .001 (see table 6.21). These results also provide evidence to support a relationship between LI and year-to-year retention.

Table 6.21

Combined year-to-year retention chi-square analysis

Retained Following Year	Received Library Instruction				
	LI Yes	*LI No*	*chi-square*	*degrees of freedom*	*p-value*
Fall 2016					
Ret Yes	887	2,030	21.500	1	< .001
Ret No	524	1,619			
Total (*N*=)	5,060				
Spring 2017					
Ret Yes	598	1,622	42.629	1	< .001
Ret No	277	1,281			
Total (*N*=)	3,778				
Fall 2017					
Ret Yes	713	1,787	15.142	1	< .001
Ret No	411	1,364			
Total (*N*=)	4,275				
Spring 2018					
Ret Yes	427	1,513	33.138	1	< .001
Ret No	191	1,172			
Total (*N*=)	3,303				
Grand Total	16,416		102.06	1	<.001

An odds ratio analysis of semester-to-semester retention across both institutions resulted in highly significant outcomes (p < .001) for each semester as well. The odds ratios varied from 1.5 to 1.9 with 95 percent CIs ranging from 1.3 to 2.2. The aggregate analysis of all students' semester-to-semester retention from all semesters produced a result of 1.73 at a significance level of less than .001 with 95 percent CIs from 1.59 to 1.87 (see table 6.22). These results indicate that odds of semester-to-semester retention were increased with LI.

Table 6.22

Combined semester-to-semester retention odds ratio test

Retained Following Term[a]	Received Library Instruction (95% CI)					
	LI Yes	*LI No*	*Odds Ratio*	*Low*	*High*	*p-value*
Fall 2016						
Ret Yes	1,342	2,977	1.505888	1.30913	1.732	< .001
Ret No	323	1,079				
Total (*N*=)	5,721					

Table 6.22

Combined semester-to-semester retention odds ratio test

Retained Following Term[a]	Received Library Instruction (95% CI)					
	LI Yes	*LI No*	*Odds Ratio*	*Low*	*High*	*p-value*
Spring 2017						
Ret Yes	738	2,046	1.779	1.51246	2.093	< .001
Ret No	239	1,179				
Total (*N=*)	4,202					
Fall 2017						
Ret Yes	1,083	2,595	1.682	1.43285	1.974	< .001
Ret No	232	935				
Total (*N=*)	4,845					
Spring 2018						
Ret Yes	559	1,917	1.850344	1.53126	2.236	< .001
Ret No	165	1,047				
Total (*N=*)	3,688					
Grand Total	18,456		1.73	1.59	1.87	<.001
a. Summers excluded						

Year-to-year odds ratios for each semester were between 1.3 and 1.7, with all results showing high statistical significance (p < .001). The 95 percent CIs ranged from 1.15 to 2.08. The overall year-to-year odds ratio was somewhat lower than the semester-to-semester ratio but still 1.46 with a statistical significance level of less than .001. The 95 percent confidence interval ranged from 1.36 to 1.58 (see table 6.23). These results suggest increased odds of year-to-year retention for students receiving in-class LI.

Table 6.23

Combined year-to-year retention odds ratio test

Retained Following Year	Received Library Instruction (95% CI)					
	LI Yes	LI No	Odds Ratio	Low	High	p-value
Fall 2016						
Ret Yes	887	2,030	1.350	1.18997	1.532	< .001
Ret No	524	1,619				
Total (*N=*)	5,060					
Spring 2017						
Ret Yes	598	1,622	1.705	1.45262	2.001	< .001
Ret No	277	1,281				
Total (*N=*)	3,778					

Table 6.23
Combined year-to-year retention odds ratio test

| Retained Following Year | Received Library Instruction (95% CI) | | | | | |
	LI Yes	LI No	Odds Ratio	Low	High	p-value
Fall 2017						
Ret Yes	713	1,787	1.324	1.15075	1.524	< .001
Ret No	411	1,364				
Total (*N*=)	4,275					
Spring 2018						
Ret Yes	427	1,513	1.731742	1.43655	2.088	< .001
Ret No	191	1,172				
Total (*N*=)	3,303					
Grand Total	16,416		1.46	1.36	1.58	<.001

A relative probability test on the combined semester-to-semester data resulted in ratios ranging from 1.09 to 1.19. The 95 percent CIs ranged from a low of 1.06 to a high of 1.25, suggesting that the probability of semester-to-semester retention increased anywhere from 6 percent to 25 percent when students were in a class that received LI. A relative probability test on the overall aggregated data for all students in all semesters resulted in a ratio of 1.52 with 95 percent CI varying from 1.42 to 1.62. Thus, students in classes that included LI were 42 to 62 percent more likely to be retained in the following semester (see table 6.24).

Table 6.24
Combined semester-to-semester retention relative probability test

| Retained Following Term[a] | Received Library Instruction (95% CI) | | | | | |
	LI Yes	*LI No*	*Relative Probability Ratio*	*Low*	*High*	*p-value*
Fall 2016						
Ret Yes	1,342	2,977	1.098139	1.06571	1.132	< .001
Ret No	323	1,079				
Total (*N*=)	5,721					
Spring 2017						
Ret Yes	738	2,046	1.191	1.13910	1.245	< .001
Ret No	239	1,179				
Total (*N*=)	4,202					
Fall 2017						
Ret Yes	1,083	2,595	1.120	1.08514	1.157	< .001
Ret No	232	935				
Total (*N*=)	4,845					

Table 6.24
Combined semester-to-semester retention relative probability test

Retained Following Term[a]	Received Library Instruction (95% CI)					
	LI Yes	LI No	Relative Probability Ratio	Low	High	p-value
Spring 2018						
Ret Yes	559	1,917	1.193794	1.13820	1.252	< .001
Ret No	165	1,047				
Total (N=)	3,688					
Grand Total	18,456		1.522062	1.428676	1.621552	<.001
a. Summers excluded						

When examining combined data from both institutions for year-to-year retention, a relative probability analysis revealed relative probability ratios of 1.11 to 1.22 with 95 percent CIs between 1.05 and 1.29. All semesters had significant results at the $p < .001$ level. This suggests an increased probability of year-to-year retention ranging from 11 percent to 22 percent with LI. An aggregate analysis of all students in all semesters resulted in a relative probability ratio of 1.33 with 95 percent CIs from 1.26 to 1.41 (see table 6.25). In other words, students in classes receiving LI were 26 percent to 41 percent more likely to be retained in the following year than those in similar classes that did not receive LI.

Table 6.25
Combined year-to-year retention relative probability test

Retained Following Year	Received Library Instruction (95% CI)					
	LI Yes	LI No	Relative Probability Ratio	Low	High	p-value
Fall 2016						
Ret Yes	887	2,030	1.130	1.07544	1.187	< .001
Ret No	524	1,619				
Total (N=)	5,060					
Spring 2017						
Ret Yes	598	1,622	1.223	1.15716	1.293	< .001
Ret No	277	1,281				
Total (N=)	3,778					
Fall 2017						
Ret Yes	713	1,787	1.119	1.05988	1.180	< .001
Ret No	411	1,364				
Total (N=)	4,275					

Table 6.25

Combined year-to-year retention relative probability test

Retained Following Year	Received Library Instruction (95% CI)					
	LI Yes	LI No	Relative Probability Ratio	Low	High	p-value
Spring 2018						
Ret Yes	427	1,513	1.226153	1.15203	1.305	< .001
Ret No	191	1,172				
Total (*N=*)	3,303					
Grand Total	16,416		1.336087	1.262175	1.414328	<.001

Conclusions

It appears that there is a positive relationship between LI being provided in a course and higher retention in the following semester and year. We were able to reject the null hypothesis in most chi-square tests of independence, revealing that it is statistically likely that LI and retention do have a relationship to each other. Furthermore, the odds ratios in almost all cases suggest improved odds of retention for students participating in courses that include LI. Finally, the relative probability analysis indicated that the semester-to-semester effect size of LI could range anywhere from 3 percent to 62 percent, meaning that students who participate in in-class LI are anywhere from 3 percent to 62 percent more likely to be retained in the following semester. The year-to-year effect size could be as low as 3 percent up to as high as 42 percent.

However, correlation does not equal causation, so it is not possible to say that LI *causes* higher retention. It may be that other factors present in the instructors or format of the sections including LI that led the students to be retained at higher rates. For example, are classes full term, late start, or compact four-week sessions? Does the course meet online only, hybrid online and in person, or exclusively face to face? Do classes meet daily, once a week, or twice a week? What time of day do classes meet? Do faculty encourage their students to use library resources or incorporate library resources into their curriculum? Perhaps instructors who include LI in their courses are more apt to introduce students to a variety of campus resources or engage in other high-impact best practices throughout the term, thereby increasing students' overall engagement. Indeed, in O'Kelly's 2017 conference proceedings, retention rates for faculty who invited LI were higher across the board, whether or not specific courses or sections included LI. As O'Kelly states,

> The hypothesis is that faculty who engage with the library via library instruction are also likely to be more effective, perhaps by engaging with other high-impact practices that positively influence retention.

For example, those faculty might be assigning undergraduate research projects or encouraging their students to use academic support services, which are known practices that contribute to student success—and are likely to require library services and resources.[52]

As mentioned in the methodology section, there could also be factors present in the students themselves that contribute to higher or lower retention, such as first-generation, traditional/nontraditional, or full-time/part-time enrollment status.

Implications

For AWC, these initial results and an upcoming librarian retirement prompted re-evaluation of current librarian job descriptions. The head reference librarian position was revised and reclassified as an outreach and instruction librarian. Preliminary steps were taken to publicize the information, market it to faculty and college administrators, and utilize it for a grant application to request more instructional space. That grant funding was awarded in October 2018 and will include a creation of a digital humanities center and an additional classroom to house library instructional activities. The AWC Academic Library also utilized this data to promote its services and become part of the first-year experience orientation, remain an integral part of new and returning faculty orientations, and join the Campus Activities Board. Drilling down further into the data and exploring practical steps to encourage faculty to request LI, as well as more formal assessment of instructional techniques and activities, will certainly be on the horizon.

At Hagerstown Community College, preliminary results of this study were presented as evidence of the library's value in 2019 unit planning meetings and also included in outreach materials to faculty. Additional insights gained through preparation of this chapter will support future marketing to faculty as well. Within the library, LI will be further developed and refined as an activity of significance not only for student learning but also for engagement. All three professional librarians currently support the LI program, so continuing professional development in pedagogy and instructional techniques can help to make LI even more effective over time.

Suggestions for Future Research

For future research, we recommend gathering the data on a section-by-section or even student-by-student basis. This would allow for statistical analyses to be performed on a variety of variables, which should allow greater predictive power for the analysis.

Further research could also be conducted to look specifically at first-generation students, freshmen, and students enrolled in developmental courses or in honors-designated courses.

Additionally, a specific campaign to reach a broader variety of courses, to engage faculty, and to thoroughly promote the instructional capabilities of the academic library should be carried out. As Mary O'Kelly proposes in her paper published in conference proceedings, "Academic Libraries and Student Retention: The Implications for Higher Education":

> Faculty influence whether a student uses the library, whether through direct assignments or cocurricular programs. Therefore, as this paper proposes, faculty engagement with the library, including encouraging student use of the library, is a contributing factor to student retention.[53]

Furthermore, she suggests that traditional LI is not alone in impacting retention, but many other services and resources provided by the library, such as guest lecturing in the classroom, offering seminars to specific high-risk groups (first-year), and even mentoring students may increase retention.[54]

As the landscape of higher education and modes of instructional delivery continue to change, implications of more online instruction, as opposed to face-to-face, and its effect on student retention will need to be investigated. LI, in general, will adapt and change as new pedagogical and technological developments arise. While many institutions may cut staff and budgets in an effort to recoup costs due to low enrollment or other factors in the future, it will be important for librarians to turn to the research that supports the relationship between retention of students and number of professional library staff, librarians' role in faculty outreach, and their work in LI and utilize it to advocate for themselves.

Lastly, the statistical methodologies utilized in this chapter require further evaluation. The approach of using methods seen in the medical world to apply to this data and to draw conclusions from those means of evaluation appears to be relatively novel. Research combining these two factors is still emerging. In this chapter, we conducted what is essentially a retrospective cohort study in that we assessed retention rates after student participation in LI. Retrospective cohort studies often include determining the risk factors associated with the two groups (retained vs. not retained). Without investigating underlying factors such as first-generation status, previous educational attainment or experience, faculty involvement, and so on that may make the student initially at more risk for not being retained, we are unsure of the ability to claim that there is an association between participation in LI and retention. Therefore, creating controls for those variables would allow for a greater confidence in reporting positive correlation between the two. Even in assessed risk case-controlled studies, no conclusive causality can be determined. We encourage future researchers conducting similar studies to assess this method and explore it further.[55]

Acknowledgments

Throughout the writing of this chapter, we have been able to rely on practitioners who graciously shared their expertise with us. We would not have been able to write this chapter without their help. We received exceptional guidance from the following individuals and would like to acknowledge their contribution to this chapter and express our gratitude:

Mary O'Kelly, associate dean for education and user services in the University Libraries at Western Michigan University, pioneer of combining library instruction and retention data to determine the positive correlation between the two. She inspired us to attempt this analysis, provided encouragement and support, and suggested ways to take our analysis further.

Karl Benedict, director of research data services/director of IT, College of University Libraries and Learning Sciences, at University of New Mexico, was our mentor throughout the writing process. He provided us with wise counsel and was available, accessible, knowledgeable, and supportive of our team. He provided us with edits, feedback, and a group demonstration of R, an essential tool used to derive our statistical analysis.

Betty Lopez, Arizona Western College's director of institutional effectiveness and research, analyzed the raw AWC data, adding additional measures and performing additional analysis as we needed it, and providing advice.

Ryan Spurrier, now assistant director of institutional research at Mount St. Mary's University; previously coordinator of institutional reporting at Hagerstown Community College, provided analysis of the original raw HCC data as well as recommendations for fine-tuning the methodology.

David Grimes, learning support specialist for STEM at Hagerstown Community College, patiently provided statistics consultation as we waded through new-to-us ideas and terminology.

Lauralea Banks Edwards, assistant vice president for strategy and analysis at Salt Lake Community College, offered helpful insights into the use of data analysis strategies across disparate fields of inquiry and most of all encouragement.

Notes

1.   Sidney Eng and Derek Stadler, "Linking Library to Student Retention: A Statistical Analysis," *Evidence Based Library and Information Practice* 10, no. 3 (2015): 50–63, https://doi.org/10.18438/ B84P4D; Dennis Krieb, "Assessing the Impact of Reference Assistance and Library Instruction on Retention and Grades Using Student Tracking Technology," *Evidence Based Library and Information Practice* 13, no. 2 (2018): 2–12, https://doi.org/10.18438/eblip29402.
2.   Mary O'Kelly, "Correlation between Library Instruction and Student Retention" (presentation, Southeastern Library Assessment Conference, Atlanta, GA, November 16, 2015); Mary O'Kelly, "Getting Started with Assessing Student Retention," Georgia Library Association Carterette Series Webinars, September 28, 2016, video, 1:00:30, https://vimeo.com/185130648; Mary O'Kelly, "Academic Libraries and Student Retention: The Implications for Higher Education," in *Proceedings of the 2016 Library Assessment Conference: Building Effective, Sustainable, Practical Assessment,* ed. Sue Baughman, Steve Hiller, Katie Monroe, and Angele Pappalardo, 485 (Washington, DC: Association of Research Libraries, 2017), Conference Proceedings, ScholarWorks@GVSU, Grand Valley State University, https:// scholarworks.gvsu.edu/library_proceedings/7/; M. O'Kelly et al., "Correlation between Library Instruction and Student Retention: Methods and Implications," manuscript in preparation.
3.   O'Kelly, "Getting Started."
4.   Elizabeth M. Mezick, "Return on Investment: Libraries and Student Retention," *Journal of Academic Librarianship* 33, no. 5 (September 2007): 564, https://doi.org/10.1016/j.acalib.2007.05.002.
5.   Mark Emmons and Frances C. Wilkinson, "The Academic Library Impact on Student Persistence," *College and Research Libraries* 72, no. 2 (2011): 143–44, https://doi.org/10.5860/crl-74r1.
6.   Emmons and Wilkinson, "Academic Library Impact," 136–38.
7.   Emmons and Wilkinson, "Academic Library Impact," 145–46.

8.   Jason M. Vance, Rachel Kirk, and Justin G. Gardner, "Measuring the Impact of Library Instruction on Freshman Success and Persistence," *Communications in Information Literacy* 6, no. 1 (2012): 54–56, https://doi.org/10.15760/comminfolit.2012.6.1.117.

9.   Boris Teske, Michael DiCarlo, and Dexter Cahoy, "Libraries and Student Persistence at Southern Colleges and Universities," *Reference Services Review* 4, no. 2 (2013): 273–76, https://doi.org/10.1108/00907321311326174.

10.   Krista Soria, Jan Fransen, and Shane Nackerud, "Library Use and Undergraduate Student Outcomes: New Evidence for Students' Retention and Academic Success," *portal: Libraries and the Academy* 13, no. 2 (2013): 155, https://doi.org/10.1353/pla.2013.0010.

11.   Soria, Fransen, and Nackerud, "Library Use," 153–60.

12.   Soria, Fransen, and Nackerud, "Library Use," 153–60.

13.   Gregory A. Crawford, "The Academic Library and Student Retention and Graduation: An Exploratory Study," *portal: Libraries and the Academy* 15, no. 1 (2015): 49–55, https://doi.org/10.1353/pla.2015.0003.

14.   Crawford, "Academic Library and Student Retention," 43–56.

15.   Amy Jo Catalano and Sharon Rose Phillips, "Information Literacy and Retention: A Case Study of the Value of the Library," *Evidence Based Library and Information Practice* 11, no. 4 (2016): 7, https://doi.org/10.18438/B82K7W.

16.   Eng and Stadler, "Linking Library," 52.

17.   Eng and Stadler, "Linking Library," 55–58.

18.   Eng and Stadler, "Linking Library," 57–58.

19.   Eng and Stadler, "Linking Library," 57–58.

20.   O'Kelly, "Academic Libraries and Student Retention," 485.

21.   O'Kelly, "Academic Libraries and Student Retention," 485.

22.   O'Kelly, "Academic Libraries and Student Retention," 486.

23.   O'Kelly, "Academic Libraries and Student Retention," 486–87.

24.   O'Kelly, "Academic Libraries and Student Retention," 486–87.

25.   O'Kelly, "Academic Libraries and Student Retention," 488–89.

26.   Carol Hargis, Jennifer Rowe, and Julie Leuzinger, "The Impact of Library Instruction on Undergraduate Student Success: A Four-Year Study" (presentation, 2018 Texas Library Association, Dallas, TX, April 4, 2018), https://digital.library.unt.edu/ark:/67531/metadc1132752/.

27.   Hargis, Rowe, and Leuzinger, "Impact of Library Instruction."

28.   Hargis, Rowe, and Leuzinger, "Impact of Library Instruction."

29.   Krieb, "Assessing the Impact."

30.   Krieb, "Assessing the Impact," 6.

31.   Krieb, "Assessing the Impact," 7–11.

32.   "Hagerstown-Martinsburg, MD-WV Metro Area," Census Reporter, accessed June 29, 2020, https://censusreporter.org/profiles/31000US25180-hagerstown-martinsburg-md-wv-metro-area/.

33.   "Hagerstown-Martinsburg, MD-WV," Data USA, accessed June 29, 2020, https://datausa.io/profile/geo/hagerstown-martinsburg-md-wv.

34.   "Fast Facts about HCC," Hagerstown Community College, accessed June 29, 2020, https://www.hagerstowncc.edu/about-hcc/fast-facts.

35.   "Why AWC?" Arizona Western College, accessed July 9, 2020, https://www.azwestern.edu/about/why-awc.

36.   "Demographics," Yuma County Chamber of Commerce, accessed July 9, 2020, https://www.yumachamber.org/demographics.html (page discontinued).

37.   "QuickFacts: Yuma County, Arizona," US Census Bureau, accessed July 11, 2020, https://www.census.gov/quickfacts/fact/table/yumacountyarizona/PST045219.

38.   "QuickFacts: Yuma County."

39.   "President's Report 2019: A Year in Review," Office of the President, Arizona Western College, 2020, https://www.azwestern.edu/sites/default/files/awc/office-of-the-president/AWC_PresidentsReport_2019.pdf.

40.   "President's Report 2019."

41.   Maher M. El-Masri, "Terminology 101: Retrospective Cohort Study Design," *Canadian Nurse*, April 1, 2014, https://canadian-nurse.com/en/articles/issues/2014/april-2014/

terminology-101-retrospective-cohort-study-design; Saul Crandon, "Case-Control and Cohort Studies: A Brief Overview," *Students 4 Best Evidence (blog)*, December 6, 2017, https://s4be.cochrane.org/blog/2017/12/06/case-control-and-cohort-studies-overview/.

42. John-Michael Gamble, "An Introduction to the Fundamentals of Cohort and Case–Control Studies," *Canadian Journal of Hospital Pharmacy* 67, no. 5 (2014): 366–77, https://doi.org/10.4212/cjhp.v67i5.1391.

43. Muriel Ramirez-Santana, "Limitations and Biases in Cohort Studies," in *Cohort Studies in Health Sciences*, ed. R. Mauricio Barría (InTechOpen, 2018), https://doi.org/10.5772/intechopen.74324.

44. O'Kelly, "Getting Started."

45. Mary L. McHugh, "The Chi-Square Test of Independence," *Biochemia Medica* 23, no. 2 (June 2013): 143–49, https://doi.org/10.11613/BM.2013.018.

46. Lisa Sullivan, "Tests for Two or More Independent Samples, Discrete Outcome," Hypothesis Testing—Chi Squared Test, last updated September 1, 2016, https://sphweb.bumc.bu.edu/otlt/MPH-Modules/BS/BS704_HypothesisTesting-ChiSquare/BS704_HypothesisTesting-ChiSquare3.html.

47. Mary L. McHugh, "The Odds Ratio: Calculation, Usage and Interpretation," *Biochemia Medica* 19, no. 2 (June 2009): 120–26, https://doi.org/ 10.11613/BM.2009.011.

48. Wayne W. LaMorte, "Confidence Intervals for Measures of Association," Random Error, Boston University School of Public Health, last updated June 16, 2016, https://sphweb.bumc.bu.edu/otlt/MPH-Modules/EP/EP713_RandomError/EP713_RandomError4.html.

49. Peter Cummings, "The Relative Merits of Risk Ratios and Odds Ratios," *Archives of Pediatrics and Adolescent Medicine* 163, no. 5 (May 4, 2009): 438–45, https://doi.org/10.1001/archpediatrics.2009.31.

50. Sourabh Dutta, "A Look at the Various Ratios in Medicine—Risk Ratio, Odds Ratio and Likelihood Ratio," *Indian Journal of Rheumatology* 9, no. 3 (July 28, 2014): 136–40, https://doi.org/10.1016/j.injr.2014.06.002.

51. R Core Team, "R: A Language and Environment for Statistical Computing," computer software, The R Project for Statistical Computing, R Foundation for Statistical Computing, 2020, https://www.r-project.org/; RStudio Team, "RStudio: Integrated Development for R," computer software, RStudio, PBC, 2020, https://rstudio.com/; Minato Nakazawa, "Fmsb: Functions for Medical Statistics Book with Some Demographic Data, R Package Version," computer software, The Comprehensive R Archive Network, 2019, https://CRAN.R-project.org/package=fmsb.

52. O'Kelly, "Academic Libraries and Student Retention," 486–87.

53. O'Kelly, "Academic Libraries and Student Retention," 485.

54. O'Kelly, "Academic Libraries and Student Retention," 485.

55. Angela Creel, Wendy Hoag, and Kendra Perry, "Code and Data to Accompany 'Investigating and Communicating Library Instruction's Relationship to Student Retention: A Study of Two Community Colleges,'" OSF, last updated February 7, 2021, https://osf.io/qarzw.

Bibliography

Arizona Western College. "President's Report 2019: A Year in Review." Office of the President, Arizona Western College, 2020. https://www.azwestern.edu/sites/default/files/awc/office-of-the-president/AWC_PresidentsReport_2019.pdf.

———. "Why AWC?" Accessed July 9, 2020. https://www.azwestern.edu/about/why-awc.

Catalano, Amy Jo, and Sharon Rose Phillips. "Information Literacy and Retention: A Case Study of the Value of the Library." *Evidence Based Library and Information Practice* 11, no. 4 (2016): 2–13. https://doi.org/10.18438/B82K7W.

Census Reporter. "Hagerstown-Martinsburg, MD-WV Metro Area." Accessed June 29, 2020. https://censusreporter.org/profiles/31000US25180-hagerstown-martinsburg-md-wv-metro-area/.

Crandon, Saul. "Case-Control and Cohort Studies: A Brief Overview." *Students 4 Best Evidence* (blog), December 6, 2017. https://s4be.cochrane.org/blog/2017/12/06/case-control-and-cohort-studies-overview/.

Crawford, Gregory A. "The Academic Library and Student Retention and Graduation: An Exploratory Study." *portal: Libraries and the Academy* 15, no. 1 (2015): 41–57. https://doi.org/10.1353/pla.2015.0003.

Creel, Angela, Wendy Hoag, and Kendra Perry. "Code and Data to Accompany 'Investigating and Communicating Library Instruction's Relationship to Student Retention: A Study of Two Community Colleges.'" OSF. Last updated February 7, 2021. https://osf.io/qarzw.

Cummings, Peter. "The Relative Merits of Risk Ratios and Odds Ratios." *Archives of Pediatrics and Adolescent Medicine* 163, no. 5 (May 4, 2009): 438–45. https://doi.org/10.1001/archpediatrics.2009.31.

Data USA. "Hagerstown-Martinsburg, MD-WV." Accessed June 29, 2020. https://datausa.io/profile/geo/hagerstown-martinsburg-md-wv.

Dutta, Sourabh. "A Look at the Various Ratios in Medicine—Risk Ratio, Odds Ratio and Likelihood Ratio." *Indian Journal of Rheumatology* 9, no. 3 (July 28, 2014): 136–40. https://doi.org/10.1016/j.injr.2014.06.002.

El-Masri, Maher M. "Terminology 101: Retrospective Cohort Study Design." *Canadian Nurse*. April 1, 2014. https://canadian-nurse.com/en/articles/issues/2014/april-2014/terminology-101-retrospective-cohort-study-design.

Emmons, Mark, and Frances C. Wilkinson. "The Academic Library Impact on Student Persistence." *College and Research Libraries* 72, no. 2 (2011): 128–49. https://doi.org/10.5860/crl-74r1.

Eng, Sidney, and Derek Stadler. "Linking Library to Student Retention: A Statistical Analysis." *Evidence Based Library and Information Practice* 10, no. 3 (2015): 50–63. https://doi.org/10.18438/B84P4D.

Gamble, John-Michael. "An Introduction to the Fundamentals of Cohort and Case–Control Studies." *Canadian Journal of Hospital Pharmacy* 67, no. 5 (2014): 366–77. https://doi.org/10.4212/cjhp.v67i5.1391.

Hagerstown Community College. "Fast Facts about HCC." Accessed June 29, 2020. https://www.hagerstowncc.edu/about-hcc/fast-facts.

Hargis, Carol, Jennifer Rowe, and Julie Leuzinger. "The Impact of Library Instruction on Undergraduate Student Success: A Four-Year Study." Presentation, 2018 Texas Library Association, Dallas, TX, April 4, 2018. https://digital.library.unt.edu/ark:/67531/metadc1132752/.

Krieb, Dennis. "Assessing the Impact of Reference Assistance and Library Instruction on Retention and Grades Using Student Tracking Technology." *Evidence Based Library and Information Practice* 13, no. 2 (2018): 2–12. https://doi.org/10.18438/eblip29402.

LaMorte, Wayne W. "Confidence Intervals for Measures of Association." Random Error, Boston University School of Public Health. Last updated June 16, 2016. https://sphweb.bumc.bu.edu/otlt/MPH-Modules/EP/EP713_RandomError/EP713_RandomError4.html.

McHugh, Mary L. "The Chi-Square Test of Independence." *Biochemia Medica* 23, no. 2 (June 2013): 143–49. https://doi.org/10.11613/BM.2013.018.

———. "The Odds Ratio: Calculation, Usage and Interpretation." *Biochemia Medica* 19, no. 2 (June 2009): 120–26. https://doi.org/10.11613/BM.2009.011.

Mezick, Elizabeth M. "Return on Investment: Libraries and Student Retention." *Journal of Academic Librarianship* 33, no. 5 (September 2007): 561–66. https://doi.org/10.1016/j.acalib.2007.05.002.

Nakazawa, Minato. "Fmsb: Functions for Medical Statistics Book with Some Demographic Data, R Package Version." Computer software. The Comprehensive R Archive Network, 2019. https://CRAN.R-project.org/package=fmsb.

O'Kelly, M., M. Hobscheid, J. Jeffryes, and R. Passarelli. "Correlation between Library Instruction and Student Retention: Methods and Implications." Manuscript in preparation.

O'Kelly, Mary. "Academic Libraries and Student Retention: The Implications for Higher Education." In *Proceedings of the 2016 Library Assessment Conference: Building Effective, Sustainable, Practical Assessment.* Edited by Sue Baughman, Steve Hiller, Katie Monroe, and Angele Pappalardo, 485–90. Washington, DC: Association of Research Libraries, 2017. Conference Proceedings, ScholarWorks@GVSU, Grand Valley State University. https://scholarworks.gvsu.edu/library_proceedings/7/.

———. "Correlation between Library Instruction and Student Retention." Presentation, Southeastern Library Assessment Conference, Atlanta, GA, November 16, 2015.

———. "Getting Started with Assessing Student Retention." Georgia Library Association Carterette Series Webinars, September 28, 2016. Video, 1:00:30. https://vimeo.com/185130648.

R Core Team. "R: A Language and Environment for Statistical Computing." Computer software. The R Project for Statistical Computing, R Foundation for Statistical Computing, 2020. https://www.r-project.org/.

Ramirez-Santana, Muriel. "Limitations and Biases in Cohort Studies." In *Cohort Studies in Health Sciences*. Edited by R. Mauricio Barría. InTechOpen, 2018. https://doi.org/10.5772/intechopen.74324.

RStudio Team. "RStudio: Integrated Development for R." Computer software. RStudio, PBC, 2020. https://rstudio.com/.

Soria, Krista. Jan Fransen, and Shane Nackerud. "Library Use and Undergraduate Student Outcomes: New Evidence for Students' Retention and Academic Success." *portal: Libraries and the Academy* 13, no. 2 (2013): 147–64. https://doi.org/10.1353/pla.2013.0010.

Sullivan, Lisa. "Tests for Two or More Independent Samples, Discrete Outcome." Hypothesis Testing—Chi Squared Test. Last updated September 1, 2016. https://sphweb.bumc.bu.edu/otlt/MPH-Modules/BS/BS704_HypothesisTesting-ChiSquare/BS704_HypothesisTesting-ChiSquare3.html.

Teske, Boris, Michael DiCarlo, and Dexter Cahoy. "Libraries and Student Persistence at Southern Colleges and Universities." *Reference Services Review* 41, no. 2 (2013): 266–79. https://doi.org/10.1108/00907321311326174.

US Census Bureau. "QuickFacts: Yuma County, Arizona." Accessed July 11, 2020. https://www.census.gov/quickfacts/fact/table/yumacountyarizona/PST045219.

Vance, Jason M., Rachel Kirk, and Justin G. Gardner. "Measuring the Impact of Library Instruction on Freshman Success and Persistence: A Quantitative Analysis." *Communications in Information Literacy* 6, no. 1 (2012): 49–58. https://doi.org/10.15760/comminfolit.2012.6.1.117.

Yuma County Chamber of Commerce. "Demographics." Accessed July 9, 2020. https://www.yumachamber.org/demographics.html (page discontinued).

CHAPTER 7

Benchmarking and Peer Assessment

Sam Suber

Libraries across the nation are facing increased scrutiny, and there is a need to prove value or face reduced hours and budgets. To tackle this threat, Moraine Valley Community College (MVCC) decided to examine ways to tell the story of its library in a meaningful and transparent way. For community college libraries, the pressure to prove their value is often applied by administration and focuses on faculty perceptions of the library's usefulness and, most importantly, how the library directly contributes to student success. Librarians at MVCC brainstormed ways to communicate value to the institution, including ideas such as statistical tracking of library resources and marketing campaigns. However, the best-received idea was benchmarking, which was proposed by the library dean. Benchmarking would demonstrate both strengths and weaknesses of the library, bring context to library operations in comparison to peer institutions, and strengthen arguments for increased funding to college administration. As a result, benchmarking was widely accepted as an assessment method within the library and identified as a strategic goal for the library's 2015–2020 strategic plan.

The benchmarking efforts remained idle until 2019, when the library dean assigned the task to the electronic services coordinator, the author of this chapter. The project was undertaken in 2019, and the analysis for that fiscal year has been completed, but the library will continue to engage in benchmarking annually as new data becomes available. How this project was completed will be presented in four sections in this chapter. The first section will detail scope and methods of data procurement and manipulation where benchmarking data was available to analyze and use. The second section will detail the results of the benchmarking analysis and why each benchmark was chosen and used to demonstrate student success at the college. The third section will detail limitations of the benchmarking project. The fourth section will be a review of concepts taken from the project and takeaways that can be used by libraries that want to work on a benchmark analysis.

Scope and Methods

A foundational planning document for this project is the *Standards for Libraries in Higher Education* published by the Association of College and Research Libraries (ACRL). The *Standards* were selected because they described specifically how an academic library can benchmark and tie the benchmarking to its institution's mission and goal. Appendix 2 of the *Standards* focuses on benchmarking and identifies a sample of nine principles for consideration in benchmarking: institutional effectiveness, professional values, educational role, discovery, collections, space, management/administration/leadership, personnel, and external relations.[1] Within each principle, there are several specific data points that can be used in library benchmarks.

Since the MVCC library chose to utilize existing professional standards for benchmarking, the remaining obstacles for the project were getting the necessary data to perform the benchmark assessment and identifying a platform to manipulate and house data. The library chose two data warehouses to serve this purpose: ACRLMetrics—now ACRL Benchmark: Library Metrics and Trends—and the Illinois Community College Board (ICCB) Data Book.

ACRL Metrics, now Benchmark, is a database of compiled data from the ACRL Academic Library Trends and Statistics Survey, which is a national survey given to academic libraries to answer questions on collections, budgeting, staffing, circulation of materials, hours the library is open and library trends.[2] This survey, given annually, corresponds to a fiscal year, and for a fee, libraries can purchase a subscription to ACRLMetrics to access and download available survey data. The library chose to use ACRLMetrics because its data matches the data points identified for benchmarking and was current to the last fiscal year. Although other sources were considered and had similar data, often these data sets did not have current information within the last five years.

The ICCB Data Book contains freely available information on Illinois community colleges at the institutional level, including staffing, budgeting, and enrollment numbers as well as college completion statistics.[3] This was chosen because it contained data that the ACRLMetrics database did not. Specifically, the ICCB Data Book has community college expenditures for a fiscal year, which was a useful data point for comparing how much each community college invested in its library each fiscal year. For example, to derive the Library Expenditures to Institution Expenditures Percentage benchmark, it required cross-comparing data points from the two databases, pulling total expenditures of each community college library from the ACRLMetrics database, and then pulling the total expenditures of the community college from the ICCB database. The only limitation of the ICCB Data Book is that it is limited to community colleges in Illinois.

To house, manipulate, and present the data to form the benchmarks, Microsoft Excel was chosen, as it contained database features and staff had experience using it for data entry. Within Excel, pivot tables were used to manipulate data and extract the significant features in a data set, while Power Pivot allowed the creation of databases from spreadsheets as needed. Pivot tables might include sums, averages, or other statistics, which are grouped together in a meaningful way.

Results

Twenty benchmarks were selected for this project in the calendar year 2019. This section will discuss four benchmarks that were used in demonstrating the library's impact on student learning:

- total library material expenditures per student FTE (full-time equivalent) and head count
- collections use per student FTE and head count
- reference transactions per student FTE and head count
- instruction sessions per student FTE and head count

MVCC chose to benchmark data with specific libraries within the Network of Illinois Learning Resources in Community Colleges (NILRC) library consortium and with a specific peer group as defined by the ICCB. The ICCB defines a peer group by FTE, budget and staffing at the specific community college. MVCC was placed in peer group VII, which represented the community colleges that had the highest FTE and budgets for community colleges within the state.[4] In our benchmarking assessment, not all colleges from peer group VII are represented. In some cases, the data was not available in ACRL-Metrics and other community college libraries were used as a substitute. Please note peer libraries were anonymized in this chapter.

The first benchmark, total library material expenditures per student FTE and head count, falls under the Collections principle of the *Standards*.[5] The formulas to derive this benchmark are shown in figure 7.1. This benchmark was chosen because collections support research, curricular foci, and instructional strengths of the institution. It could be argued that the more a library spends on collections, the wider the scope of its collection and thus higher use by patrons. Conversely, if a library spends less on collections, it could indicate collections spending is more targeted and library budgetary funding is directed to other areas of the library. Results showed that MVCC spent the least per student among peer group colleges in FY15–FY18 reporting years, as shown in table 7.1.

$$\frac{\text{total library material expenditures}}{\text{student FTE}} \quad \text{and/or} \quad \frac{\text{total library material expenditures}}{\text{student head count}}$$

Figure 7.1

Formulas used to derive the first benchmark: total library material expenditures per student FTE and head count

In comparison, Community Colleges 1 and 2 spent significantly more on materials per student. In FY18, the MVCC library spent $31.70 per student FTE, as opposed to $65.22 spent by Community College 1 and $61.06 spent by Community College 2. It was noted that MVCC library spent less per student, and it highlighted that MVCC collection budget lines did not have the flexibility to allow for growth in comparison to budget lines at peer institutions. This disparity was presented to MVCC administration to argue for more funding in collections to align with peer libraries collections spending. The administration

Table 7.1

Total library material expenditures per student FTE and headcount

Row Labels	Total Library Material Expenditures per Student FTE	Total Library Materials Expenditures per Student Headcount
VII		
Community College 1		
FY15	$45.83	$26.07
FY16	$57.67	$32.44
FY17	$60.25	$33.70
FY18	$65.22	$35.82
Community College 2		
FY15	$66.59	$37.22
FY16	$65.30	$36.29
FY17	$61.71	$34.53
FY18	$61.06	$34.50
Community College 3		
FY15	$59.98	$34.48
FY16	$64.06	$36.83
FY17	$62.17	$35.76
FY18	$63.46	$36.30
Community College 4		
FY15	$53.58	$28.84
FY16	$47.29	$25.30
FY17	$61.51	$33.35
FY18	$56.54	$31.16
Moraine Valley Community College		
FY15	$28.51	$17.74
FY16	$29.04	$17.70
FY17	$30.35	$18.32
FY18	$31.70	$19.21
Grand Total	**$53.47**	**$30.47**

considered the results but believed they did not tell the whole story. Collections spending tells only how much the library is spending on resources for students, but it does not show if students are using the resources, contributing to student success. An institution could be spending more per student, but that does not mean collections are being used. Since collections spending did not necessarily equate to student use, the MVCC library's initial request for increased collections funding was declined. Due to the denial of the library's request, the benchmark collections usage per student FTE and head count was used to address administration's questions about collection usage.

The benchmark collections use per student FTE and head count is from the Collections principle from the *Standards*.[6] Collections use can be defined by electronic resource use (including e-book and e-audio statistics), physical collections use (physical checkouts of books, DVDs, periodicals), or both combined together in one metric. The MVCC library chose to use physical collections use as the data showed the best comparison against peer colleges and would bring the best argument for funding to administration. The formulas to create those benchmarks are shown in figure 7.2. The results are shown in table 7.2.

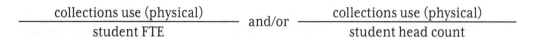

$$\frac{\text{collections use (physical)}}{\text{student FTE}} \quad \text{and/or} \quad \frac{\text{collections use (physical)}}{\text{student head count}}$$

Figure 7.2

Formulas used to derive the second benchmark: physical collections use per student FTE and head count

Table 7.2

Collections use per student FTE and headcount

Row Labels	Collections Use Per Student FTE (Physical)	Collections Use Per Student Headcount (Physical)
VII		
Community College 1		
FY15	6.11	3.47
FY16	6.98	3.92
FY17	4.99	2.79
FY18	6.14	3.37
Community College 2		
FY15	2.88	1.61
FY16	3.14	1.75
FY17	3.90	2.18
FY18	4.37	2.47
Community College 3		
FY15	3.28	1.89
FY16	3.63	2.09
FY17	1.62	0.93
FY18	1.17	0.67
Community College 4		
FY15	2.99	1.61
FY16	2.87	1.54
FY17	2.75	1.49
FY18	2.44	1.35
Moraine Valley Community College		
FY15	5.47	3.41
FY16	7.47	4.55
FY17	7.30	4.41
FY18	7.11	4.31
Grand Total	**4.75**	**2.71**

In FY18, the MVCC library had more physical usage than any other in college in peer group VII. Specifically, the MVCC library had 7.11 physical usage per student FTE, while other colleges, like Community College 4, which had 2.44, and Community College 1, which had 6.14. This benchmark in combination with the material expenditures per student FTE benchmark demonstrated that the MVCC library spent less on collections but received a greater return in collections usage. After these results were shared, administration approved a budget increase in physical collections for the next fiscal year. These benchmarks verified for administration that students were using the collection and that MVCC librarians' selection of materials were meeting student needs, despite their limited budget.

These two benchmarks were presented as discrete requests to administration as the MVCC library and other departments within MVCC make one budget request per fiscal year. As benchmarks were formed, they were presented to administration to back up claims in future funding requests. Data from the benchmarks better informed decision-making for both the library and administration.

The next benchmark was reference transactions per student FTE and head count. This benchmark is from the Discovery principle from the *Standards*.[7] The formulas to create this benchmark are shown in figure 7.3. This benchmark was chosen because reference transactions indicate patrons are seeking information to learn how to navigate college resources and to support their coursework. The library facilitates this by teaching students how to access resources needed to support their coursework. We hoped that this benchmark would reflect a high number of transactions per student, supporting an argument for increased staffing at the MVCC Library. Table 7.3 shows the results of this benchmark.

$$\frac{\text{reference transactions}}{\text{student FTE}} \quad \text{and/or} \quad \frac{\text{reference transactions}}{\text{student head count}}$$

Figure 7.3

Formulas used to derive the third benchmark: reference transactions per student FTE and head count

Table 7.3

Total reference transactions per student FTE and headcount

Row Labels	Sum of 64 Transactions	Reference Transactions per Student FTE	Reference Transactions per Student Headcount
VII			
Community College 1			
FY15	37,779	2.32	1.32
FY16	31,122	2.06	1.16
FY17	16,025	1.10	0.61
FY18	12,487	0.91	0.50
Community College 2			
FY15	4,280	0.51	0.29
FY16	3,209	0.39	0.22
FY17	3,981	0.49	0.27
FY18	4,799	0.60	0.34
Community College 3			
FY15	19,541	2.34	1.34
FY16	20,998	2.58	1.48
FY17	11,256	1.42	0.82
FY18	13,663	1.77	1.01
Community College 4			
FY15	7,244	1.36	0.73
FY16	6,424	1.27	0.68
FY17	5,748	1.19	0.65
FY18	5,576	1.20	0.66
Moraine Valley Community College			
FY15	6,663	0.71	0.44
FY16	6,158	0.67	0.41
FY17	6,005	0.68	0.41
FY18	5,393	0.65	0.39
Grand Total	**22,8351**	**1.27**	**0.72**

Among peer group VII institutions, the MVCC library came in second to last in respect to reference transactions per student FTE. For example, the MVCC library, in FY18, had .65 reference transactions per Student FTE, while Community College 4 had 1.20 reference transactions per FTE, and Community College 1 had .91 reference transactions per FTE. These results showed that MVCC students were not using reference as often as students at other college libraries. Different librarians at MVCC had theories as to why the results showed such low usage of reference services. One librarian posited that it could be an effect of lower enrollment at the college, while another librarian thought that students were becoming more self-reliant as the internet makes it easier to find information. Though there was not consensus among the librarians, we decided to explore the benchmark instruction sessions per student to examine if students might be learning these skills through other library services. The higher the number of Instruction Sessions per Student, the more likely students have already been introduced to information-seeking techniques by the library, allowing them to begin finding information themselves. Correlation does not equal causation, but in order to have meaningful context, the additional benchmark was needed.

The benchmark instruction sessions per student falls under the Educational Role principle of the *Standards*.[8] The formula to create the benchmark is shown in figure 7.4. The results of this benchmark are shown in table 7.4.

$$\frac{\text{instruction sessions}}{\text{student FTE}} \quad \text{and/or} \quad \frac{\text{instruction sessions}}{\text{student head count}}$$

Figure 7.4

Formulas used to derive the fourth benchmark: instruction sessions per student FTE and head count

Table 7.4

Total presentations and instruction sessions per student FTE and headcount

Row Labels	Sum of Number of presentations - total (calculated)	Instruction Sessions Per Student (FTE)	Instruction Sessions Per Student (Headcount)
VII			
Community College 1			
FY15	874	0.05	0.03
FY16	804	0.05	0.03
FY17	790	0.05	0.03
FY18	714	0.05	0.03
Community College 2			
FY15	409	0.05	0.03
FY16	413	0.05	0.03
FY17	238	0.03	0.02
FY18	245	0.03	0.02
Community College 3			
FY15	307	0.04	0.02
FY16	306	0.04	0.02
FY17	251	0.03	0.02
FY18	290	0.04	0.02

Row Labels	Sum of Number of presentations - total (calculated)	Instruction Sessions Per Student (FTE)	Instruction Sessions Per Student (Headcount)
VII			
Community College 4			
FY15	249	0.05	0.03
FY16	234	0.05	0.02
FY17	242	0.05	0.03
FY18	238	0.05	0.03
Moraine Valley Community College			
FY15	614	0.07	0.04
FY16	548	0.06	0.04
FY17	580	0.07	0.04
FY18	565	0.07	0.04
Grand Total	**8911**	**0.05**	**0.03**

For reference, ACRL defines *Presentations* as a combination of instruction sessions given to students and any type of educational, recreational, and cultural presentations such as guest authors or speakers.[9] MVCC had to take that into account because the benchmarked results did not reflect total instructions sessions but a combination of all presentations within a library. Absent a metric specific to library instruction, the data was analyzed for Presentations. In FY17 and FY18, the MVCC library had 0.7 instruction sessions per student, while other colleges like Community College 1 had 0.5. MVCC ranked highest among the peer group, which helped us explain the results of reference transactions per student. In addition, the higher number of instruction sessions demonstrated that faculty valued the library to teach students about resources available. This also supports the argument that the library supports student success through instruction by teaching students how to use library resources, helping them become more self-reliant. Ultimately, the latter two benchmarks were not shown to administration to argue for additional staffing but instead were used internally to improve services for the library. Part of the reasoning for this was because the Presentations metric was not specific enough to instruction sessions and could therefore be misleading.

Limitations

Limitations that hindered project completion included a lack of data and inconsistencies in the data available. Depending on the fiscal year, we found that two to three institutions within peer group VII did not have data available in ACRLMetrics. Data consistency was also an issue, as we found that some data from other institutions were outliers, with abnormally high or low values. Since there was no way to determine the cause of these outliers, these institutions were removed in the data analysis for the specific benchmark where the outlier was present. In situations with missing or inconsistent data, other community colleges outside of peer group VII were used as substitutes.

Review and Takeaways

This project involved gathering, presenting, and manipulating data to create benchmarks in order to demonstrate value and to argue for additional resources. To do this, the MVCC library used the ACRLMetrics database and the ICCB Data Book to examine four out of twenty benchmarks used to measure the library's contributions to student learning. The material expenditures per student FTE/head count benchmark combined with the collections usage per student FTE/head count benchmark demonstrated how MVCC library supported student learning through physical collections despite lack of adequate funding in this area. The reference transactions per student FTE/head count benchmark in conjunction with instruction sessions per student FTE/head count supported the theory that students learned foundational research skills through library instruction, making them more independent library users and reducing the frequency of reference transactions. It should be noted that the number of reference transactions is not reflective of depth and scope of assistance requested.

When pursuing a benchmarking project, one has to consider the audience viewing the data and the means to warehouse the data. These steps created unique challenges as different staff had different learning styles and levels of data literacy. It is recommended to have internal meetings and educational workshops to keep staff informed. The MVCC library used benchmarking to demonstrate value and argue for additional resources. While not all results necessarily shone a positive light on MVCC, they still served a meaningful purpose and were used as opportunities for improvement. This removed the guesswork in determining where to focus efforts, with results highlighting areas to improve services and resource allocation. Libraries undertaking a benchmark analysis will want to recognize that this exercise is useful not only in demonstrating value but also in finding opportunities to grow internally.

Notes

1. Association of College and Research Libraries, *Standards for Libraries in Higher Education* (Chicago: Association of College and Research Libraries, 2011, rev. 2018), 5.
2. Association of College and Research Libraries, ACRLMetrics login page, accessed April 1, 2020, https://www.acrlmetrics.com. ACRLMetrics became ACRL Benchmark: Library Metrics and Trends in late 2021, https://www.ala.org/acrl/proftools/benchmark.
3. Illinois Community College Board, "Data Book," accessed April 1, 2020, http://www2.iccb.org/data/data-characteristics/.
4. Illinois Community College Board, "ICCB Peer Group List," accessed April 1, 2020, http://www2.iccb.org/pods/other/iccb-peer-group-list/.
5. Association of College and Research Libraries, *Standards*, 23.
6. Association of College and Research Libraries, *Standards*, 23.
7. Association of College and Research Libraries, *Standards*, 23.
8. Association of College and Research Libraries, *Standards*, 23.
9. Association of College and Research Libraries, ACRL Academic Library Trends and Statistics Annual Survey Instructions and Definitions, accessed Oct 13, 2021, https://acrl.countingopinions.com/docs/acrl/2018_Instructions.pdf

Bibliography

Association of College and Research Libraries. ACRLMetrics login page. Accessed April 1, 2020. https://www.acrlmetrics.com. ACRLMetrics became ACRL Benchmark: Library Metrics and Trends in late 2021, https://www.ala.org/acrl/proftools/benchmark.

———. *Standards for Libraries in Higher Education.* Chicago: Association of College and Research Libraries, 2011, rev. 2018.

———.*ACRL Academic Library Trends and Statistics Annual Survey Instructions and Definitions.* Chicago: Association of College and Research Libraries, 2010, rev. 2018.

Illinois Community College Board. "Data Book." Accessed April 1, 2020. http://www2.iccb.org/data/data-characteristics/

———. "ICCB Peer Group List. Accessed April 1, 2020. http://www2.iccb.org/pods/other/iccb-peer-group-list/

CHAPTER 8

Exploring Modern Baseball Analytics to Reinvent Library Assessment

Joseph Eshleman

Introduction

There are many reasons community college librarians pour resources into assessment. Most likely, the primary reason would be to provide measurements that demonstrate the value of the library and help improve its services. However, there may be less of a consensus around the idea of what and how to measure. Certainly, there is overlap on a number of statistics and other measures that libraries use to assess. For example, quantitative compiling on checkouts, reference transactions, and library instruction classes is usually standard, and some of those numbers make sense to collect as a way to fulfill data needs for accreditation. In addition to these numbers, there may be qualitative assessments that individual libraries use to support and supplement their data. Community college libraries generally assess how their library and their library workers contribute to student success, yet the methods to measure how these goals are achieved can vary greatly. There is a field that is almost obsessed with assessment to which libraries can look that may allow an expansion into new ways to measure worth, and that field is a baseball field.

The history of baseball statistics is quite interesting and offers an instructive glimpse into how to measure contribution and worth. In the same way that libraries have changed

121

through the years, the way the game has been played and how player contribution has been measured have gone through several different eras. Baseball always seems to have had a healthy obsession with statistics, and in comparison to other major sports, statisticians and record keepers seem to gravitate to this historic fascination.[1] There is conjecture as well as sound evidence around why baseball seems to draw in those concerned with numbers and records. One idea is that baseball's leisurely style of play allows for more introspection, which adds emphasis to a commitment to recording the game. Additionally, the long history of the game has elevated it to something that is historically and culturally important to record and reflect upon. This long history of tracking different facets of the game for statistical purposes aligns with librarians' ongoing efforts to evolve assessment efforts in order to improve service to students.

This chapter will provide a short overview of how libraries have collected information and the parameters they have used to record statistics about their value. In conjunction with this, and as a way to shed light on how assessment evolves, a brief look at baseball's history of record keeping and assessment of player value will be looked at in tandem. The objective is to reflect on the evolution of assessment in both endeavors to demonstrate how changing the parameters and method of assessment sheds new light on value. In addition, the chapter will highlight how community college libraries can potentially begin to assess using new parameters in a stark break with their past assessment practices, using examples from the Central Piedmont Community College (CPCC) libraries.

Foundations of Baseball Statistics and Library Assessment

Going through the history and evolution of statistical assessment with regard to both baseball and libraries can be an illuminating endeavor. Taking liberties with how certain eras can be classified, the breakdown can be generously divided in this way: the tallying eras, the expansion on tallying, the deeper assessment eras, and the future era. Abstaining from adding strict dates that match these eras is due to the fact that both baseball and libraries have large, ever-changing data sets and parameters, and the chronological histories of both institutions do not necessarily match up perfectly. Despite this, journeying thorough some highlights can lead to ideas on how to advance assessment for libraries.

Early Statistics and Assessment

During the same time that baseball began in the late 1880s, libraries were assessing by tallying the number of visitors and the number of books checked out.[2] Using large paper binders (similar to the way accounting was accomplished), libraries would record for recording's sake and would not often asses their value apart from how often their collection was used. Libraries had a type of monopoly on knowledge storage and use and therefore did not have their value come into question very frequently. At this time, baseball was interested only in recording the game and not in using the statistics of players in team measurements or deep assessments. This disinterest in a focus on individual contributions may have aligned with the prevailing notion of the importance of collective efforts in the sport. That is to say, the major value was whether one team outscored another, not individual player accomplishments.

Like baseball, with its early era priority of simply keeping score of the actual game, libraries also demonstrated their value with rudimentary number compiling, one of the best examples of that being collection size, "Rightly or wrongly, collection size has long been considered an indicator of collection quality."[3] For years, academic libraries would boast of the number of books they held, which appeared to directly imply the amount of knowledge stored within the stacks. This look at knowledge accumulation in the form of bound volumes has since been proven to be somewhat limited. Collection size is not indicative of the diversity of voices within the collection and its ability to support the specific educational needs of its campus community. However, at the time, collection size was touted with pride. This position aligns with the way in which team efforts in baseball obscured individual contributions and reflects the historic lack of inclusivity that defined and shaped baseball in the beginning of the twentieth century.

The importance placed on the size and standardization of the collection may have undervalued the public's understanding of the contribution of the workers in the library in the same way that players were not considered to be stars when baseball began. That concept changed drastically in baseball, and the case could be made that a similar impactful event that elevates the role of the library worker has not yet occurred in librarianship.

Evolution of Baseball Statistics and Library Assessment

At the turn of the century, for baseball, numerous individual statistics began to gain importance, such as batting average (how many times a player got a hit in relation to how many times they batted), runs scored by a player, and runs batted in.[4] Expansion into more categories such as types of hits (singles, doubles, triples, home runs) and pitching statistics began to take hold and serve as important assessment measures through the 1980s.

"A Numbers Revolution" by ESPN writer Alan Schwarz is a fascinating and pertinent article that details over fifty chronological data points of baseball record keeping.[5] This article is associated with Schwarz's book *The Numbers Game: Baseball's Lifelong Fascination with Statistics*, which was published in 2004.[6] Initiating his list with "1845—First box score appears in New York Morning News. Batters' columns include only runs and outs."[7] and closing out with "2003—MLB.com decides to begin outfitting stadiums with sophisticated camera systems to capture pitch and throw velocities, runner speeds, batted-ball trajectories and more, in part to build an entire new set of fielding statistics, ETA 2006,"[8] this rundown is a helpful and illuminating record of how baseball statistics progressed throughout the years.

One of the interesting trends that this 160-year review shows is that in many cases, baseball fans were the catalysts for improving methods and changing the parameters of how to assess the game. In libraries, this would be similar to patrons playing a role in how the library measures itself and makes improvements. Patron-driven assessments typically provide qualitative data and can be done using various assessment tools such as student surveys. One such tool that libraries can use to gather this type of patron-driven data is Project Outcome.

Project Outcome is an online assessment platform for libraries created by the Association of College and Research Libraries.[9] This survey-based site allows academic and public libraries to assess themselves based on numerous service area measurements. For academic libraries, these areas are digital and special collections, instruction, research, teaching support, events/programs, library technology, and space. These uniform surveys promote consistency with four preloaded questions and the option to add three open-ended questions. The surveys primarily assess student dispositions, such as confidence and awareness of resources, and provide libraries the opportunity to create reports that show comparisons to other library scores, including national and Carnegie class averages. Although the assessment tool here is of primary interest, rather than contemplating the measurement parameters used, the tool is a great leap forward in gathering relevant library data. This is similar to the numbers revolution in baseball touched on earlier, and a line can be drawn to how libraries must continue to reevaluate their methods for measuring their academic contributions and value.

At the CPCC libraries, librarians have utilized the instruction, teaching support, and events/programs surveys to assess our library's offerings. Although the libraries previously surveyed students, the Project Outcome library assessment platform allowed CPCC to provide context to administration, demonstrating how our libraries performed in comparison to other libraries. As an example of how these surveys and the data are designed, the four questions in the instruction surveys put forward to students measure their knowledge, confidence, application/new skills, and awareness of resources. Collectively, using a total of 184 surveys, 91 percent learned something new to help succeed in classes, 94 percent intend to apply what they learned, 85 percent felt more confident about completing assignments, and 91 percent were more aware of resources and services provided by the library. These numbers aligned with the Carnegie class of Associate's Colleges/2-year Institutions and national averages. This type of library instruction assessment goes beyond tallying students in classes and allowed us to shift to a more meaningful assessment of our instruction efforts.

Applying New Measures to Old Statistics

An interesting addendum to compiling baseball statistics occurred when newer measurements were applied to earlier scorekeeping to re-evaluate the information to more modern standards. As summed up by John Thorn in his *Our Game* blog post "Major League Baseball Record Keeping," old records were pored through with an eye for new assessment parameters. This created a situation where the "group not only found new data to correct old inaccuracies but also applied new yardsticks to men who had gone to their graves never having heard of an RBI or a save."[10] Similarly, libraries would benefit from taking new approaches, such as using new teaching practices to make new meaning out of previous student learning assessment efforts, or applying new collection development approaches to evaluate existing collections for diversity and inclusion.

How do libraries measure up when they look at how their communities are served? Are certain groups ignored or not included? An emphasis on inclusive teaching practices at the CPCC libraries and how to assess these is a constant talking point. Currently, libraries could be said to be doing a better job thinking about their communities, whereas some feel as if baseball has recently ignored its communities.[11] This idea maps to community college libraries assessing their services, resources offered, and physical spaces to measure the satisfaction and needs of all of their patrons. Taking their name seriously and emphasizing the service to their myriad patron groups, a question for community college libraries when assessing their services and resources would seem to be self-evident: Are they serving their communities? Baseball has come under a great deal of justified criticism for abandoning its connections to youth and separating the sport from its formerly blue-collar audience. Criticisms have included high ticket prices that shut out those who could formerly see a game and showing games too late at night to develop younger fans' interest. Even in regard to appealing to girls and women who love the sport, football has been thought to have reached out to this audience in a much better way.

Technology and Deeper Assessments

Computers have obviously affected almost every facet of life and have contributed greatly to assessment. This technological leap also was felt by libraries and is demonstrated by the amplification of assessment in libraries during this time. This is also noted in the Value of Academic and Research Libraries section of the Association of College and Research Libraries (ACRL) website:

> ACRL has long been concerned with accountability, assessment, and student learning. In the early 1980s, ACRL was on the cutting edge of these issues with a publication on assessment to "stimulate librarians' interest in performance measures and to provide practical assistance so that librarians could conduct meaningful measurements of effectiveness with minimum expense and difficulty."[12]

Sabermetrics, which is often credited to baseball analyst Bill James, also coincides with the advent of computers in the 1980s and has been seen as the breakthrough for the largest advance in baseball assessment:

> The term itself was coined in 1980 …by renowned baseball analyst Bill James…. [It was] named in honor of the Society for American

Baseball Research (SABR) of which James is a member.... He called sabermetrics "the search for objective knowledge about baseball." However, that's not where the story begins. From simple scorekeeping to the more complex statistics that define the game today, statistics have long been important in baseball.[13]

The interesting use of the terminology *objective knowledge* belies the notion that individual player statistics were now considered obsolete and using the statistics holistically to assess the team's ability to win or lose was the main focus. In fact, as will be shown later, sabermetrics have limitations in relation to concepts such as intangibles and the human element. This is an important distinction to make as it relates to libraries because there should always be an understanding that assessment does not necessarily provide conclusive answers but gives guidelines for decisions. In the same way that libraries are "growing organisms"[14] and are subject to an ever-evolving community, baseball's strict reliance on numbers alone did not lead to ultimate success. This notion is even more important to consider at a community college, where the student population is much more varied and ever-changing than at other institutions of higher learning. It has been pointed out in many sources that even though Bill James is considered to be the founder and major progenitor of sabermetrics, there were numerous antecedents that paved the way for his new look at baseball statistical measurement.[15] A way to map out how this era parallels library assessment is to focus on how assessment has gained in stature comprehensively within education. Community colleges have taken a much more serious look at assessment in the last few decades, some of which has been driven by the continuing questions around the value of education. Moving away from quantitative assessment and into qualitative was the trend. Parameters such as instruction classes taught and reference desk interactions made way for deeper insight into metrics that measured the diversity of a collection and an interest in learning analytics that showed correlation between library use and GPAs. While learning analytics have not been used in the library at Central Piedmont, collective efforts when looking at chat statistics, use of library study rooms, and computer reservations in tandem with one-on-one appointments and embedded librarians in classes in the school's LMS can help to form ideas on how to support student success. For example, embedded librarians can use their understanding of class assignments to help students in chat and offer help when assignments are due. One-on-one appointments often offer unique opportunities to ask students directly about library resources and services needed.

One fascinating recent sidebar to this discussion about baseball statistical gathering is the well-known case of *Moneyball*.[16] *Briefly, this story involved the general manager of the Oakland A's, Billy Beane, and his emphasized use of different and newer statistics (sabermetrics) to measure player worth, more so than anyone in the past. Beane*

performed data mining on hundreds of individual players, ultimately identifying statistics that were highly predictive of how many runs a player would score. These statistics weren't necessarily numbers that baseball scouts traditionally valued. Instead of competing for

high-priced home-run hitters with high batting averages, he sought
lower-cost players with high on-base percentages.[17]

A book and movie followed the season Beane strongly relied on this method and in
which he had some success with this strategy (The A's won twenty games in a row during
the season.) Ultimately, his team did not gain the desired outcome. (The A's did not win
the World Series that year, or any year from then to the present day, for that matter, using
these methods.) It should be noted that although his team did not gain the ultimate goal,
the theories created admiration because of the financial angle. That is, Beane's team was
successful by some measurements because the organization did not spend as much money
as others that were less successful. Therefore, his newer strategy was deemed to be better
than an old one in some ways. Applying this analogy to libraries, could a library be more
successful serving its community than others in such a way that it would spend less money
and meet some desired goals?

Could a library perform a parallel version of moneyball (moneylibrary)? It is an interesting thing to think about, and of course, some of the aspects of the comparison don't fit
well, such as the fact that libraries don't generate their own money in the same way that
baseball does. Despite this, are some libraries structured so that they can look at assessment in new and interesting ways to achieve their goals? Have some libraries realized that
a diverse collection can be more important to their community than the largest budget or
than building a redundant collection? Are some community college libraries modeling
the value of the economic impact they have on upward mobility in their community as a
priority rather than showing their patrons how they have more databases than the previous year? What numbers and impact are the most important? All of these questions can
lead to different strategies for different community colleges and ideally each can lead to
renewed discussion on the value of the library.

An early era rudimentary statistic such as batting average, which could be said to
correspond to the number of books in a library collection, morphed half a century later
to the sabermetric wins above replacements (WAR). The WAR statistic "measures a player's value in all facets of the game by deciphering how many more wins he's worth than a
replacement-level player at his same position."[18] Using this type of assessment advance-
ment, could libraries measure the value of their entire contribution to a community college
in a more holistic way? Could they calculate the loss a community college would experience if the library was not there or all of its services needed to be replaced by another
campus entity?

Turning to other timely topics, the current expansion of surveillance and decision-making using artificial intelligence continue to be major influencers in assessment
across professions. How will both baseball and libraries respond to data collection and
assessment that remove some of the human element and rely more on decisions made by
algorithms and machine learning? Some of this change has already begun to occur, much
to the dismay of library advocates who point out the dangerous and transgressive aspects
of relying on these systems. As has been pointed out in the past with search engines, social
media advertising, and targeting, as well as an issue within library software systems, the

underlying algorithms and coding that run these systems are created by humans with built-in biases and lack of foresight on how the systems may be used in negative ways.[19] Reidsma's deep dive into how library system algorithms create bias stemmed from earlier studies on search engines by authors such as Cathy O'Neil and Safiya Noble.[20]

As a way to unite all of these disparate ideas (understanding the diverse community college student population, focusing on the collective value of the community college library rather than just separate services and resources, and spending more time assessing how library systems may reinforce inequality), it is interesting to see how they all point away from technological solutions toward the importance of library workers. A refocus on how library workers impact student success may be the most important lesson here as a move from quantitative to qualitative continues to be a priority. At Central Piedmont's main campus, a new library is set to open in 2022, and it is being built with an adjoining student success center. Reinforcing the idea of a library as a type of student success support system with library workers who have student success at the forefront of their goals may be the most important measurement that proves the value of the library and will continue to improve library services.

Future of Statistics and Assessment

In the same way that moving from more static and generic statistic taking evolved in baseball to a system that focused on how deeper meaning was derived from how a player can contribute in multiple ways, libraries should consider this concept when assessing their value. A rather large subset of librarians and those who are interested in baseball appear to have an inordinate enthusiasm for monitoring and recording specific aspects in their fields. For librarians, the historical drive (and need) to keep track of collections ideally allows for insight into how to best share information. For baseball statisticians and avid followers of the game, including those within the sport, keeping track of statistics and records allows for quantitative debate about how players and teams rate during their current playing time and comparatively against historical numbers. Each of these groups desires to show value and has used different methods through history to do it.

Using baseball as a way to parse out ways to compare and contrast assessment of libraries can be enlightening, but like many analogies and comparisons, it has limitations. The one that initially crops up is the competitive nature of baseball as a sport versus the service-oriented nature of librarianship. Despite this, the assessment inclinations of both endeavors are a core feature, and the idea of using the assessment information to create improvement and value overlaps. As articulated in this chapter, baseball (and its infatuation with statistical assessment) serves as an example of how to continually reevaluate parameters of assessment and creatively change ways to assess. The impetus for baseball is to gain a competitive edge and, although at first glance it would appear that the goal would be different for libraries, parallels do exist. Although libraries (and librarians) are not prone to competitive natures (or at least in the same way as baseball), there is still a drive within libraries to perform well. Part of this drive should be a motivating factor to move away from direct tallying measurement and toward more meaningful measures that focus on how libraries contribute to the overall student experience. Should community college libraries put more consideration into the different ways students (and other patrons) are affected by the library? Is there a way to record and measure the impact that the library has on their lives? Although this chapter merely scratched the surface on new ways to think about how to measure the library's impact on students by using baseball's innovative approaches to assessment, the conceptual pointers are there.

Notes

1. Alan Schwarz, "A Numbers Revolution." ESPN, July 8, 2004, https://www.espn.com/mlb/columns/story?columnist=schwarz_alan&id=1835745.
2. Scott W. H. Young, "On the Imperial History of Library Assessment," Scott W. H. Young website, April 30, 2020, https://scottwhyoung.com/posts/imperial-library-assessment.
3. Mary F. Casserly, "Research in Academic Library Collection Management 1990–2007," in *Academic Library Research: Perspectives and Current Trends*, ed. Marie Radford and Pamela Snelson, ACRL Publications in Librarianship No. 59 (Chicago: Association of College and Research Libraries, 2008), p. 83, University Libraries Faculty Scholarship, Scholars Archive, University at Albany, State University of New York, http://scholarsarchive.library.albany.edu/ulib_fac_scholar/27.
4. Schwarz, "Numbers Revolution."
5. Schwarz, "Numbers Revolution."
6. Alan Schwarz, *The Numbers Game* (New York: T. Dunne, 2004).
7. Schwarz, "Numbers Revolution."
8. Schwarz, "Numbers Revolution."
9. Association of College and Research Libraries, "Project Outcome: Measuring the True Impact of Libraries," 2018–2019, https://acrl.projectoutcome.org/.
10. John Thorn, "Major League Baseball Record Keeping," *Our Game,* July 14, 2014, https://ourgame.mlblogs.com/major-league-baseball-record-keeping-3fd036a44072.
11. Stephen L. Carter, "Baseball Fans Are Too Old, Too White and Too Few," Bloomberg Opinion, October 31, 2019, https://www.bloomberg.com/opinion/articles/2019-10-31/baseball-s-diversity-problem-fans-are-older-whiter-and-fewer.
12. Association of College and Research Libraries, "ACRL History," https://www.ala.org/acrl/aboutacrl/history/history.
13. Thorn, "Major League Baseball Record Keeping."
14. Scott Piepenburg, "The Five Laws of Library Science," *Librarian to Librarian* (blog), October 18, 2019, https://librariantolibrarian.wordpress.com/2019/10/18/the-five-laws-of-library-science/.
15. Thorn, "Major League Baseball Record Keeping."
16. Michael Lewis. *Moneyball: The Art of Winning an Unfair Game* (New York: W.W. Norton, 2004). *Moneyball,* directed by Bennett Miller. (Columbia Pictures, 2011).
17. Alan Schwarz, "Darwins of the Diamond," ESPN, July 8, 2004, https://www.espn.com/mlb/columns/story?columnist=schwarz_alan&id=1835736.
18. Major League Baseball, "Wins above Replacement (WAR)," http://m.mlb.com/glossary/advanced-stats/wins-above-replacement.
19. Matthew Reidsma, *Masked by Trust* (Sacramento, CA: Library Juice Press, 2019).
20. Reidsma, *Masked by Trust*; Cathy O'Neil, *Weapons of Math Destruction* (New York: Crown, 2016); Safiya Umoja Noble, *Algorithms of Oppression* (New York: New York University Press, 2018).

Bibliography and Additional Resources

Association of College and Research Libraries. "ACRL History." https://www.ala.org/acrl/aboutacrl/history/history.

———. "Project Outcome: Measuring the True Impact of Libraries." 2018–2019. https://acrl.projectoutcome.org/.

Bogan, Kelsey. "Diversity Audit: A Practical Guide." *Don't Shush Me! Adventures of a Future Ready High School Librarian* (blog), June 15, 2020. https://dontyoushushme.com/2020/06/15/diversity-audit-a-practical-guide/.

Carter, Stephen L. "Baseball Fans Are Too Old, Too White and Too Few." Bloomberg Opinion, October 31, 2019. https://www.bloomberg.com/opinion/articles/2019-10-31/baseball-s-diversity-problem-fans-are-older-whiter-and-fewer.

Casserly, Mary F. "Research in Academic Library Collection Management 1990–2007." In *Academic Library Research: Perspectives and Current Trends*. Edited by Marie Radford and Pamela Snelson, 82–137. ACRL Publications in Librarianship No. 59. Chicago: Association of College and Research Libraries, 2008. University Libraries Faculty Scholarship. Scholars Archive, University at Albany, State University of New York. http://scholarsarchive.library.albany.edu/ulib_fac_scholar/27.

Leis, Michael. *Moneyball : The Art of Winning an Unfair Game*. New York : W.W.Norton, 2004.

Major League Baseball. "Wins above Replacement (WAR)." http://m.mlb.com/glossary/advanced-stats/wins-above-replacement.

Miller, Bennet, director. *Moneyball*. Columbia Pictures, 2011.

Noble, Safiya Umoja. *Algorithms of Oppression: How Search Engines Reinforce Racism*. New York: New York University Press, 2018.

O'Neil, Cathy. *Weapons of Math Destruction: How Big Data Increases Inequality and Threatens Democracy*. New York: Crown, 2016.

Piepenburg, Scott. "The Five Laws of Library Science." *Librarian to Librarian* (blog), October 18, 2019. https://librariantolibrarian.wordpress.com/2019/10/18/the-five-laws-of-library-science/.

Project READY: Reimagining Equity and Access for Diverse Youth, Institute of Museum and Library Services. "Library Collection Shelf Audit for Diversity and Inclusion." January 1, 2019. https://ready.web.unc.edu/.

Reidsma, Matthew. *Masked by Trust: Bias in Library Discovery*. Sacramento, CA: Library Juice Press, 2019.

Schwarz, Alan. "Darwins of the Diamond." ESPN, July 8, 2004. https://www.espn.com/mlb/columns/story?columnist=schwarz_alan&id=1835736.

———. *The Numbers Game: Baseball's Lifelong Fascination with Statistics* (New York: T. Dunne, 2004).

———. "A Numbers Revolution." ESPN, July 8, 2004. https://www.espn.com/mlb/columns/story?columnist=schwarz_alan&id=1835745.

Thorn, John. "Major League Baseball Record Keeping." *Our Game*, July 14, 2014. https://ourgame.mlblogs.com/major-league-baseball-record-keeping-3fd036a44072.

Young, Scott W. H. "On the Imperial History of Library Assessment." Scott W. H. Young website. April 30, 2020. https://scottwhyoung.com/posts/imperial-library-assessment.

CHAPTER 9

Assessing User-Centeredness with Focus Groups

A Study of Commuter Students in a Community College Library

Sharell Walker and Joanna Thompson

Introduction

While surveys tend to be the most frequently used research method in libraries, focus groups are growing in popularity in library research. Using focus groups as an assessment tool can be an interesting and informative way to gather information in a student-centered process. During the 2019–2020 academic year, the A. Philip Randolph Library, which serves the Borough of Manhattan Community College (BMCC), City University of New York (CUNY), ran a series of focus groups in hopes of gathering qualitative data pertaining to student use of the library space. In the past, the library faculty and staff have used a variety of methods to assess their services and their space, including observational studies and surveys. The most recent period of using focus groups is an attempt to expand upon past assessment methods to incorporate broader student voices. This chapter will explore whether focus groups are an effective method for evaluating physical library spaces and whether the BMCC library space meets the needs of its exclusively commuter patrons.

Background

It is important to understand the student body of BMCC in order to understand their unique library space needs. BMCC is one of seven CUNY community colleges that work to provide high-quality associate degree programs in order to transition New York City students into four-year degree programs or professional success. A summary of the most recent demographic data (spring 2019) is available on BMCC's website. The demographic data reveals that many BMCC students are:

- International and multilingual. A total of 156 countries and 103 languages are represented at BMCC. As of spring 2019, the top ten countries represented, outside of the United States, are the Dominican Republic, Mexico, China, Jamaica, Ecuador, Guyana, Bangladesh, Haiti, Trinidad and Tobago, and Colombia. The top ten languages represented, other than English, are Spanish, Chinese, Bengali, French, Arabic, Russian, Creole, Albanian, Cantonese, and Korean.
- A nontraditional age demographic. The average age of students at BMCC is twenty-four. Of students, 10.5 percent are eighteen years and under, 63.9 percent are nineteen to twenty-five years old, and 25.6 percent are twenty-six years and older.
- Low-income. Of students, 64.7 percent are Pell Grant recipients, and 31.3 percent are Tuition Assistance Program grant recipients. New York State's Tuition Assistance Program (TAP) helps eligible New York residents pay tuition at approved schools in New York State.
- Part-time. Of BMCC students, 31.7 percent attend the college part-time. As of fall 2018, BMCC had the second largest part-time population in the CUNY system.
- Commuters. BMCC does not offer dorming options on the school campus. Roughly 85 percent of BMCC students commute to the campus from and hold residency in one of the five boroughs that make up New York City (Brooklyn, Bronx, Manhattan, Queens, Staten Island).[1]

The Randolph Library, located on the fourth floor at 199 Chambers Street, is named after the African American labor leader and social activist A. Philip Randolph (1889–1979). The library serves over 23,000 undergraduate students from over 150 countries. It offers 113,000 volumes of books, 169 databases, 114,000 e-journals, and 580,000 e-books. The library has not undergone any major structural changes since its erection in 1983. The library has designated areas for the stack, reserve, and reference collections, a library instruction classroom, approximately 300 carrels for individual student work, two group study rooms, and a front area with group tables and a circular sofa for comfortable seating. The library space continues to evolve around student needs in minor ways, such as alternative seating options, but further and larger scale change should reflect the needs of the students.

Purpose of the Study

The library's mission is to serve the BMCC community by "providing high-quality services, collections, spaces, and experiences—both virtual and physical—that create an environment of transformation and growth."[2] Along with the mission, the BMCC library has four goals in which it strives to achieve, one of which is to "create user-centered spaces and services in the Library."[3] The purpose of the focus groups is to ensure that the library is in fact user-centered. Do the students feel comfortable in the library space? Do they find the space useful? What would they change if given the option? In order to successfully achieve these ideals, the library must study how students are using the spaces and services, if the spaces and services are providing quality experiences, and how the library can improve services to adequately satisfy the needs of the BMCC community.

Methodology

To investigate students' perceptions and needs in the BMCC library space, the library organized five student focus groups. Students were recruited via a weekly e-mail blast to all BMCC students sent out by BMCC Student Affairs. A flyer was designed by the library specifically for recruiting students (figure 9.1).

Students then filled out a Google Form to indicate interest in a specific focus group date. A fifth focus group date was later added in an attempt to recruit more students. The intake Google Form consisted of the following intake questions and guidelines:

1. Email Address

2. Name

3. Choice of Preferred Date of Focus Group

4. By clicking the SUBMIT button I agree to the following:

    a. I understand that my responses will be analyzed and transcribed for informational use.

    b. I understand that my participation is completely voluntary and that I can withdraw from the study at any time.

    c. I understand that my participation is in no way related to my academic record at BMCC.

    d. I understand that my responses will potentially be published.

    e. I understand that my name and all identifying characteristics will be removed before any publication of study results.

Only students who had been at BMCC for longer than two semesters were eligible for participation to increase the likelihood that students had significant experience in the library. Twenty students were accepted for the focus groups in an effort to keep the focus group sizes manageable during this first phase of what could be a series of focus groups. When recruitment exceeded capacity, students were accepted on a first come, first served basis. All students who participated were offered refreshments and a thirty-day Unlimited MetroCard (card used for fare payment on public transportation in New York City)

BMCC Library Focus Groups!

Would you like to take part in a focus group for
the library? Come tell us your opinions and concerns
for the chance to get a wonderful prize.

October 17th,
2PM-4PM

October 24th,
10AM to 12PM

November 6th,
2PM-4PM

November 20th,
10AM-12PM

LARGE STUDY ROOM
S410N

To sign up for the focus group please fill out the form linked
here: https://forms.gle/pEUCxW9XEoJhf9317

You can also use the QR code to get to the form directly
from your phone.

We are looking for 20 participants. Each participant will
receive a **30 day unlimited MetroCard** and will be entered
into a raffle to win **one of 4 brand new Chromebooks from Dell!**

Figure 9.1

Flyer to recruit students for focus groups

and were entered into a raffle for one of four Dell Chromebooks. These incentives were
chosen specifically for commuter students at BMCC, who are in need of technological
and travel support.

The focus groups were held in a private group study room in the library space. All focus
group sessions were recorded using Otter, a free application that records and transcribes

audio. Notes were also taken to ensure clarity. All participants were assigned numbers for anonymity and gave verbal consent to be recorded. In addition to participants, there were two to four librarians present at each focus group. One librarian asked questions and facilitated discussion, while another librarian recorded the conversation and took notes.

During the focus groups, students were asked about their feelings on the library space. Focus group questions consisted of the following:

1. In a typical semester, describe how you use the Library, specifically the physical space.

2. How do you feel when you use the library space? Please describe specific situations when you were frustrated or pleased.

3. What needs do you see BMCC Library filling in your college community?

4. In your opinion, what are the most beneficial resources, services or programs offered by the Library?

5. Do you find the library space comfortable?

6. In a world with no restrictions on funding and space, describe what your ideal library looks like.

7. What is one thing we can do or change about the library space to make your life as a student easier?

8. Do you have any suggestions for us or anything else you would like to add?

The focus groups were semi-structured, allowing students to address issues with the library and library space beyond our list of questions and to bounce ideas off of each other. Unlike a more structured, rigid survey typical of library research, this design allowed students to suggest library space changes that librarians might not think of. The focus groups were casual and conversational, and facilitators encouraged students to be honest about both positive and negative feelings regarding the library space. The research team built a climate of trust by reassuring students that their answers would remain confidential and there would be no retaliation against them for negative feedback. Between focus groups, the research team met to reflect on focus groups and reevaluate questions. They discussed some overarching themes that emerged throughout each focus group and reworded focus group questions for clarity if needed.

At the conclusion of the focus groups, the research team created a preliminary list of codes based on initial impressions of themes in the focus groups. While codes about the collection were included, an effort was made to focus on codes related primarily to the library space. The team then used Taguette, an open-source, browser-based data analysis tool, to code all focus group transcripts. Taguette is a simple but powerful tool that allows users to create projects, upload documents or text files, and create codes and descriptions of codes. Users can highlight words or sentences and add a previously created code or can add codes as they work through each document. The transcripts of the focus group conversations were uploaded and scanned, and individual sentences and statements were assigned a relevant code or codes. Sentences about irrelevant topics such as the group refreshments were omitted from coding. After an initial round of coding, the research team reconvened to discuss adding codes. During this meeting, the team added additional codes and developed more detailed descriptions of codes as needed (table 9.1).

Table 9.1

Codes and descriptions

Tags	Description	Examples
Atmosphere	The mood, tone, and ambiance of the library	Decor, cleanliness, temperature, comfort
Basic operations	The basic rules and regulations of the library	Rules of the library, hours, signage
Collection	References to the physical collections of the library	Books, stacks, reserves, fiction, nonfiction
Community equipment	References to computer bays, printers, and copy machines; nonmobile equipment	Printers, copy machines, paper cutter, computer bays
Electronic equipment	References to electronic devices provided for individual mobile use	Laptops, tablets, calculators, DVDs
Group seating	Areas available for multiple students to sit together and work	Couches, long tables
Individual seating	Individual desk available for single student use	Carrel, chair, desk
Noise	Sound level of the library space	Loud, quiet
Online sources	Specific to sources available from the library website	Catalog, OneSearch, databases, website
Personnel	Library and school employees	Librarian, security guard, staff
Privacy	Reference to being monitored or watched by employees or other students	Cameras, privacy
Programming	Events that happen inside the library	Events, displays, workshops

Using Focus Groups in Library Planning

Various resources were consulted in the decision to conduct focus groups as a way to garner student opinions. Focus groups have proven to be useful tools in procuring information. In the article "The Importance of User-Centered Design: Exploring Findings and Methods," Rosalie Lack gives an explanation of how focus groups have become a useful way to gather input on services to meet user needs. Lack described focus groups as a "group dynamic [which] generates ideas."[4] Our purpose in these focus groups is to not only understand how students use our space and services but also to generate new ideas on how the space and services can be improved. Lack states,

> The give and take of focus group conversations is useful for learning what participants think about a particular topic and for uncovering why they think as they do… focus groups provide insight into the user's current environment—what works well or not with their current system and what are the glaring omissions. In addition to providing a good tool for gathering feedback about a service currently in use, focus groups can also reveal user expectations regarding new services.[5]

The flow of conversation will prove helpful in getting students to be honest about their use of the library and what they hope to see in the library as future services and resources. The conversational quality will get in-depth information that a survey may not, such as deep reasoning for why students feel certain ways or think certain things about the library and its usefulness.

Christina Hillman and colleagues, in the article "User-Focused, User-Led: Space Assessment to Transform a Small Academic Library," describe the use of focus groups in an effort to understand student use of the library space. Hillman and colleagues state, "Findings from focus groups provided better understanding of what users think about library spaces, including their intended use and desire for these spaces."[6] Hillman and colleagues also demonstrated the important information gathered from commuter students in their use of the library space. Hillman and colleagues state, "Commuters indicated coming to the library most often between classes to connect with friends, not to engage in serious work…. For group work and projects, both commuters and residents commonly use library spaces."[7] As BMCC has only commuter students, it is important to understand the difference between resident students and commuter students in their library needs. Hillman and colleagues' use of a focus group was beneficial to help discover these important differences in library habits. However, the student body at Hillman's small academic library is very different from the large community at BMCC.

Results and Implications

The focus groups garnered a plethora of suggestions on how to improve the library space for student use. The most frequently mentioned code was "atmosphere," referring to the mood, tone, and ambiance of the library. Many students complained about the temperature of the library, the cleanliness of the space, and the decor. Students felt the library needed updating to its decor to match the more updated areas of the school. Suggested changes included painting the walls brighter colors, more windows, and regular carpet shampooing. These items would make the library a more comfortable space for students.

Seating, both group and individual seating, proved to be a large issue for students as well. Many students requested more options for comfortable seating so students could relax, and even take naps, in the library. Requests included more soft couches or even a separate meditation room for students to have a calm quiet space. This proved to be a valuable suggestion as many students use the library as their only study space. Students indicated that they felt uncomfortable studying at home due to a variety of reasons. In addition, as BMCC is a campus of only commuter students, students do not have the luxury of a dorm room to return to if they need to study during a break in classes. Returning home to study could require a commute of anywhere from thirty minutes to two hours depending on where the student lives. BMCC students often schedule classes in between their work schedule and often need a quiet place to relax for a minute or two or to do schoolwork.

The variety of responses gave a plethora of tips and suggestions that the library could use to advocate for future changes to the library space. In addition to the issues outlined above, students also commented on their desire for more programming, newer computer equipment, and more welcoming and understanding personnel. The fact that students prioritized a welcoming atmosphere and comfortable seating over collections and programming points to the needs of commuter students, who often do not have another place to study or relax. For many BMCC students, the library provides respite, and changes should be made to the space with this in mind. The results of this study could serve as a successful bargaining tool during requests to administration for changes to the library space. This study is meant to be the beginning of a longer series of assessments aimed at understanding the needs of commuter students in the academic library.

Limitations of Focus Groups

Some limitations of the focus groups should be noted. Though the focus groups allow for in-depth conversation during the focus group session, the possibility for follow-up conversation is limited. Focus groups are considered to be one-shot sessions. Follow-up conversations or interaction would require additional steps and meetings. In addition, while multiple incentives were offered for participation, the number of participants was still smaller than the potentially greater number of survey responses that could be achieved. Focus groups have a smaller scale of participants though they allow for in-depth conversation.

Tips on Successful Focus Groups

One of the most important tips to be offered for successful focus groups is to create an environment of comfort and safety for the participants. As previously stated, it was important to make the students feel comfortable during the focus group so they would be open and honest with their answers. The research team attempted to achieve a good level of comfort in multiple ways:

1. Be clear with your representation. The research team attempted to make the purpose of the focus group very clear to all participants. The goals for the focus group, and why and how students were recruited were made explicitly clear. The research team answered all questions and concerns from participants to ensure they understood the focus group process and how their responses would be used.

2. Be clear with consent and security. From the beginning of the recruitment process it was made clear to the students their involvement was completely voluntary. As seen in the intake Google Form, students had to agree to a multitude of privacy and information use rules in order to participate in the study. These rules and conditions were reiterated at the beginning of each focus group and recorded in the transcripts. Each participant was also recorded agreeing to their responses being recorded and transcribed for publication. Each participant was given a number as an identifier to avoid the use of their actual names during the focus groups. This was done to give students the assurance that their responses would not be held against them in any way.

3. Be understanding and friendly. It was important for participants to feel comfortable, welcome, and at ease with those conducting the study. For this reason, the research team was carefully chosen to include a mix of library faculty and library science graduate students. If possible, librarians should employ a graduate student or student library worker to assist in facilitating focus groups. Participants responded well to discussing their concerns with someone close in age that they could relate to. Students were encouraged to take snacks as the focus group progressed and make themselves comfortable with the research team.

The question of how to successfully recruit participants for the focus groups was considered from the very beginning of the research and assessment process. As is well known to most outreach and assessment librarians, getting people to participate is one of the major battles, if not the hardest. The BMCC students have a history of difficult recruitment for library events. One of the common challenges is often scheduling conflicts. All BMCC students are commuter students, and many have other responsibilities that take away from their time to be on campus for extracurricular activities. With this in mind, the research team knew the incentives needed to be worth the time of the students. Previous outreach and engagement events proved that a free MetroCard was a great lure to the commuter student body. In addition, free food often proved to be a useful recruitment tool. Lastly, the Dell Chromebooks were offered as extra incentive and as an aid to students who often lack technological access at home.

Even with the plethora of offers, student involvement was still a challenge. Though five students would be scheduled for each focus group, often not all five showed up at the appointed time. Some arrived late and thus missed questions, and others failed to show up at all. This led to doing an additional focus group as opposed to the original number of focus groups scheduled in the hopes of getting more participation. The research team also had a multitude of date options for students to pick from in the hopes they could find a focus group time to fit into their busy schedules.

Conclusion

The purpose of the focus groups was to investigate whether or not the library space is adequately user-centered and caters to commuter students. Did the students feel the library was a welcoming space available for their use? Did the students feel the library was "their" space? In short, our results indicate that the library is less user-centered than desired. Students felt a variety of updates and changes could be made to the library space to transform it into the welcoming environment they were seeking. The focus groups provided a list of different suggestions that could be enacted to help modify the space for student use. Though focus groups can have some limitations, they are useful tools for getting in-depth and focused information from a subject group. Focus groups allow for a conversational and informal session of information sharing that adds qualitative depth to the previous quantitative library assessments. When a comfortable environment is created, you will find the subject group ready and willing to give honest information about the topic at hand. These focus groups proved to give very useful information to the research team about the desires of the BMCC commuter student body in regard to their library space, but also pointed to the need for continued assessment as the library makes changes. This assessment will be used to advocate for future changes and transitions in the library space to continue in the goal to create a user-centered space for the BMCC student body.

Notes

1.   BMCC Office of Institutional Effectiveness and Analytics, "BMCC Enrollment Fact Sheet," Borough of Manhattan Community College, last updated June 11, 2019, https://www.bmcc.cuny.edu/wp-content/uploads/2019/06/Spring-2019-Factsheet.pdf.
2.   BMCC Library, "Vision, Mission and Goals," Borough of Manhattan Community College, last updated September 2016, https://www.bmcc.cuny.edu/library/about/vision-mission-goals/.
3.   BMCC Library, "Vision, Mission and Goals."
4.   Rosalie Lack. "The Importance of User-Centered Design: Exploring Findings and Methods," *Journal of Archival Organization* 4, no. 1–2 (2006): 72, https://doi.org/10.1300/J201v04n01_05.
5.   Lack, "User-Centered Design," 72.
6.   Christine Hillman et al., "User-Focused, User-Led: Space Assessment to Transform a Small Academic Library," *Evidence Based Library and Information Practice* 12, no. 4 (2017): 46, https://doi.org/10.18438/B83X00.
7.   Hillman et al., "User-Focused, User-Led," 46.

Bibliography

BMCC Library. "Vision, Mission and Goals." Borough of Manhattan Community College. Last updated September 2016. https://www.bmcc.cuny.edu/library/about/vision-mission-goals/.

BMCC Office of Institutional Effectiveness and Analytics. "BMCC Enrollment Fact Sheet." Borough of Manhattan Community College. Last updated June 11, 2019. https://www.bmcc.cuny.edu/wp-content/uploads/2019/06/Spring-2019-Factsheet.pdf.

Hillman, Christine, Kourtney Blackburn, Kaitlyn Shamp, and Chenisvel Nunez. "User-Focused, User-Led: Space Assessment to Transform a Small Academic Library." *Evidence Based Library and Information Practice* 12, no. 4 (2017): 41–61. https://doi.org/10.18438/B83X00.

Lack, Rosalie. "The Importance of User-Centered Design: Exploring Findings and Methods." *Journal of Archival Organization* 4, no. 1–2 (2006): 69–86. https://doi.org/10.1300/J201v04n01_05.

From *Standards* to *Framework*

What Are Your Students Learning?

Joy Oehlers, Joyce Tokuda, and Erica Dias

This chapter details Kapiʻolani Community College Library's shift from focusing on student performance indicators and checking off what students can do (figure 10.1) toward an attempt to guide students to question and explore the information landscape. Previously, our goals were to make sure students could and would use the library databases and the library catalog. Our assessment rubric (figure 10.2) was a checklist to confirm that students could identify pertinent keywords and synonyms, distinguish the Boolean "and" from the Boolean "or," operate the databases' limiters, find a book on our shelves, apply the CRAAP test to websites, and know where to grab the citation. We focused on the how-to processes. Our assessment results, on paper, showed that in the past decade, we were successful in teaching our students these skills, and so our students must be information-literate and competent. But in reality, we continued to be dissatisfied with our students' information-seeking and -using behaviors and attitudes.

The attractiveness of the ACRL *Information Literacy Competency Standards for Higher Education* lies in its textbook simplicity: it is easy to comprehend and even easier to operationalize.[1] It encapsulates the information consumption of a pre-internet, pre-crowdsourcing, and pre–social media era. The information-literate student in that era relied on traditional markers of authority, used traditional sources of information, and produced traditional research. This is not to say that the 2000 *Standards* were lacking in any way; the *Standards* sought to "create student-centered learning environments where inquiry is the norm, problem-solving becomes the focus, and thinking critically is part of the process."[2] These familiar themes continue in our adaptation of the *Framework for Information Literacy for Higher Education* at Kapiʻolani Community College.[3] Our information literacy vision (figure 10.3) is for our students to:

- dive deeper and dig for evidence (authority and inquiry frames)
- think critically and choose strategically (authority, inquiry, strategic exploration, and value frames)
- practice open-ended problem-solving and generate solutions (using any aspects of the six frames)

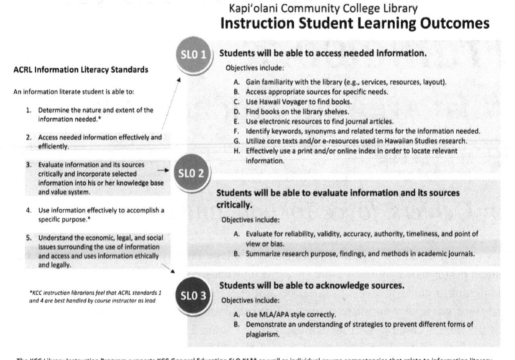

Figure 10.1

Student learning outcomes based on ACRL *Information Literacy Competency Standards for Higher Education*

RESEARCH CHALLENGE LIBRARY ENG 100 RUBRIC

Instructions:

Use a random sampling of six students' Research Challenge worksheets per class. Use one rubric per student. Compile and summarize results in the Library's student learning outcomes (SLO) assessment form.

	Objective	Strong	Approaching	Not Strong	N/A
SLO 1 Access	Identifies keywords, synonyms and related terms for the information needs	Creates 4 adequate search terms.	Creates 3 adequate search terms.	Creates 1-2 adequate search term(s).	
	Use Hawaii Voyager/ebrary to find books	Found one book/ebook	←	Did not complete this quest	
	Use electronic sources to find journal [and/or magazine, news] articles	Met Task Sheet requirement for # of articles.	←	Did not meet Task Sheet requirement for # of articles.	
SLO 2 Evaluation	Evaluate for reliability, validity, accuracy, timeliness, and point of view or bias	Applied CRAAP for all sources accurately, with passing scores for all.	Applied CRAAP for all sources with passing scores. However, scoring is not accurate.	Did not apply CRAAP scores with passing scores for all. OR Scores are overly inflated.	
	Determine if the information found meets their information needs	Articulates how three or more sources meet their information needs.	Articulates how two sources meet their information needs.	Articulates how one source meets their information needs.	
SLO 3 Acknowledge Sources	Use MLA/APA correctly	Citations have little to no errors. Works Cited/ References page is properly formatted.	Citations have capitalization and formatting errors. Works Cited/ References page has some formatting errors.	Citation style is not recognizable. Works Cited/ References page has no formatting at all.	

Figure 10.2

Student learning outcomes learning rubric based on ACRL *Information Literacy Competency Standards for Higher Education*

Kapiʻolani Community College Library Student Learning Outcomes

Updated June 2019

SLO #1	**Students will be able to search strategically to find needed information.** *Objectives include:* A. *Persist in searching until the information need is satisfied. [inquiry]* B. *Modify search terms or strategies in a meaningful way as a result of a previous search. [strategic exploration]* C. *Revise research questions in response to new information or understandings. [inquiry]*
SLO #2	**Students will be able to identify diverse perspectives within their research topic.** *Objectives include:* A. *Seek to understand the larger conversation about a research topic before looking for sources that support an argument. [conversation]* B. *Develop an awareness of their own biases and worldview. [value]* C. *Describe how and why some groups are underrepresented or marginalized within systems that produce and disseminate information. [value]*
SLO #3	**Students will be able to assess information and its sources critically.** *Objectives include:* A. *Articulate how and why a source may be considered "authoritative". [authority]* B. *Fact-check or scrutinize evidence put forward by an author, which includes recognizing quoting out of context, bias, and deceptive statistics. [authority, inquiry]*
SLO #4	**Students will be able to identify and acknowledge others' ideas.** *Objectives include:* A. *Summarize extended passages. [inquiry]* B. *Identify the claim, thesis, or hypothesis of a work. [inquiry]* C. *Give credit to the original ideas of others through proper attribution and citation. [value]*

The Library's learning outcomes are an adaptation of the Association of College and Research Libraries' Framework for Information Literacy for Higher Education. The Framework consists of six frames: (1) Authority is Constructed and Contextual; (2) Information Creation as a Process; (3) Information Has Value; (4) Research as Inquiry; (5) Scholarship as Conversation; (6) Searching as Strategic Exploration. Each Library SLO objective is labeled with the most relevant frame(s) in [brackets].

SLOs 4A and 4B are inspired by the results of the Citation Project.*

The Library Instruction Program supports the College learning outcomes:
- *ILO #1: Use critical and creative thinking and reasoning.*
- *GE SLO #1: Thinking/Inquiry - Make effective decisions with intellectual integrity to solve problems and/or achieve goals utilizing the skills of critical thinking, creative thinking, information literacy, and quantitative/symbolic reasoning.*

* The Citation Project, accessed September 13, 2020, http://www.citationproject.net/resources.

Figure 10.3

Student learning outcomes based on the ACRL *Framework for Information Literacy for Higher Education*

Dive Deeper and Dig for Evidence

Show Me the Evidence

In our *Show Me the Evidence* (figure 10.4) assignment, the librarian and psychology instructors combine two student learning outcomes (SLOs) from the psychology curriculum with one SLO from the library:

- PSY 100 Survey of Psychology SLOs:
  - Compare and contrast the major perspectives of psychology: behavioral, neuroscience, cognitive, evolutionary, humanistic, psychodynamic, and sociocultural.
  - Apply psychological concepts, theories, and research findings as these relate to everyday life.
- Library SLO 3B: Students will be able to assess information and its sources critically: fact-check or scrutinize evidence put forward by an author, which includes recognizing quoting out of context, bias, and deceptive statistics (authority and inquiry frames).

We provide a choice of five magazine articles on a pop psychology topic or popular psychology myth that relates to everyday life. Topics include predicting marriage success, infant memories, popular people live longer, Facebook and jealousy, and trustworthiness and eye color. These five articles are short with lower Lexile levels to capture our students' attention. Students select one article and are tasked with tracking down one of the scientific studies mentioned within the article. Students must:

- Access the full text of that scientific study. This provides learning opportunities in using library databases or Google Scholar, including the use of automated APA citations. For many students, this is also their initial encounter with an original research article. As a result, we require students to read only the abstract and the discussion sections in this initial foray into scholarly communications.
- Assess the differences between how information is packaged in magazines versus research articles. In addition to practicing fact-checking, we want students to "realize that information sources vary greatly in content and format and have varying relevance and value."[4] We assess their notations on the differences between the popular magazine and the scientific study to check what they learned and how it might influence their choice of sources for future college papers. We hope that by the time our community college students are ready to transfer to a four-year college, they will choose research studies, not because their instructors require that all sources cited must be from scholarly academic journals[5] but because they understand the relevance and value of research articles.
- Apply a major perspective of psychology to a study that relates to everyday life. By collaborating with psychology instructors to incorporate their subject SLOs into the library assignment, instructors begin to see that library instruction is not necessarily busywork. Hence, our library instruction efforts are always linked to course outcomes and curriculum needs (figure 10.5).

To challenge your students further, choose sources that quote out of context or use deceptive statistics. You may replace the magazine articles with social media posts or blogs for this exercise. Look for emotionally driven or highly opinionated articles in disciplines such as economics, food sciences, sustainability, and women's studies to get student attention. We recognize that students cite what they read—in particular, what they read in their social media posts—and they cite what their filter bubble directs.[6] Instead of adopting the traditional route of introducing library search techniques, explaining the intricacies of library databases, and finding scholarly peer-reviewed journal articles, we let students have this information literacy experience at their own pace in an environment they are familiar with. Because this exercise is placed in their curriculum context and popular media articles are used as the starting point, students see the relevance of engaging with the assignment.

Our hope is that students will learn not to believe everything at face value or let their preconceived beliefs and emotions dictate what they choose to read and cite in their papers. Moreover, we want students to think critically about where evidence comes from, especially in their everyday encounters on popular media, and that information literacy is not just for writing their college papers. The very non-prescriptive nature of the *Framework* allows us to "choose the most relevant ones [frames] …in ways that make sense"[7] to focus on assessing the change in student learning, instead of how well they understand library jargon. Students already have so much new information from their course curriculum, they have "precious little headspace for information literacy to sink into."[8]

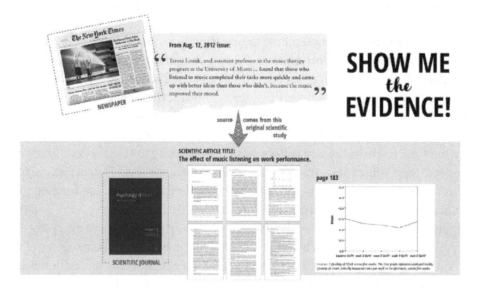

Figure 10.4
Show Me the Evidence

ASSESSMENT RUBRIC

Learning Outcomes	Meets	Approaching
10 pts: • Students will be able to identify the claim of a work. • Students will be able to search strategically to find needed information.		
Design and refine search strategies.	Identify the search words that refer to a scientific study.	Identify some search words that refer to a scientific study.
Gain familiarity with research databases.	Determine appropriate databases to search.	Attempt to use one or more databases.
10 pts: • Students will be able to assess information and its sources critically. • Students will be able to fact-check or scrutinize evidence put forward by an author		
Identify findings in scientific research.	Explains additional findings in their own words.	Basic understanding of the findings.
Differentiate between leisure and scientific articles.	Use examples to illustrate 3-5 differences between leisure and scientific articles.	Highlight 1-2 differences between leisure and scientific articles.
6 pts: • Students will be able to give credit to the original ideas of others through proper attribution and citation.		
Provide citations for sources.	Provide the correct citation format for both the leisure article and the scientific study article.	Provide a citation for at least one source.
4 pts: PSY SLO: Explain a perspective of psychology as it relates to the scientific article.	A detailed explanation of a perspective related to the scientific article.	State perspective without explanation.

Figure 10.5

Show Me the Evidence assessment rubric based on the ACRL *Framework for Information Literacy for Higher Education*

Claims versus Evidence

Another example of using Wiggins and McTighe's backward design approach is our three-part information literacy unit to help our health instructors introduce evidence-based research to first-year community college students.[9] To unpack the complexities and levels of evidence-based research, students first need to understand what scientific evidence is, then understand how the different levels of evidence are constructed along with their different applications, before finally trying to locate an example of an evidence-based study. The three parts build on each other to get to the final student learning outcome. We use:

1. Well-known advertisements to highlight the differences between claims and evidence. Our animated video of well-known personalities and products includes claims[10] from:

    a.   Dr. Oz, a physician with his own television talk show, who claims that his product will repair cartilage without providing adequate evidence to support his claims.[11]

    b.   Joe Montana, a celebrity footballer, who claims in a YouTube advertisement that "a bottle [of Joint Juice] each day lets me do the things I love."[12]

2. Personas to illustrate how different research methodologies lead to different levels of evidence-based research and their related uses.[13]

3. The PIO (Patient, Intervention, Outcome) framework to break down their clinical question [14] and then use their PIO question to practice finding one evidence-based research article in PubMed Central.[15] Students then practice using the abstract of the article retrieved from PubMed Central to identify the claim and the level of evidence.

We use quizzes to assess what students learn about evidence and types of evidence-based research which aligns with the following SLOs:

- Library SLO 3A: Students will be able to assess information and its sources critically: Articulate how and why a source may be considered "authoritative" (authority frame).

- Library SLO 4B: Students will be able to identify and acknowledge others' ideas: Identify the claim, thesis, or hypothesis of a work (inquiry frame).

We also assess how they *apply* what they have learned to their reading of the evidence-based research article abstract. To engage students, we must move beyond search and retrieve, step outside our traditional comfort zone, and use media and sources that students can relate to. In turn, our assessment must focus more on metaliteracy attitudes and behavior and less on how they find their sources. The mark of our success is when students can apply what they learn to different clinical questions.

Think Critically and Choose Strategically

Website Evaluation

Community college students use Google and Wikipedia a lot; based on anecdotal observation at our community college, even students who use library databases would almost always start and end their search exploration at Google. Georgas summed it succinctly: "Undergraduates use Google to do research and, for many of them, it may be the *only* search tool they use."[16] Google is fast and efficient, and its natural language algorithms are far superior to library databases' controlled vocabulary precision. Students completing their very first general education writing paper or submitting their subject weekly assignments do not have the time to conduct or understand the concept of a thorough literature review. While most students acknowledge that library sources are more credible and reliable,[17] this does not translate to the same students choosing to use library sources.

To help students use Google more efficiently, we work with English composition faculty to offer a web evaluation class early in the semester for both their online and in-class students. Instead of librarians lecturing and demonstrating how to identify suitable websites for citing in college papers, students work in groups to evaluate a range of preselected websites that on the surface looks suitable for research:

- "The Dakota Access Pipeline: The Facts":[18] This professional-looking organization (the pipeline developer) prompts students to examine and be aware of their own political and economic biases and worldview.
- "Lead-Laced Water in Flint: A Step-by-Step Look at the Makings of a Crisis":[19] A time line of events from a national media source as reported in 2016.
- "Dakota Access Pipeline":[20] A time line of legal challenges from a well-known .edu site.
- "22 Dead Bodies Discovered in Flint River Found to Be the Source of Water Contamination":[21] A fake news site added for humor and a reminder of the importance of fact-checking and scrutinizing evidence in context.
- "Critical Access: Reckoning with a Shrinking Water Supply":[22] A sponsored content article published in the respectable *Atlantic*.
- "Development of a Model to Simulate Groundwater Inundation Induced by Sea-Level Rise and High Tide in Honolulu, Hawaii":[23] Published in a peer-reviewed scholarly journal, *Water Research*, but highly technical for a beginning English composition paper.

Students have to think critically and question if what they find on the website is appropriate, authoritative, reliable, and credible for their informational needs. Each group then presents its investigations and justifications to the class. At the end of each group presentation, we compile a list of the questions it raised. After the final presentation, the class works on codifying the types of questions into four to five different criteria that they can use in the future when selecting websites. Students enjoy this self-questioning bottom-up approach to learning; they feel in control of their learning and they find the learning more meaningful.[24] We also round out the session by showing some advanced Google search tips, which students really enjoy. Three months later, these students return for a series of annotated bibliography classes, and we get to see the quality of their web sources. Overall assessment of their annotated bibliographies indicates that these students are able to select and summarize authoritative, balanced, credible, current, and reliable websites. By delaying our assessment, we are able to see how students put into practice the evaluation questions raised at the start of the semester.

Pilot Observational Study

Our pilot study used Zoom screen capture and concurrent think-aloud audio recording to gather insights into how students actually do research. We want to understand their attitudes and search habits, how they modify their search strategies, and their rationale for selection of sources; in particular, how they meet the two SLOs:

- Library SLO 1B: Students will be able to search strategically to find needed informa-tion: Modify search terms or strategies in a meaningful way as a result of a previous search (strategic exploration frame).
- Library SLO 3A: Students will be able to assess information and its sources critically: Articulate how and why a source may be considered "authoritative" (authority frame).

Library student workers volunteered for this pilot assessment in exchange for work hours. They represented the range of students at our community college, from a recent high school graduate who has not yet taken an information literacy class to a mature student who has completed many research papers, from undecided majors to a STEM major and a recent four-year college transferee, as well as students who attended private and public high schools.

Using our mock assignment sheet (figure 10.6) and a draft outline (figure 10.7) for an English composition research project on whether coffee is good or bad for your health, students demonstrated how they would start on their research and logged problems and difficulties encountered, how they might use the information they found, and how they decided whether the sources are good enough, all the while speaking aloud what they were thinking and the rationales behind their actions and choices. All the worksheets contained a high level of ambiguity to allow for different student search pathways. This assessment provided rich and surprising data:

- Students can and do search strategically. They modify their search terms as they change their perspectives. They are proficient with basic Google search skills, and this is where library instruction can fill a gap by getting students to feel more comfortable using advanced Google operators and strategies.
- Another key observation is that students are not able to differentiate between self-validating internal links and links to original sources. This is one area we have not discussed in our library instruction but is important as many leisure websites generate business by promoting internal links.
- Some students are critical that the evidence offered is not strong, that the article makes bold claims, or that the article is good for generating ideas; they are quick to note that it would be better to cite the original sources cited in the article. An astute

student noted that "everything has bias." This is certainly a frame that we need to incorporate into our instruction classes. Students mention that they are wary of .com sites because of what their instructors have said, but this is not reflected in their choice of websites to pursue.

- Students' definition of an authoritative source is correlated to their trust in Google that the best results will be displayed first; they also like the Featured Snippets and People Also Asked features. The more observant students look at the reference links, the author's credentials, and the publication date. Even though we often ask students to check the About Us section whenever they encounter an unfamiliar site, it seems not every student is aware of the significance of questioning the authority or host of the website.
- They use natural language query and, given the nature of the research question, they end up with listicles, blogs, news features, and leisure articles in their search results. Going forward, we will introduce Google Scholar or put together an exercise to show the differences between natural language queries and using research concepts and advanced Google limiters.

ENG 100 ASSIGNMENT: ARGUMENTATIVE ESSAY

Argumentative Research Essay Topic: Is coffee good or bad for your health

Minimum requirements: 2 credible sources and essay not to exceed 3 pages.

In an Argumentative Essay, the writer:
- Presents an issue.
- Takes a position on the issue.
- Develops an argument to convince the reader that this position is correct.

Argumentative essays often require research: collect evidence that relates to the topic, such as facts, statistics, and quotations from expert sources.

Your goal is to convince readers that your opinion about this issue (your thesis statement) is valid and important. **Your introduction should:**
- Grab your readers' attention with a hook.
- Introduce and define your topic.
- Provide background information.

Then persuade the readers that your position is right. **Your body paragraphs should:**
- Present the main arguments that support your thesis statement.
- Include facts, evidence, and examples that support each argument.
- Acknowledge counterargument(s) where appropriate and respond to them with refutations.

Your conclusion should summarize all the arguments you have stated.

Figure 10.6
Mock assignment sheet

- An interesting observation is that students remarked on how the aesthetics of a website influence their choice to use it as a resource. Another mentioned that Healthline and Medical News Today sound like medical journals so these must be credible, without any verification. Students also scan headers and look for statistics or numbers to decide if a website is good.
- Finally, after an hour, even the students who looked in library resources ended up selecting only Google-sourced websites.

Coding the assessment data is very time-consuming, but the cost is worth the insights into usability behavior. Observation studies provide a more accurate indicator of where students are at in terms of information literacy skills and applications compared to formative and summative assessments. Institutional review board (IRB) approvals are not needed for pilot studies, but if we intend to expand this methodology or publish our findings, we would factor in time for IRB approvals.

DRAFT OUTLINE TO ACCOMPANY MOCK ASSIGNMENT SHEET

Name:

Introduction & Thesis Statement
Hook about coffee consumption.
Background info on different types and preparation of coffee.
Common myths and misconceptions.
Thesis Statement: Coffee is a healthy beverage when consumed in moderation.

Paragraph 1
Background info about coffee.

Paragraph 2
Benefits and impacts.

Paragraph 3
Harmful effects.

Conclusion
Benefits outweigh the harmful effects.

Figure 10.7
Draft outline to accompany mock assignment sheet

Practice Open-Ended Problem-Solving and Generate Solutions

In spring 2016, we designed a three-credit course, IS 297P Information, Power, and the Internet, as a response to the *Framework*.[25] The five learning outcomes are:

1. Question traditional markers of authority.
2. Identify multiple perspectives in cultural, political, and social contexts.
3. Explain the value of information.
4. Describe issues of access and barriers to information.
5. Make informed choices regarding their online actions.

The course critically analyzes the power structures implicit in the creation, dissemination, and consumption of information covering themes such as media literacy, misinformation, the deep web, surveillance, and the commodification of information. It examines the intersectionality of power and information in an online world, specifically:

- The power of crowdsourced information on our decision-making process. Students evaluate the implications and impacts of their crowd-powered activities.
- The power of portable and personalized news curated by our filter bubble and how it plays to the biases of the media on the political spectrum, as well as the hidden power of native advertising or sponsored content. Students assess their media online platforms to see if they are getting balanced, complete, and factual information.
- The power of an anonymous online persona and how anonymity breeds disinhibition and trolling or flaming; the deep dark web and using Tor to access information censored by prevailing regimes. Students weigh the threats to their online identity and their implications.
- The power of the published in terms of diversity, cultural appropriation, Indigenization, and differing perspective on intellectual property. Students identify the barriers affecting marginalized voices and different worldviews and ethical dimensions of intellectual property and access.
- The power of corporations, their commodification of our data, and the significance of online reputation management. Students explore ways to limit or detox their data, examine racist algorithms, and look for fake reviews in crowdsourced sites.
- The power of the government and its quest for security surveillance. Students are challenged to regard their online actions in terms of digital tracking and open government, the normalizing of data surveillance, and their preference for convenience over privacy.
- The power of the connected and issues of equitable access and censorship of information. Students examine the barriers to information for underrepresented or marginalized populations versus the information-privileged.
- The power of the informed to personalize their online information landscape and its consequences; to scrutinize misinformation in the information creation, dissemination, and perpetuation process. Students critically analyze their filter bubble

for confirmation bias and echo chambers to ensure that they do not let emotions dictate what they read and to debunk claims that they support or believe, not just the outrageous claims.

For their final action project, students identify an information problem in their life, research and develop a plan to solve the problem, and share their processes, results, and impacts through any medium (figures 10.8 and 10.9). This project is linked closely to two of our college's general education SLOs:

IS 297P

ACTION PROJECT

General Guidelines

The Action Project allows you to dive deeper into one of the issues/problems covered in IS 297P and actually DO SOMETHING about it. We don't expect you to change the world, but your impact must be visible and certainly greater than mere slacktivism.

There are five major parts to the Action Project:

1.	2.	3.	4.	5.
Research	**Plan**	**Do**	**Reflect**	**Share**
Learn more about the problem	Create your plan of action to ameliorate the problem	Execute your plan. Collect evidence to show proof of completion	Evaluate your impact and reflect on your learning	Informally present your project to the class

There are five options (see attached option pages for full detail):

1. Add diversity in voices represented online by gathering an oral history interview of a local community member
2. Add gender diversity to Wikipedia by holding a mini women-only Wikipedia edit-a-thon
3. Explore the scientific research to debunk a celebrity fad diet, then broadcast your findings
4. License your high-quality art with a Creative Commons license for others to be able to share, use, and remix your work
5. Organize and conduct a hands-on workshop to teach others information security tips

If you don't like any of the above options, you can create your own! Here are some additional ideas:

- Contribute to Terms of Service; Didn't Read (https://tosdr.org/)
- Serve as a moderator in an online community
- Make a public, shareable YouTube/Vimeo video delivering a compelling argument for _____.

Figure 10.8

IS 297P action project general guidelines

- Make effective decisions with intellectual integrity to solve problems and/or achieve goals utilizing the skills of critical thinking, creative thinking, information literacy, and quantitative/symbolic reasoning.
- Ethically, compose, convey, and interpret varied perspectives with respect to an intended audience using visual, oral, written, social, and other forms of communication.

IS 297P		
ACTION PROJECT		
Grading Rubric		
	Exceeds	**Meets**	**Approaching**
Research 100 pts	Research shows depth and comprehensiveness, showing consideration of alternative points of view. References 3 or more authoritative and relevant sources. APA style is correct. (80-100 pts)	Research shows some depth and comprehensiveness References 2 authoritative and relevant sources. APA style is acceptable. (50-79 pts)	Research lacks depth and comprehensiveness. References 0-1 authoritative and relevant sources. APA style is not recognizable. (0-49 pts)
Plan 50 pts	Plan is thoughtful and detailed. Rigor is at a challenging, yet realistic level. (40-50 pts)	Plan shows some thought and detail. Rigor is at an appropriate, yet realistic level. (25-39 pts)	Plan lacks thought and detail. Rigor is too low to create a meaningful impact. (0-25 pts)
Do 100 pts	Evidence clearly shows that the plan was executed and that a measurable positive impact was made. (80-100 pts)	Evidence shows that the plan was executed and that some positive impact was made. (50-79 pts)	Evidence does not clearly show that the plan was executed. It is questionable whether or not there was any impact made. (0-49 pts)
Reflect 50 pts	Evaluation of impact and reflection on learning is thoughtful and in-depth. (40-50 pts)	Evaluation of impact and reflection on learning shows some thought and depth. (25-39 pts)	Lacks evaluation of impact or reflection on learning. Appears to be hastily written. (0-25 pts)
Share 50 pts	Clearly explains with details the significance of the problem that was addressed, how the plan was carried out, and the results of the action. (40-50 pts)	Explains the problem that was addressed, how the plan was carried out, and the results of the action. (25-39 pts)	Explanation lacks sufficient detail to convey the problem, plan, and results to the audience. (0-25 pts)

Figure 10.9

IS 297P action project grading rubric

Action projects include:

- Designing an online security and data privacy awareness brochure and tutorial for TRIO students.
- Overcoming the obstacles in the remixing music culture by creating splices of music for others to share freely through a Creative Commons license.
- Contributing to a Wikipedia entry on celebrity fad diet with evidence-based research sources.
- Exploring issues of fair use and DMCA (Digital Millennium Copyright Act) copyright infringement by creating an instructional YouTube video.
- Dispelling myths about veganism and providing local context information by developing a website and using search engine optimization best practices to promote the site.
- Filling a gap in shareable local photography of local icons, places, and history by posting and curating a freely available and searchable resource of high-resolution photos.

IS 297P

EXIT ESSAY

General Guidelines

In **at least four pages** (1" margin, 12 pt. font, double-spaced, APA style), address the following five learning outcomes for this course using specific concepts, names, and examples. Quote from or reference at least one course reading for each learning outcome (total of at least five course readings). You can choose to address each learning outcome separately in five different sections, or all together in one narrative.

Address each of the following outcomes:

1. Name three traditional markers of authority. Explain why we should not always follow these traditional markers.
2. Pick an issue we focused on this semester. Identify multiple perspectives in cultural, political, and/or social context.
3. Explain why and how information is valuable. Provide three examples to explain the value of information.
4. Describe at least three issues of access and barriers to information. Use examples to support each issue.
5. Describe three informed choices you have made this semester or plan to make in the future regarding your online actions. Explain the rationale behind each choice.

Figure 10.10

IS 297P exit paper assessment

As an assessment tool, the exit paper is designed to capture the depth of what the students learned and their ability to effect a change in their online behavior (figures 10.10 and 10.11). This conscious reflection of the learning process provides rich data to help us assess authentic learning. Our five question stems are based on the *Framework,* and they provide pathways for students to think critically about information literacy and their self-corrective actions at the conclusion of this course. Our assessment found that students struggle with identifying multiple perspectives in cultural, political, and social contexts and tend to gravitate to obvious answers when asked to share their viewpoints on the value of information.

IS 297P			
EXIT ESSAY			
Grading Rubric			
	Exceeds	**Meets**	**Approaching**
Learning outcome 1 (15 pts)	Explains three traditional markers of authority in detail.	Explains two traditional markers of authority, or explains three with shallow detail.	Explains one traditional marker of authority.
Learning outcome 2 (15 pts)	Picks a critical issue and identifies three significant perspectives in detail.	Picks an appropriate issue and identifies two significant perspectives, or explains three with shallow detail.	Picks an issue and identifies one significant perspective.
Learning outcome 3 (15 pts)	Provides three detailed examples to explain the value of information.	Provides two examples to explain the value of information or explains three with shallow detail.	Provides one example to explain the value of information.
Learning outcome 4 (15 pts)	Identifies three issues of access in detail.	Identifies two issues of access or explains three with shallow detail.	Identifies one issue of access.
Learning outcome 5 (15 pts)	Develops three choices or plans. Provides details in the rationale.	Develops two choices or plans, or explains three with shallow detail.	Develops one choice or plan. Rationale lacks details.
Sources (25 pts)	For each learning outcome, incorporates at least one relevant source accurately. Includes sources in the References list using APA style.	For each learning outcome, demonstrates an attempt to incorporate relevant sources. Sources in the References list have some formatting errors.	Cites mostly irrelevant sources. Lacks understanding of how to cite sources. Sources are not recognizable or are missing from the References list.

Figure 10.11

IS 297P exit paper grading rubric

Reflecting on the *Framework* and Its Impact on Student Learning Outcomes

Our goals, guided by the *Framework,* focus on outcomes, not outputs; on a change in information-seeking behaviors and permanence of transferable skills, rather than discrete skills. Measuring outputs tells us what students can do: they can find a book with a complicated call number. Measuring outcomes provides some assurance that students will apply critical framing and be aware of cultural, social, and political dimensions in the information landscape. Surely information literacy in the research process must be more than shopping for four sources to fulfill their assignment requirement, which "becomes an exercise in justification of prior beliefs rather than a transformative learning opportunity."[26]

Throughout the different classes, we use a variety of assessment tools to get a 365 degree view of what and how students are learning and applying what they learned. This practice of gathering evidence from multiple sources provides a holistic view to help us pivot if in midstream we need to re-chart our course, provide more indirect support, or work with a new faculty member in a new subject area.

In our assessment experience, students can find good sources but need our support to provide an environment to help them read, take notes, and think through the information. Setting transferrable learning outcomes that transcend the one-shot session and reflecting on the *Framework* steers us toward unlearning our output-based information literacy assessment. To sum up, successful student learning is the resulting intersection of their learning environments, intentional learning outcomes, and information literacy frames. In the end, the question we constantly ask ourselves is whether we are just skirting the complex dimensions of information literacy and if, in fact, we really understand enough of this multidimensional complexion to be able to assess accurately? Perhaps we need to accept the uncertainty and not presume from the start that we will achieve our outcomes. Self-doubt is not a bad thing: it stops us from being complacent when our assessment results indicate that our students are doing a good job with our library assignments.

Notes

1. Association of College and Research Libraries, *Information Literacy Competency Standards for Higher Education* (Chicago: Association of College and Research Libraries, 2000), https://alair.ala.org/handle/11213/7668. The Standards were rescinded by the ACRL Board of Directors on June 25, 2016.
2. Association of College and Research Libraries, *Standards,* 5.
3. Association of College and Research Libraries, *Framework for Information Literacy for Higher Education* (Chicago: Association of College and Research Libraries, 2016), http://www.ala.org/acrl/sites/ala.org.acrl/files/content/issues/infolit/framework1.pdf.
4. Association of College and Research Libraries, *Framework,* 9.
5. Mónica Colón-Aguirre and Rachel A. Fleming-May, "'You Just Type In What You Are Looking For': Undergraduates' Use of Library Resources vs. Wikipedia," *Journal of Academic Librarianship* 38, no. 6 (2012): 395, https://doi.org/10.1016/j.acalib.2012.09.013.

6.   Eli Pariser, *The Filter Bubble* (New York: Penguin Press, 2011).
7.   Jillian Collier, "Pick Your Battles: Re-examining the Framework for Community Colleges," *College and Research Libraries News* 80, no. 9 (October 2019): 495, https://doi.org/10.5860/crln.80.8.494.
8.   Collier, "Pick Your Battles," 496.
9.   Grant P. Wiggins and Jay McTighe, *Understanding by Design*, 2nd ed. (Alexandria, VA: ASCD, 2005), 13–34.
10. Kapiʻolani Community College Library, "Evidence," YouTube video, 3:01, June 27, 2019, https://youtu.be/7n4kDlu7euQ.
11. "3 Easy Steps to Reduce Joint Pain," accessed September 28, 2021, https://www.doctoroz.com/gallery/3-easy-steps-reduce-joint-pain/step-1-reverse-inflammation-through-your-diet.
12. JointJuiceTV, "Joint Juice Commercial ft. Joe Montana "Extraordinary Joe"," YouTube video, 0:30, June 22, 2012, https://youtu.be/EYN-hoTYELE
13. Kapiʻolani Community College Library, "Levels of Evidence," YouTube video, 2:36, July 18, 2019, https://youtu.be/gSsg1h5OqMU.
14. Joy Oehlers, "Formulating and Answering Clinical Questions," last updated March 30, 2020, https://docs.google.com/document/d/16r-r6F_b0lJOXirLgJhwwCxQoEPzunaH60XvoN3oHB8/.
15. Kapiʻolani Community College Library, "Finding Evidence," YouTube video, 1:54, July 19, 2019, https://youtu.be/7nXwjcebhJ4.
16. Helen Georgas, "Google vs. the Library (Part III): Assessing the Quality of Sources Found by Undergraduates," *portal: Libraries and the Academy* 15, no. 1 (January 2015): 133, https://doi.org/10.1353/pla.2015.0012.
17. Colón-Aguirre and Fleming-May, "You Just Type In," 394.
18. Energy Transfer, "The Dakota Access Pipeline: The Facts," accessed September 13, 2020, https://daplpipelinefacts.com/The-Facts.html.
19. Merrit Kennedy, "Lead-Laced Water in Flint: A Step-by-Step Look at the Makings of a Crisis," NPR, April 20, 2016, https://www.npr.org/sections/thetwo-way/2016/04/20/465545378/lead-laced-water-in-flint-a-step-by-step-look-at-the-makings-of-a-crisis.
20. Environmental and Energy Law Program, "Dakota Access Pipeline," Harvard Law School, October 24, 2017, https://eelp.law.harvard.edu/2017/10/dakota-access-pipeline/.
21. "22 Dead Bodies Discovered in Flint River Found to Be the Source to Water Contamination," News4, accessed September 13, 2020, http://news4ktla.com/22-dead-bodies-discovered-flint-river-found-source-water-contamination.
22. BASF, "Critical Access: Reckoning with a Shrinking Supply of Fresh Water," *Atlantic*, sponsor content, accessed September 13, 2020, https://www.theatlantic.com/sponsored/basf-2016/critical-access-reckoning-with-a-shrinking-supply-of-fresh-water/909/.
23. Shellie Habel et al., "Development of a Model to Simulate Groundwater Inundation Induced by Sea-Level Rise and High Tides in Honolulu, Hawaii," *Water Research* 114 (2017): 122–34, http://www.soest.hawaii.edu/coasts/publications/HabelEtal_WR_2017.pdf.
24. Christine Chin, "Student-Generated Questions: Encouraging Inquisitive Minds in Learning Science," *Teaching and Learning* 23, no. 1 (June 2002): 59–67.
25. Joy Oehlers and Joyce Tokuda, IS 297P: Information, Power, and the Internet, course website, Kapiʻolani Community College, accessed September 13, 2020, https://is297p.wordpress.com.
26. Susan Woods, "No Room for Argument: Researching Politicized Topics as a Learner," in *Critical Approaches to Credit-Bearing Information Literacy Courses*, ed. Angela Pashia and Jessica Critten (Chicago: Association of College and Research Libraries, 2019), 18.

Bibliography

Association of College and Research Libraries. *Framework for Information Literacy for Higher Education*. Chicago: Association of College and Research Libraries, 2016. http://www.ala.org/acrl/sites/ala.org.acrl/files/content/issues/infolit/framework1.pdf.

———. *Information Literacy Competency Standards for Higher Education*. Chicago: Association of College and Research Libraries, 2000. https://alair.ala.org/handle/11213/7668. The Standards were rescinded by the ACRL Board of Directors on June 25, 2016.

BASF. "Critical Access: Reckoning with a Shrinking Water Supply." *Atlantic*, sponsor content. Accessed September 13, 2020. https://www.theatlantic.com/sponsored/basf-2016/critical-access-reckoning-with-a-shrinking-supply-of-fresh-water/909.

Chin, Christine. "Student-Generated Questions: Encouraging Inquisitive Minds in Learning Science." *Teaching and Learning* 23, no.1 (June 2002): 59–67.

Collier, Jillian. "Pick Your Battles: Re-examining the Framework for Community Colleges." *College and Research Libraries News* 80, no. 9 (October 2019): 494–97. https://doi.org/10.5860/crln.80.8.494.

Colón-Aguirre, Mónica, and Rachel A. Fleming-May. "'You Just Type In What You Are Looking For': Undergraduates' Use of Library Resources vs. Wikipedia." *Journal of Academic Librarianship* 38, no. 6 (2012): 391–99. https://doi.org/10.1016/j.acalib.2012.09.013.

Energy Transfer. "The Dakota Access Pipeline: The Facts." Accessed September 13, 2020. https://daplpipelinefacts.com/The-Facts.html.

Environmental and Energy Law Program. "Dakota Access Pipeline." Harvard Law School, October 24, 2017. https://eelp.law.harvard.edu/2017/10/dakota-access-pipeline/.

Georgas, Helen. "Google vs. the Library (Part III): Assessing the Quality of Sources Found by Undergraduates." *portal: Libraries and the Academy* 15, no. 1 (January 2015): 133–61. https://doi.org/10.1353/pla.2015.0012.

Habel, Shellie, Charles H. Fletcher, Kolja Rotzoll, and Aly I. El-Kadi. "Development of a Model to Simulate Groundwater Inundation Induced by Sea-Level Rise and High Tides in Honolulu, Hawaii." *Water Research* 114 (2017): 122–34. http://www.soest.hawaii.edu/coasts/publications/HabelEtal_WR_2017.pdf.

Kapiʻolani Community College Library. "Evidence." YouTube video, 3:01. June 27, 2019. https://youtu.be/7n4kDlu7euQ.

———. "Finding Evidence." YouTube video, 1:54. July 19, 2019, https://youtu.be/7nXwjcebhJ4.

———. "Levels of Evidence." YouTube video, 2:36. July 18, 2019. https://youtu.be/gSsg1h5OqMU.

Kennedy, Merrit. "Lead-Laced Water in Flint: A Step-by-Step Look at the Makings of a Crisis." NPR, April 20, 2016. https://www.npr.org/sections/thetwo-way/2016/04/20/465545378/lead-laced-water-in-flint-a-step-by-step-look-at-the-makings-of-a-crisis.

News 4. "22 Dead Bodies Discovered in Flint River Found to be the Source of Water Contamination." Accessed September 13, 2020. http://news4ktla.com/22-dead-bodies-discovered-flint-river-found-source-water-contamination.

Oehlers, Joy. "Formulating and Answering Clinical Questions." Last modified March 30, 2020. https://docs.google.com/document/d/16r-r6F_b0lJOXirLgJhwwCxQoEPzunaH60XvoN3oHB8/.

Oehlers, Joy, and Joyce Tokuda. IS 297P: Information, Power, and the Internet. Course website. Kapiʻolani Community College. Accessed September 13, 2020. https://is297p.wordpress.com/.

Pariser, Eli. *The Filter Bubble: What the Internet Is Hiding from You*. New York: Penguin Press, 2011.

Wiggins, Grant P., and Jay McTighe. *Understanding by Design*, 2nd ed. Alexandria, VA: ASCD, 2005.

Woods, Susan. "No Room for Argument: Researching Politicized Topics as a Learner." In *Critical Approaches to Credit-Bearing Information Literacy Courses*. Edited by Angela Pashia and Jessica Critten, 13–34. Chicago: Association of College and Research Libraries, 2019.

CHAPTER 11

Mind the Gap

Using Reflective Practice for Reference Consultations

Amanda M. Leftwich

> *"Observe the changes that take place in your mind under the light of awareness."*
>
> —*Thích Nhất Hạnh*

Introduction

In today's world, it seems gratuitous to pause, even if only for a moment. Our collective attention isn't focused just on today, but tomorrow, and sometimes the following weeks and years. Each time our attention is diverted, it takes a bit longer to bring our awareness back to the present moment. As community college librarians, we're constantly on the go to and from committee meetings to information literacy (IL), reference desk, and back again. Are we really focused on doing any of these tasks well if our awareness is elsewhere? Do you remember the last time your attention was fully focused on the present moment during a reference shift? Reflective practice allows us the opportunity to slow down, intentionally.

Take a deep breath. Find a comfortable position. Good, now relax your shoulders and your jaw. When ready, bring your attention to your breath and keep it there for two to three minutes (set a timer, if needed). Try practicing non-judgment during this time and just breathe. When time is up, slowly bring your attention back to this chapter. In a notebook or in the margins of this book, write down what you experienced during this exercise. Where was your awareness during this exercise? Were you thinking about work, life, or what to eat later? Were you nervous that you weren't "doing this practice right"? Did any random thoughts come to mind? How did your body feel? Believe it or not, this is an example of reflective practice!

Donald A. Schön, described this phenomenon as "reflection in action."[1] He explained, "A practitioner's reflection-in-action may not be very rapid. It is bounded by the "action-present", the zone of time in which action can still make a difference to the situation. The action-present may stretch over minutes, hours, days, or even weeks or months, depending on the pace of the activity and the situational boundaries that are characteristic of the practice."[2] It is through continuous practice that we begin to see our repeated patterns and processes. As our practice grows, we notice not only when our attention drifts but also how to bring our awareness back in a thoughtful and deliberate way. Michelle Reale echoes this thought: "Reflection is deliberate and intentional.... It is a process that we consciously undertake, in the professional sense, in order to take stock of our practice by interpreting, analyzing, and questioning the way we work."[3] One becomes a reflective practitioner by practicing. Mindfully setting our intentions to reflect in our work is the first step to improving our work patterns and awareness. Bringing this intentionality into our theories, practices, and procedures grounds ourselves into our work—instead of our work grinding us.

During reference consultations, librarians' attention could be focused on completing another task. Therefore, if no one comes, we can say we completed some task. Reference consultations require unique focus and attention. The utmost care and awareness must be present during these appointments to create a sense of connection and understanding between us and our students. Symphony Bruce explains its importance: "These moments can be harnessed to cultivate connection and relationship. Because of the one-on-one nature of such interactions and the vulnerability required, librarians can either provide care or perpetuate the practices that lead to the disconnection a student may experience."[4]

Remember, *it is not* the job of librarians to take on the emotional labor of students! Nor should librarians be tasked with managing community college students' stressors,[5] while stifling their own emotions.[6] However, providing intentional consultations allows students to opt out of the "one-size fits all model of most library instruction programs [which] rarely suffices for the student with a complex research problem, or for the student who is out of step with his fellow students."[7] Community college students often rely on social networks for research assistance[8] and utilize the library as a meeting and study space.[9] Therefore, changing the way we approach reference services through reflective and awareness practices could shift perspectives on community college libraries as a whole. The last of Ranganathan's five laws of library science notes that "a library is a living organism."[10] Although Ranganathan spoke on the importance of the library being flexible and open to change and growth,[11] we can lend these ideas to our reference services as well. Reference services must change and grow as often as the library does. Connecting reflection and Ranganathan's laws reminds us not to remain stagnant in our work. Any services we provide should reflect the livingness of the libraries, but also our awareness of reasonable actions to make library services happen. We are also living and working in these spaces!

Bringing our awareness to building this connection and away from our busy distractions, we form roots into intentional practices. The constant need to stay busy, or grind culture, draws our focus away from our mission to support the informational learning needs of students, faculty, and staff. Grind culture "is a culture of raw achievement where longer and longer hours are not just the norm, they are the metric for success."[12] This notion is a fallacy. One cannot consistently *grind* and be mindful or reflective. It is only through intentional reflective practice that we can shift our attention to the work that matters. This chapter explores reflective practice as a framework for building better connections with students while bringing our awareness to closing gaps in reference services.

Reference Services and Reflection: Closing the Gap

As a reflective practitioner, I noticed something troubling in my reflective journal. Although I had constant and frequent individual research consultations, I never reflected on the student consultations again. Much like our IL sessions and reference shifts, it was a one-and-done meeting—therefore, and I had no means of observing my work. The students I saw noted the value of one-on-one consultations and frustration in trying to evaluate and discover resources on their own. The act of providing consultations, however, is not enough for my own work growth. Although most of the literature on the subject has justified the means of consultation as an important tool in combination with instruction,[13] my institution had no assessment guidelines in place to review our processes. Nor were any processes available for making changes based on living experiences in reference services. One question I kept writing in my reflective journal: "What happened during my consultation sessions?" My writing after noticing the pattern:

> I seem to be the only one with weekly (repeated) appointments and have *a system (for lack of a better word)* for it. I've been asked (by the Dean) to share my system in order to help the other librarians, so that we'll all use the same format (to communicate with students and faculty). I'm honestly surprised by this revelation. How are my colleagues recording processes with faculty and students about their reference consultations? The "system" is really just sharing information with students and faculty about the appointment and resources found, if requested (based on my own reflective process—not perfect by any means—ever-changing as I do). And keeping detailed reflective notes on the consultation right afterwards. If you don't reflect regularly, will you forget about it? How will we close the reference gap if this is the case?[14]

John Dewey challenged educators to reflect daily on practical issues.[15] He believed that reflective practitioners would be able to "gain control in a troubled situation (and thus has a practical or utilitarian force), it is also instrumental to the enrichment of the immediate significance of subsequent experiences."[16] In other words, practitioners would be able to connect what they learned from their reflections to their work and daily lives. Without consistent reflection, we lose track of what we're trying to accomplish in the first place. For community college librarians, it is imperative that we have a strong foundation in whatever we're trying to accomplish and its importance because of the fast-paced nature of our institutions and student learning. This helps center us beyond our work. Otherwise, we begin to struggle on a treacherous road toward burnout and low morale. *Reflect on your last reference interaction. Where was your attention during this interaction? Were you focused on the question asked of you? Did your attention drift at any moment, or were you interrupted by another something or someone else?*

The Reference and User Service Association's (RUSA's) *Guidelines for Behavioral Performance of Reference and Information Service Providers* (RUSA *Guidelines*) provides little assistance on centering or reflecting on reference outside of following up.[17] This is troublesome for any librarian looking to reflect on their work. If the only means for assessment is outward-facing and behavioral-based, what does this mean for the emotional welfare of librarians? The RUSA *Guidelines* currently state that "the librarian is responsible for determining if the patron is satisfied with the results of the searchset."[18] Emmelhainz, Pappas, and Seale strongly critique this notion as "aspirational standards for ideal reference encounters."[19] We do not need to aspire to be greater, but should strive to develop a better understanding of ourselves and our reactions in our work. Therefore, questions or reflections should be focused on *why we do what we do*. Reflective practitioners examine themselves as a whole and sit in a new understanding without judgment. The old systems and guidelines of reference should be updated to reflect the whole person, not just their behavior. Carol Rogers explains, "Reflection is a meaning-making process that moves a learner from one experience into the next with deeper understanding of its relationship with and connections to other experiences and ideas."[20] Beginning to shift focus to making connections changes your perspective on everything around you. *Reflect on any barriers, guidelines, or policies in place that no longer make sense for your work or workplace. Why are these guidelines or policies in place? Are they supporting your work goals? If not, how can you pivot or break barriers in order to thrive?*

New Strategies for Reference

Before Your Shift

As with anything new, we need to select a process in which to start. For the purposes of this chapter, we're focusing solely on reference services. Now, you'll need to decide what type of technique you will use to reflectively write and think. O'Connell and Dyment offer several suggestions to educators for types of journal entries, including personal reflection (how we understand and interact with things), professional development (how we grow in the workplace or in our learning), and sense of place and connection to place (how you grow or thrive in a particular place or how you aren't growing in that place).[21] In reference services, we aim to understand and engage students (personal reflection), find best practices to engage students through webinars or conferences, pedagogies (professional development), and evaluate the results (sense of place). For example, reflect on previous experiences during your reference shifts. How did you feel? Did you engage the students as critical thinkers,[22] or do you just provide the answer? Do you note any changes that need to be made for your own comfort during your shifts? For example, during a meeting, my colleagues noted students' discomfort around sitting at the reference desk. We also noted our own discomfort around sitting waiting for questions and being frequently interrupted during reference consultations. We all shared the same experiences and opted not to sit at the desk unless students request it and moved consultations to more comfortable seating in the library. This seems small. However, it changed our dynamic in the library and with the students. We separately noted a problem, gently reflected on the issue, and asked for a change to be made based on previous experiences. Before we can cultivate new relationships with students, we must observe how we've interacted with them in the past.

During Your Shift

Relax your body and remember to breathe. Gently center yourself; don't rush to your consultation or reference shift. Moving with intention helps set a calmed mind and pace. Use the facilities, grab some water, coffee, or tea and a notebook. When a student arrives, remember to introduce yourself and invite them to do the same. This doesn't have to be an emotional or life dump, a simple "My name is _____ and I'm here for your appointment" will suffice. Review with the student why they made an appointment for a consultation with you and what they are hoping to find. It is vital at this moment to remind the student that you are working together to find this information. You alone aren't required to know all the answers as a librarian, but rather to provide a pathway to information. Encourage students to take notes, pictures, or recordings of your sessions. This asks them to gently reflect on what works for them. It also connects with treating students as critical thinkers and active learners.[23] They must take part in the learning process, as this is a community of practice.

As a Black librarian, I have found this critical to my own wellness. As the only Black Indigenous People of Color (BIPOC) librarian on staff, I found that most of my consultations and reference shifts were booked by BIPOC students. At first, this was a thrilling and exciting opportunity to connect with students. After a few weeks, it became tiring, and I began to burn out. Kawanna Bright explains this phenomenon in her study:

> I have had other people come and say "I've been looking for you on the reference desk for days and I kept coming back." And I was like "well why didn't you ask the person?" And they were like "well cause it wasn't you."[24]

Although we want to assist all students, especially those who remind us of ourselves, it's not always possible. Do the best you can with what you have. Ask for help when you need it. Remember, your intention and awareness are what matter most. Focus your attention on what you can do, and gently reflect on everything else.

After Your Shift

Right after your shift, write down what happened and any feelings that arose. Again, this will assist you in highlighting any work patterns you've been questioning. In order to create daily patterns for reflection, add some cushion between your consultations and other duties. I usually have a ten-to-fifteen-minute window between my consultations for reflection. You can always allocate less or more time as fits with your schedule. Here's a note from my reference consultation,

> I've worked with [student R] for a few sessions more. I've noted previously that they need to visit the Writing Center for more assistance. I'm not a grammar wizard, and really need to focus on assisting with resources only. It makes me a bit uncomfortable to provide any structural assistance. I'll need to refer R to the Writing Center, or ask if I can bring a tutor during one of our consultations. R needs to learn the importance of using resources outside of myself for assistance. I cannot keep being the only person offering all of the library and academic support to students of color.[25]

In the same journal or a separate calendar, remember to follow up with students, *if requested*. At the end of each shift or session, I'll ask if students need an e-mail documenting what we've worked on together. Most students will say no and opt to take their own notes or use another method of recording during your consultations. Following up is not the role of just the librarian.[26] You must allow students to reach out to you as well. Whatever means they used to contact you for a consultation would be the same means with which they could reach you again. Remember, the point of reflection is to engage in continuous learning. Use this time to really dig into your own processes. You aren't writing to find a solution but rather to view reactions to your daily processes. Whether you change them based on your writing is up to you. *Reflect on what's working, what's not, and your feelings on the topic. What do you notice from students during your reference shifts and consultations? How can you further student active learning? What barriers are in place to make this a reality?*

Practice Reflections

Reflection is indeed a practice. It takes continuous exploration of our thoughts, actions, and processes in order for this practice to find a place in our daily routines. We must continually make time for reflection. The process won't start if we don't. Promoting reflective practice isn't a one-time occurrence, but a lifetime practice. Once you've grabbed a journal, reflect on the unanswered questions to bring your own reflective practice. This list is just something to start. As your practice grows, add your own questions.

1. Why am I choosing to reflect? What is the purpose of reflective practice to my work or life?

2. How will I make time to reflect (e.g., blocking off time on calendars and providing cushions between consultations)?

3. What am I looking to learn about myself or my work processes?

4. How can I be honest with myself during my reflective practices?

5. How will I observe patterns or behaviors without judgment in my work (e.g., reviewing the journal biweekly, monthly, yearly)?

6. What barriers are in place that will make reflective practice difficult? How will I break these barriers?

7. What will I do with any information I've learned during my reflective practice afterward?

Conclusion

Reflective practice is an ever-changing process. It requires us to allow for growth, curiosity, and gentleness in our lives and work. As you continue on this journey, you will note changes with articulated compassion. When challenges arise, welcome them without judgment, and continue on the path. Allow reflective practice to shine a light into the unknown without reservation. Practice with openness. Practice with humor. Practice with awareness. Just remember to practice.

Notes

1. Donald A. Schön, *The Reflective Practitioner How Professionals Think in Action* (New York: Basic Books, 1983), 62.
2. Schön, *The Reflective Practitioner How Professionals Think in Action*, 62.
3. Michelle Reale, *Becoming a Reflective Librarian and Teacher* (Chicago: ALA Editions, 2017), 2.
4. Symphony Bruce, "Teaching with Care: A Relational Approach to Individual Research Consultations," *In the Library with Lead Pipe*, February 5, 2020, http://www.inthelibrarywiththeleadpipe. org/2020/teaching-with-care/.
5. Emily A. Pierceall and Marybelle C. Keim, "Stress and Coping Strategies among Community College Students," *Community College Journal of Research and Practice* 31, no. 9 (October 2007): 706, https:// doi.org/10.1080/10668920600866579.
6. Celia Emmelhainz, Erin Pappas, and Maura Seale, "Behavioral Expectations for the Mommy Librarian: The Successful Reference Transaction as Emotional Labor," in *The Feminist Reference Desk: Concepts, Critiques, and Conversations*, ed. Maria T. Accardi (Sacramento, CA: Library Juice Press, 2017), 42.
7. Crystal D. Gale and Betty S. Evans, "Face-to-Face: The Implementation and Analysis of a Research Consultation Service," *College and Undergraduate Libraries* 14, no. 3 (September 2008): 90, https:// doi.org/10.1300/J106v14n03_06.
8. Christine Wolff-Eisenberg and Braddlee, *Amplifying Student Voices*, research report (New York: Ithaka S+R, August 13, 2018), https://doi.org/10.18665/sr.308086.
9. Stephen R. Porter and Paul D. Umbach, *What Challenges to Success Do Community College Students Face?* RISC (Revealing Institutional Strengthens and Challenges), (Raleigh, NC: Percontor, January 2019), https://www.risc.college/sites/default/files/2019-01/RISC_2019_report_natl.pdf.
10. S. R. Ranganathan, *The Five Laws of Library Science*, HathiTrust edition (Madras, India: Madras Library Association, 1931), 397, https://hdl.handle.net/2027/uc1.$b99721.
11. Ranganathan, *Five Laws*, 397.

12. Lewis Nathaniel, "Grind Culture," Medium, November 26, 2019. https://medium.com/@lewisibdp/grind-culture-e2aa2b84ab5c#:~:text=Grind%20or%20Hustle%20culture%20is,are%20the%20metric%20for%20success.

13. Tina J. Magi and Patricia E. Mardeusz, "Why Some Students Continue to Value Individual, Face-to-Face Research Consultations in a Technology-Rich World," *College and Research Libraries* 74, no. 6. (November 2013): 607, https://doi.org/10.5860/crl12-363.

14. Amanda M. Leftwich, "Reflection Journal" (unpublished manuscript, September 13, 2018), typescript.

15. John Dewey, *John Dewey: The Later Works, 1925–1953, Volume I: 1925* (Carbondale and Edwardsville: Southern Illinois University Press, 1981), 340.

16. John Dewey, *Intelligence in the Modern World* (New York: Modern Library, 1939), 934.

17. Reference and User Services Association, *Guidelines for Behavioral Performance and Information Service Providers* (Chicago: Reference and User Services Association, 1996, rev. 2004, 2011, 2013), http://www.ala.org/rusa/resources/guidelines/guidelinesbehavioral.

18. Reference and User Services Association, *Guidelines*.

19. Emmelhainz, Pappas, and Seale, "Behavioral Expectations," 28.

20. Carol R. Rodgers, "Defining Reflection: Another Look at John Dewey and Reflective Thinking," *Teachers College Record* 104, no. 4 (June 2002): 845, https://doi.org/10.1111/1467-9620.00181.

21. Timothy S. O'Connell and Janet E. Dyment, *Theory into Practice* (Charlotte, NC: Information Age Publishing, 2013), chap 5, EBSCOhost.

22. Sharon Ladenson, "Feminist Reference Services: Transforming Relationships through an Ethic of Care," in *The Feminist Reference Desk: Concepts, Critiques, and Conversations*, ed. Maria Accardi (Sacramento: Library Juice Press, 2017), 77.

23. Emmelhainz, Pappas, and Seale, "Behavioral Expectations," 42.

24. Kawanna Bright, "A Woman of Color's Work Is Never Done: Intersectionality in Reference and Information Work," in *Pushing the Margins: Women of Color and Intersectionality in LIS*, ed. Rose L. Chou and Annie Pho (Sacramento: Library Juice Press, 2018), 186.

25. Amanda M. Leftwich, "Reflection Journal" (unpublished manuscript, November 19, 2019), typescript.

26. Emmelhainz, Pappas, and Seale, "Behavioral Expectations," 28.

Bibliography

Bright, Kawanna. "A Woman of Color's Work Is Never Done: Intersectionality in Reference and Information Work." In *Pushing the Margins: Women of Color and Intersectionality in LIS*. Edited by Rose L. Chou and Annie Pho, 163–95. Sacramento, CA: Library Juice Press, 2018.

Bruce, Symphony. "Teaching with Care: A Relational Approach to Individual Research Consultations." *In the Library with a Lead Pipe*, February 5, 2020. http://www.inthelibrarywiththeleadpipe.org/2020/teaching-with-care/.

Dewey, John. *Intelligence in the Modern World: John Dewey's Philosophy.* New York: Modern Library, 1939.

———. *John Dewey: The Later Works, 1925–1953; Volume I: 1925.* Carbondale and Edwardsville: Southern Illinois University Press, 1981.

Emmelhainz, Celia, Erin Pappas, and Maura Seale. "Behavioral Expectations for the Mommy Librarian: The Successful Reference Transaction as Emotional Labor." In *The Feminist Reference Desk: Concepts, Criticisms, and Conversations.* Edited by Maria Accardi, 27–45. Sacramento, CA: Library Juice Press, 2017.

Gale, Crystal D., and Betty S. Evans. "Face-to-Face: The Implementation and Analysis of a Research Consultation Service." *College and Undergraduate Libraries* 14, no. 3 (September 2008): 85–101. https://doi.org/10.1300/J106v14n03_06.

Ladenson, Sharon. "Feminist Reference Services: Transforming Relationships through an Ethic of Care." In *The Feminist Reference Desk Concepts, Critiques, and Conversations*, edited by Maria Accardi, 73-83. Sacramento: Library Juice Press, 2017.

Leftwich, Amanda M. "Reflection Journal." Unpublished manuscript, September 13, 2018, typescript.

———. "Reflection Journal." Unpublished manuscript, November 19, 2019, typescript.

Magi, Trina J., and Patricia E. Mardeusz. "Why Some Students Continue to Value Individual, Face-to-Face Research Consultations in a Technology-Rich World." *College and Research Libraries* 74, no. 6 (November 2013): 605–18. https://doi.org/10.5860/crl12-363.

Nathaniel, Lewis. "Grind Culture." Medium, November 26, 2019. https://medium.com/@lewisibdp/grind-culture-e2aa2b84ab5c#:~:text=Grind%20or%20Hustle%20culture%20is,are%20the%20metric%20for%20success.

O'Connell, Timothy S., and Janet E. Dyment. *Theory into Practice: Unlocking the Power and the Potential of Reflective Journals*. Charlotte, NC: Information Age Publishing, 2013. EBSCOhost.

Pierceall, Emily A., and Marybelle C. Keim. "Stress and Coping Strategies among Community College Students." *Community College Journal of Research and Practice* 31, no. 9 (October 2007): 703–12. https://doi.org/10.1080/10668920600866579.

Porter, Stephen R., and Paul D. Umbach. *What Challenges to Success Do Community College Students Face?* RISC (Revealing Institutional Strengthens and Challenges). Raleigh, NC: Percontor, January 2019. https://www.risc.college/sites/default/files/2019-01/RISC_2019_report_natl.pdf.

Ranganathan, S. R. *The Five Laws of Library Science*, HathiTrust edition. Madras, India: Madras Library Association, 1931. https://hdl.handle.net/2027/uc1.$b99721.

Reale, Michelle. *Becoming a Reflective Librarian and Teacher: Strategies for Mindful Academic Practice*. Chicago: ALA Editions, 2017.

Reference and User Services Association. *Guidelines for Behavioral Performance of Reference and Information Service Providers*. Chicago: Reference and User Services Association, 1996, rev. 2004, 2011, 2013. https://www.ala.org/rusa/resources/guidelines/guidelinesbehavioral.

Rodgers, Carol R. "Defining Reflection: Another Look at John Dewey and Reflective Thinking." *Teachers College Record* 104, no. 4 (June 2002): 842–66. https://doi.org/10.1111/1467-9620.00181.

Schön, Donald A.. *The Reflective Practitioner: How Professionals Think in Action*. New York: Basic Books, 1983.

Wolff-Eisenberg, Christine and Braddlee. *Amplifying Student Voices: The Community College Libraries and Academic Support for Student Success Project*." Research report. New York: Ithaka S+R, August 13, 2018. https://doi.org/10.18665/sr.308086.

CHAPTER 12

Building Librarian Assessment Confidence through Communities of Research Practice

Aryana Bates, Mary Ann Lund Goodwin, Jacquelyn Ray, and Melinda McCormick Coslor

Introduction

Librarians serve a key role in the fabric of an academic institution. This value is not always clearly visible, making it vital for librarians to demonstrate their contributions to student learning as well as to institutional assessment efforts. Assessment is essential to the enhancement of librarian-led (or -facilitated) work, and engagement in assessment can improve how the library is perceived institution-wide. Librarians in the Washington State community and technical college system participated in two yearlong cohorts designed to teach librarians how to conduct assessment projects using the Association of College and Research Libraries (ACRL) Assessment in Action (AiA) framework. Funded by a

Library Services and Technology Act (LSTA) grant,[1] the project provided participants with mentors, evolving into a supportive assessment community as librarians planned and implemented assessment or action research projects through an entire research cycle.

The authors of this chapter conducted a phenomenological study, based on interviews with twenty-two of the grant participants, to discover, "What did grant participants learn by engaging in independent research projects?" In doing so, we gained insight into participants' experiences implementing an action research project, the results of their work, and the impact they felt it had on their practice and perceived value within the context of their institutions. Understanding how librarians view assessment work provides a model for other librarians and equips library administrators to support and advocate for their work.

Literature Review

While academic librarians are familiar with the changing higher education environment and have added new services and resources in response to student and faculty needs,[2] they have been slower to see new opportunities to ask and answer questions related to the value that libraries bring to higher education.[3] Indeed, the role of librarians and their place in the academy has long been questioned, with Hopkins noting early graduates of library schools were taught practical skills like typing and "library hand," and "most of the new library school graduates were neither the intellectual nor social equals of academic faculty."[4] Academic libraries and librarians tend to be taken for granted as few others within the higher education community fully understand the roles they play within the educational enterprise.[5]

Recognizing the need to help academic libraries and librarians validate the importance of their contributions to institutional mission fulfillment, ACRL initiated the Value of Academic Libraries program. The program was designed to help academic librarians develop the skills necessary to articulate the value of libraries in measurable ways.[6] Professional development for academic librarians was identified as a key element in helping them with the development of assessment skills that can be used to demonstrate the library's value to the institution.[7] ACRL facilitates AiA RoadShow workshops, teaching librarians how to apply action research methodology to library assessment projects.[8]

One promising approach to professional development is cultivating communities of practice, or "groups of people who share a concern or a passion for something they do and learn how to do it better as they interact regularly."[9] Communities of practice provide participants with the opportunity to build common understandings of practice and competency as well as professional identity.[10] Sustainable communities of practice attract and engage members by generating a sense of relevance, energy, and excitement.[11] They are guided by seven principles, including four pertinent to this study: (a) the ability to evolve over time, (b) a focus on value, (c) openness to insider and outsider knowledge, and (d) the ability to accommodate all members regardless of their level of commitment to the community. Communities of practice also support transformative learning.[12]

Evaluating transformative learning outcomes requires learners to consider how their perceptions and understanding have changed over time.[13] Our data analysis section explores whether the action research project led to a transformative learning experience, or "learning that transforms problematic frames of reference to make them more inclusive, discriminating, reflective, open, and emotionally able to change"[14] among the participating librarians.

Methodology

Grant participants were invited to engage in individual or group semi-structured, qualitative interviews conducted by the coinvestigators. Twenty-two librarians out of a total of forty-three grant recipients volunteered to participate. Informed consent was obtained from participants, and interviews were conducted synchronously via Zoom. Interviews were recorded, transcribed, coded, and analyzed. As recommended by Guba and Lincoln,[15] member checks and rounds of peer calibration around coding conventions were done to provide a level of trustworthiness in the data analysis and a verification of the overall results of the research findings.

Data Analysis

Seven themes emerged from the study data, broadly organized into three overarching concepts, namely communities of practice, transformative learning, and value of academic libraries. In the following sections, we discuss the concepts and themes to illustrate the effect that participation in the assessment research projects had on the librarians and their institutions.

Concept One: Communities of Practice

Participating in the grant provided librarians with the opportunity to recognize and to build common understandings around assessment practices and competencies as well as to build professional identity. They discovered common barriers and ways of overcoming them and developed a shared awareness of how and with whom to collaborate.

THEME ONE—BARRIERS

Librarian researchers encountered barriers ranging from issues related to the grant project design to mixed messaging within and across institutions, as well as complications related to their own projects. The grant project timeline (essentially six months) was a significant barrier. The timeline was out-of-sync with librarians' nine-month contracts and the academic cycle. The six months left little room for error or risk taking, making production of deliverables stressful, and some participants felt the timeline made it hard to cultivate relationships with collaborators or to develop effective research instruments. Those interested in conducting longitudinal assessment projects lacked the time to do so, and one team opted not to apply for a grant project in the second year because of the tight timeline.

Several projects involved librarians working at two or more colleges, which created a unique set of barriers related to lack of communication, mixed messages, and uneven levels of support. Inconsistent practices among college institutional review boards (IRBs) complicated the collaborative work among at least one group of college researchers. Administrative turnover and concomitant librarian workload shift disrupted at least one project, and there was inconsistency in support and expectations among library administrators overall.

The design of some projects created barriers as well. Some teams experienced logistical issues related to coordinating work among large teams, separating outcomes on a dual-track project with two funding sources, or aligning assessment goals with the grant criteria. Others experienced unexpected staffing shortages that impeded their project's progress, or because their project involved small, intensive stakeholder sessions, found their projects difficult to scale up or sustain. Some observed that their project took considerably longer than they expected, and grant funding notwithstanding, had a heavy impact on their workload. The tight grant cycle came up again as a limiting factor because it restricted findings to one set of data. More than one participant mentioned struggling with how to make meaning out of the data gathered. Finally, a couple of groups were left puzzling over what work to carry on after the grant, and especially what to do, given the results of the research.

Sustaining assessment work and ensuring the continuity of the communities of practice created by the participants were also points of concern. Several participants expressed regret that without ongoing systemic support, the community of practice they created was ending. One remarked, "We have this image of what we could have, and then there's the reality of 'it's over.'" Some articulated the desire for sustained efforts, and one participant noted, "How do we still keep this conversation with all community college librarians up when we are kind of a little fragmented." Of particular concern is how to keep smaller and less affluent libraries involved in the ongoing community of practice.

THEME TWO—COLLABORATION

Two key threads emerged on the theme of collaboration: cross-pollination of skills within the project team, and development of trust and intellectual community with colleagues. Participants talked about the value of working together to define the team's project, identify campus partnerships, develop research questions, and divide the labor according to team members' strengths. As a result, they became aware of what they did and did not know as a group, what they needed to prioritize to complete the project, and of the wealth and depth of their peers' knowledge, both within and beyond the library.

Working with faculty in other disciplines cultivated relationships between departments by strengthening already existent relationships or sparking new ones. One newly hired librarian at a small library noted that the grant "really helped cement that in some very tangible ways." Another stated that the project helped other faculty "see the library and librarians as a connection to other folks on campus," which allowed for a convergence of interests that sparked additional funding from the institution's vice president of instruction to expand the project.

Participants found that the opportunity to work with others both within, across, and outside the libraries was one of the more valuable takeaways of the project. In particular, several commented on the value of partnering with institutional researchers, finding that their assistance made the research process more understandable. One researcher summed it up, saying, "I really enjoyed the collaboration with all the different colleges and librarians that participated in the grant. Learning what they did and what they got out of it …I see it as …librarians being more recognized in helping students achieve success."

Concept Two: Transformative Learning

Participant interviews revealed that many had transformative learning experiences as a result of participating in the grant and developed new understandings of the importance of assessment and their responsibility to engage in assessment work. The transformative learning concept consisted of three themes: participants' growing awareness of the assessment culture they created, their teaching praxis, and increased levels of professional confidence.

THEME ONE—ASSESSMENT CULTURE

Although most participants did not have previous assessment research experience, others had considerable experience. Several had developed targeted instructional assessments; one had written an article on discourse analysis; one described themself as bringing a programmatic approach toward assessment to their new institution; and one had even participated in the 2015 national AiA project.

Participants noted that their original perception was that assessment is a burden or hassle, inauthentic to the real purpose of teaching. One commented that assessment felt like a forced exercise for the sole purpose of proving librarians' worth and that it framed libraries as "less than" other instructional areas of the college. However, participants came to appreciate that the grant project provided time and space to conduct assessment research in a way that would otherwise not have been feasible.

To be of most value, assessment should be integrated into daily work, especially the work of teaching. For some participants, engaging in the process of action research reinforced this previously held ideal; for others, it broadened views on the nature of and approach to assessment. As one participant put it, "My understanding really disintegrated …from a very ideal sense of what assessment is …as rigid or set in stone …[to] being a lot more messy and a lot more social. It shows the gritty reality of how this all goes down." Several came to understand that assessment is most valuable when understood as an iterative process. Participants also learned how important it is to frame an assessment project by identifying the information being sought, the reason it is needed, and how the results can be used to improve services or instruction.

The grant project immersed participants in the language of assessment, making the concept more relevant to instruction and librarianship. One participant found themself reflecting about the inherent tension between protecting student privacy and the need for data to assess services and engage in continuous improvement. One participant even stated that assessment could be a "fun and rewarding" way of understanding the library's contribution to the college.

Theme Two—Teaching Praxis

Many participants described how the grant changed their work. The project provided a timeline, guidelines, an opportunity to think about how to gather data, permission to fail (the tight grant cycle notwithstanding) and figure out solutions, and the chance to work within the larger institution and cultivate cross-department relationships.

Researchers used the project timeline to stay on track: to prioritize what needed assessing, to think about types of assessment that could be conducted, to be thoughtful about how data collection surveys were framed, to be intentional about how assessment of an initiative's growth was being conducted, and to think strategically about how and why the evidence could be used. The grant project's guidelines provided a framework to organize the project from preplanning projects to implementing and concluding the research. By gathering and analyzing multiple types of data, the researchers could refine their data gathering tools, reframe questions to better serve the research question, and consider how to sustain the research into the future.

In some cases, researchers discovered their results were not what they had hoped for. Nevertheless, by conducting the research and doing rigorous data analysis, they gained (*a*) a clearer understanding of their own work and its effectiveness, (*b*) greater facility with the research process, and (*c*) a more nuanced sense of the library's effectiveness within the larger institution. For example, one group of researchers found their library's services were not as effective at closing equity gaps as they expected although their data was congruent with their institution. The team took the results as a data-driven cue to acknowledge the need to improve their services in order to meet their own goals of equity and inclusion.

Some participants reported changes in their consciousness and concomitant approach to their practice as a result of their research project. One project that included student-developed content based on their identities, cultures, and personal stories expanded the participant's understanding about how information literacy is acquired. Another multi-college team collaborated to create a suite of online information literacy modules to share across the state. The effort helped participants not only realize their aspirations to support students and faculty with high-quality, accessible learning content based on open education principles and instructional design best practices, but it also reduced their workload in a systematic way. As one mentioned, the new modules serve "students that we can't reach face to face in our classroom …or who like to do things differently." The project also incorporated inclusion-focused design, providing one participant with a deeper understanding of the principles of inclusion as the team chose to use *we* instead of *I* as they constructed the modules in consideration of students coming from collectivist rather than individualist cultures and societies.

For some, the assessment project cultivated a shift of focus from quantity to quality of topics covered in library instruction sessions. Some expanded their instructional focus from individual class sessions toward grounding the lesson in the curriculum for the "quarter, more holistically and across the board." Another participant reoriented their teaching to integrate library instruction across the full arc of a course instead of providing a traditional one-shot instruction session. In the case of a longitudinal project comparing outcomes between courses taught with and without embedded information literacy lessons, the findings inspired a participant to think more programmatically: "I'm thinking about as a group of librarians who teach the same course, how can we come together and …talk about what we're doing, streamline things, improve it at a higher level versus …specific day-to-day teaching that I do."

THEME THREE—CHANGE IN CONFIDENCE

Participants' change in confidence emerged in four threads: relationship building, capacity for conducting assessment, depth of understanding of the research process, and professional maturity. Several referred to the value of collaborating with colleagues, with collaborative work increasing the visibility of the library and librarians. One participant commented that a workshop offered by the librarians in connection with their project "helped other faculty connect with us, and with each other," and cultivated conversations that helped them do their work better. Another participant, on tenure track at the time, reported that being involved with the project "helped the VPI remember who I am, and how to say my name correctly."

Participants reported a deepened understanding of the research process, and for many, engaging in the project brought a greater level of confidence in being able to conduct future research projects. One began thinking more critically about the tension between librarianship and research, specifically the conflict between the charge to protect privacy and the need to collect data for research purposes. One developed confidence in their own thinking capacity; another reported their ability to construct a research question had improved; several realized that research is "messy" and iterative, that it is "ok to have a process that is no process," and that even just being able to figure out what questions to ask can be valuable. One summed up the attitudinal shift, saying, "I've never done research like this before …so I was kind of hesitant…. But then …it was like, yeah, we can do this, this is great. It was a lot of work …a lot of fun too, and I did learn a lot. Throw this lobster in!"

Professional maturity was another thread, either in the form of social cohesion through collaborative work or in the form of taking a leadership role, managing the project. Some gained an understanding of the interdependence of different college departments, coming to value the expertise of institutional researchers and faculty skilled in data analysis. Others appreciated seeing what other grant recipients were working on at their colleges as a way to better "build our collective abilities." One participant applied for and participated in the second year of the grant as their confidence level increased.

As participants' confidence increased, their research skills also increased. Participants noted an improvement in their ability to think deeply and flexibly about the scope and purpose of research questions and how to effectively implement research projects. A common reflection was the value of "learning from our mistakes," such as not getting buy-in from stakeholders before moving forward with a research project, or not identifying the factors having the biggest effect on findings. A significant area of growth was in gravitas or having the professional self-assurance to set hard limits around the parameters of a project; to take enough time to think through the merits and relevance of a new method before adopting it; to embrace the idea that effective assessment can be small and focused; or to accept that tools selected at the start of a project may not be the right ones after all and adjusting the next iteration of research accordingly.

Concept Three: Value of Academic Libraries

Participating in the project helped academic librarians recognize that their work contributes to institutions' mission fulfillment. Participation in the project also helped them gain recognition across their institutions.

THEME ONE—CONTRIBUTION

One participant observed that the Washington State community college system libraries now have "a bunch of research output to show for ourselves and our work" and that this sets the stage for community college librarians to become better represented in the "literature in our field." Two groups pointed out that even though they had strong reputations at their institutions, participating in the grant helped them reinforce the value and respect they already enjoyed and helped them introduce library services to new users. A fourth researcher referenced increased interest among faculty as evidence of growing esteem for the work they were doing around assessment, and another mused on being recognized as knowledgeable. Another pointed out that it was the actual work they completed, designing library instruction modules to support the curriculum, rather than the fact of participating in the grant that raised their profile with other faculty. One reported that their project amplified use of the library's "book a librarian" service, increasing the number of students accessing the research help service. One appreciated that the grant allowed for "doing more intentional, larger scope assessment work that would contribute to the profession."

THEME TWO—RECOGNITION

Recognition garnered by the participants came primarily from project collaborators, especially faculty partners. While some participants saw little or no change in how others perceived their work on campus, there was the general sense of a growing appreciation among faculty for partnering with librarians. Additionally, participants were invited to share their work at professional conferences where they received positive feedback from attendees. Two participants noted their libraries received credit for producing meaningful, evidence-based practice and assessment work during accreditation visits, with one of the libraries developing "a reputation on campus now, that we are the ...gold model for assessment."

Summary

The interviews revealed that participants experienced meaningful personal and professional change while undertaking a grant-funded assessment project. As noted earlier, professional development focused on assessment is important for increasing librarians' capacity to engage in making evidence-based continuous improvement. Likewise, embarking on assessment work with partners outside the library provides greater visibility into the library's role supporting student success. As one participant noted, "My picture of assessment ...has totally changed. It's not just about the story ...but it's about the legacy that our assessments can leave and the practice change that it can lead to with our collaborators."

By working in a team-based community of practice, participants were able to work through common issues and share expertise with less experienced researchers. Collaborations between participants were powerful and led to enhanced trust, improved knowledge of self and others, and a culture of problem-solving and peer learning. The communities of practice allowed participants to work together to improve student and institutional success. As projects evolved, participants also evolved, growing professionally by developing new skills and participating in cultures of assessment with their research partners.

Assessment is a useful tool that can inform and transform librarians' work and increase others' perception of the library as a partner in fulfilling institutional missions. Rather than an add-on or "must do," assessment is a valuable process that helps librarians ask questions, seek answers, and improve efforts. Even if project results proved unexpected or not what was hoped for, undergoing the action research project itself built confidence, helped participants cultivate new practices, improved flexibility and depth of thinking, and positioned the library as a valued contributor to impactful, evidence-based work. Indeed, integrating assessment into instruction is essential for librarian-led efforts to catalyze change, improve library resources and services, and support student success.

Our findings indicate that structured professional development activities related to assessment leads to librarian self-efficacy, increases capacity to conduct meaningful and useful assessment work, and informs practices as librarians anticipate and work to meet the needs of their students and institutions. The research work afforded through the grant transformed the practices of many grant participants. In some instances, there was clear and immediate impact, while in other cases, ongoing assessment research has become part of their professional ethos. This experiment has changed our shared work and inter-institutional collegiality.

Notes

1. The project was made possible in part by the Institute of Museum and Library Services, Washington State Library OSOS No. IG-5939. Study findings will be shared with the Washington State Library and with the participants.
2. Sharon Gray Weiner, "The History of Academic Libraries in the United States: A Review of the Literature," *Library Philosophy and Practice* 7, no. 2 (2005): 10, https://digitalcommons.unl.edu/libphilprac/58.
3. Megan Oakleaf, "What's the Value of an Academic Library? The Development of the ACRL Value of Academic Libraries Comprehensive Research Review and Report," *Australian Academic and Research Libraries* 42, no. 1 (2011): 1–2, https://doi.org/10.1080/00048623.2011.10722200.
4. Frances L. Hopkins, "A Century of Bibliographic Instruction: The Historical Claim to Professional and Academic Legitimacy," *College and Research Libraries* 43, no. 3 (1982): 194, https://core.ac.uk/download/pdf/10206725.pdf.
5. Oakleaf, "What's the Value," 2; Weiner, "History of Academic Libraries," 2.
6. Association of College and Research Libraries, *Value of Academic Libraries*, researched by Megan Oakleaf (Chicago: Association of College and Research Libraries, 2010): 7–8, http://www.ala.org/acrl/sites/ala.org.acrl/files/content/issues/value/val_report.pdf.
7. Association of College and Research Libraries, *Value of Academic Libraries*, 17.
8. Association of College and Research Libraries, "Assessment in Action: Demonstrating and Communicating Library Contributions to Student Learning and Success," program description, ACRL Road-Show, accessed April 4, 2020, http://www.ala.org/acrl/conferences/roadshows/aiaroadshow.

9.   Etienne Wenger, "Communities of Practice: A Brief Introduction," Scholars' Bank, University of Oregon Libraries, October 20, 2011, 1, http://scholarsbank.uoregon.edu/xmlui/handle/1794/11736.
10. Andrew Whitworth, et al., "Mapping the Landscape of Practice across Library Communities," *portal: Libraries and the Academy* 16, no. 3 (2016): 562, https://doi.org/10.1353/pla.2016.0034.
11. Etienne Wenger, Richard McDermott, and William M. Snyder, "Cultivating Communities of Practice: A Guide to Managing Knowledge—Seven Principles for Cultivating Communities of Practice," Working Knowledge, Harvard Business School, March 25, 2002, https://hbswk.hbs.edu/archive/cultivating-communities-of-practice-a-guide-to-managing-knowledge-seven-principles-for-cultivating-communities-of-practice.
12. Wenger, McDermott, and Snyder, "Cultivating Communities of Practice."
13. Alessandra Romano, "Transformative Learning: A Review of the Assessment Tools," *Journal of Transformative Learning* 5, no. 1 (2018): 54, https://jotl.uco.edu/index.php/jotl/article/view/199/139.
14. Jack Mezirow, "Transformative Learning Theory," in *Transformative Learning in Practice: Insights from Community, Workplace, and Higher Education*, ed. Jack Mezirow and Edward. W. Taylor (San Francisco: Jossey-Bass, 2009), 22.
15. Egon G. Guba and Yvonna S. Lincoln, *Effective Evaluation* (San Francisco, CA: Jossey-Bass, 1981).

Bibliography and Additional Resources

Association of College and Research Libraries. "*Assessment in Action: Demonstrating and Communicating Library Contributions to Student Learning and Success.*" Program description, ACRL RoadShow. Accessed April 4, 2020. https://www.ala.org/acrl/conferences/roadshows/aiaroadshow.

———. *Value of Academic Libraries: A Comprehensive Research Review and Report.* Researched by Megan Oakleaf. Chicago: Association of College and Research Libraries, 2010. http://www.ala.org/acrl/sites/ala.org.acrl/files/content/issues/value/val_report.pdf.

Guba, Egon G., and Yvonna S. Lincoln. *Effective Evaluation: Improving the Usefulness of Evaluation Results through Responsive and Naturalistic Approaches.* San Francisco: Jossey-Bass, 1981.

Hopkins, Frances L. "A Century of Bibliographic Instruction: The Historical Claim to Professional and Academic Legitimacy." *College and Research Libraries* 43, no. 3 (1982): 192–98. https://core.ac.uk/download/pdf/10206725.pdf.

Mezirow, Jack. "Transformative Learning Theory." In *Transformative Learning in Practice: Insights from Community, Workplace, and Higher Education.* Edited by Jack Mezirow and Edward. W. Taylor, 18–32. San Francisco: Jossey-Bass, 2009.

Oakleaf, Megan. "What's the Value of an Academic Library? The Development of the ACRL Value of Academic Libraries Comprehensive Research Review and Report." *Australian Academic and Research Libraries* 42, no. 1 (2011): 1–13. https://doi.org/10.1080/00048623.2011.10722200.

Renton Technical College. "Assessment in Action Grant Reports." LibGuide. Last updated March 26, 2021. https://libguides.rtc.edu/aia/2018.

Romano, Alessandra. "Transformative Learning: A Review of the Assessment Tools." *Journal of Transformative Learning* 5, no. 1 (2018): 53–70. https://jotl.uco.edu/index.php/jotl/article/view/199/139.

Weiner, Sharon Gray. "The History of Academic Libraries in the United States: A Review of the Literature." *Library Philosophy and Practice* 7, no. 2 (2005): 1–12. https://digitalcommons.unl.edu/libphilprac/58.

Wenger, Etienne. "Communities of Practice: A Brief Introduction." Scholars' Bank, University of Oregon Libraries, October 20, 2011. http://scholarsbank.uoregon.edu/xmlui/handle/1794/11736.

Wenger, Etienne, Richard McDermott, and William M. Snyder. "Cultivating Communities of Practice: A Guide to Managing Knowledge—Seven Principles for Cultivating Communities of Practice." Working Knowledge, Harvard Business School, March 25, 2002. https://hbswk.hbs.edu/archive/cultivating-communities-of-practice-a-guide-to-managing-knowledge-seven-principles-for-cultivating-communities-of-practice.

Whitworth, Andrew, Maria-Carme Torras Calvo, Bodil Moss, Nazareth Amlesom Kifle, and Terje Blåsternes. "Mapping the Landscape of Practice across Library Communities." *portal: Libraries and the Academy* 16, no. 3 (2016): 557–79. https://doi.org/10.1353/pla.2016.0034.

CHAPTER 13

Development by Design

Fostering Growth through Collaboration

Jamie Holmes and Amy Lagers

Introduction

Librarians face myriad challenges when attempting to assess information literacy instruction efforts at the community college level, including the hit-or-miss nature of scheduling, the one-shot format, and the wide variance in both students' prior knowledge and instructors' desired outcomes. A team of librarians at Tulsa Community College (TCC) was tasked by their dean to develop an assessment plan that could overcome these and other challenges. Instead of testing the students' knowledge and abilities, which is problematic simply from a logistical standpoint, they decided to take a different approach. They wanted to find a way for their instruction librarians to learn from each other, be reflective, and assess and improve their own teaching practice. The library management team (LMT) fully supported this approach and gave the team creative freedom, providing that the end product would honor and maintain collegial relationships, consider and incorporate feedback from the entire group of instruction librarians, and include a tool for the LMT to use when observing the instruction librarians on staff.

 The process for creating the program involved a review of best practices and existing programs at other institutions. Most of the existing programs found in the literature were from university libraries that serve four-year undergraduate or graduate programs;

however, the team looked for ways to adapt ideas for a community college program. The process also included a survey of peer institutions, multiple presentations to the instruction librarians and LMT to gain incremental feedback, and a pilot of the program before full implementation. This chapter will describe the program created, including the research and thought process behind each piece, with the goal that the reader will be equipped to customize an instruction assessment program for their own institution.

Purpose of Assessment

When developing any kind of assessment, it is important to identify what that assessment is going to measure, what kind of data will be collected, and how the data will be used. In this case, the team wanted to measure the effectiveness of existing instructional practices. They knew they needed to create an observation form for the library leadership, and they were interested in trying to create a model for peer observation. However, before moving on, they needed to know what was going to be done with the information. Was this assessment meant to be evaluative, or simply meant to provide feedback and opportunity for growth?

Summative versus Formative

While the actual practice of observing and giving feedback in both summative and formative programs can be similar, the differences lie in what is done with the feedback. Summative assessment typically occurs on a set schedule, and the results are quantified in some way and used as part of an instructor's annual evaluation, as is necessary in some university settings where librarians have faculty ranking and need quantifiable evidence for tenure review.[1] Meanwhile, formative assessment can occur any time, and the results are intended to provide feedback to the instructor being observed for the purpose of improving their practice. Some tenure-track, summative assessment models have an aspect of formative assessment that is provided along the way, with the summative evaluation coming at the end of the process.

In formative peer observation programs, the role of the observer should be to provide an objective lens through which the teaching librarian can reflect on the session "in a way that informs future thinking and practice."[2] Some programs are formal in nature, while others take an informal approach in which colleagues agree to collaborate and provide feedback to one another.[3] Unlike summative evaluation, feedback from formative assessments such as peer observation is shared only between the subject of the observation and the observer. These notes do not become part of an instructor's evaluation, but rather are used as a reflection tool to improve one's own practice. It is recommended in much of the literature that the feedback remain confidential.[4]

At TCC, instruction librarians do not have faculty status. Since tenure is not a consideration, the team decided to make the entire program, even the LMT observation tool, formative in nature. Annual performance evaluations are based on individual goals and performance of the job as a whole, with instruction being only one portion of a librarian's duties. While an observation by the library director will naturally inform the performance evaluation, it is not inherently tied to it, and none of the notes would become part of the official employee record.

The TCC IDeA Program

With the purpose determined, the TCC Library Instruction Development and Assessment (IDeA) program was created with three main components: a professional learning community (PLC), collaborative mentoring groups (CMGs), and teaching observations, by both peers and library directors, following a specified protocol.

Professional Learning Community (PLC)

When thinking of the TCC Library instruction program, the assessment team recognized the diversity in backgrounds, training, and experience of our instruction librarians. Some were trained as teachers in the K–12 environment, a few had been instruction librarians for many years, and others were brand new with undergraduate degrees and experience in disciplines less focused on teaching. Before assessing instructional practices, it was important to ensure that all instruction librarians were aware of best practices and felt prepared for the classroom. The group needed to develop a shared vocabulary and shared knowledge of learning theory.[5] Additionally, to successfully implement peer observation of teaching, training on giving and receiving of feedback was imperative. To address these concerns, the professional learning community (PLC) was formed.

The PLC consists of all instruction librarians participating in large-group activities every month for thirty to forty-five minutes as part of the monthly department meeting. Two librarians serve as co-facilitators each academic year, and they are responsible for planning PLC content each month. The activities, often centered upon a reading assigned before the meeting, can help enrich knowledge and skills in any instruction-related area, but they primarily focus on development in three key areas: the ability to successfully give and receive feedback in a useful and meaningful way, engaging in reflective practice, and learning theory and effective pedagogy.

Collaborative Mentoring Groups (CMGs)

As stated previously, part of the task of creating this program was to do it in a way that would preserve collegial relationships. The dean of libraries recognized that a peer observation or group mentoring process could yield unintended consequences. The TCC Library strives for a climate in which each employee feels valued and contributes their individual strengths to the missions of both the library and the college. If mentoring groups were not structured properly, differences in experience, tenure, or personality style could create the perception of unbalanced partnerships. Librarians with less experience and tenure, or those who feel less comfortable sharing in groups, could be overlooked in discussions. The team recognized that this could result in the loss of important perspectives. The collaborative mentoring group component of the IDeA program is based on the idea that, regardless of experience or background, everyone has something to learn and everyone has something to share.[6]

In the CMGs, three to four instructors gather to reflect upon teaching experiences with their peers in order to bring self-awareness, troubleshoot areas of weakness, and learn from each other's experiences. The CMGs often meet during the monthly large-group PLC time when small-group work or discussions are assigned. The assessment group liked the idea of mentors but wanted a way to structure the relationships non-hierarchically. Based on a model of Reflective Peer Mentoring, collaborative mentoring differs from traditional mentoring in that each member "functions as both mentor and mentee: bringing knowledge, questions and ideas to the group and benefiting equally from discussion, reflection, and exploration."[7] Smaller groups of three to four people help to keep mentoring relationships balanced, instead of falling into traditional roles that favor seniority or experience.[8]

Observation of Teaching

The third component of the IDeA program is observation of teaching, both by peers and by library management. From the beginning, the assessment team was tasked with creating some sort of observation form for library management to use when observing their instruction staff, with the goal of creating consistency and equity among the four campuses. A standardized form was created, providing a structure that aligned session learning outcomes with TCC's Institutional Learning Outcomes, as well as with specific concepts in the Association of College and Research Libraries (ACRL) *Framework for Information Literacy for Higher Education*.[9] The form is intended for use by supervisors when observing instruction librarians, but it is also available for use by peers if both partners choose to use it. While containing some elements of a rubric or a checklist,[10] it stays true to its formative purpose by not including any way to quantify behaviors or provide any kind of numeric score.[11] Observable behaviors on the form are organized by themes and pose several guiding questions that are based on pedagogically themed categories, such as lesson design, reflection, and engagement.[12] The IDeA team plans to review the form after its first year of use in order to reduce any unnecessary or overly complex components (see appendix).

PEER OBSERVATION PARTNERS

Within the CMGs, librarians are paired with an observation partner. Figure 13.1 shows the relationships of the IDeA components.

The peer-observation partners are paired for the duration of an academic year. Partners are required to observe one another at least once, and more observations are certainly encouraged as time permits. Librarians are assigned a new observation partner each year, and new partnerships are determined and announced near the beginning of summer, to provide more flexibility in scheduling.

The literature supports assigning observation partners in several different ways, and the IDeA team considered them all before determining a good fit for their program. One option calls for names to be drawn at random, but with the option to trade with other colleagues.[13] Another option allows for participants to choose their own partners for observation.[14] Yet a third suggests that a program coordinator assign partners in pairs or triads.[15] The IDeA team took parts of the strategies recommended by different authors, and

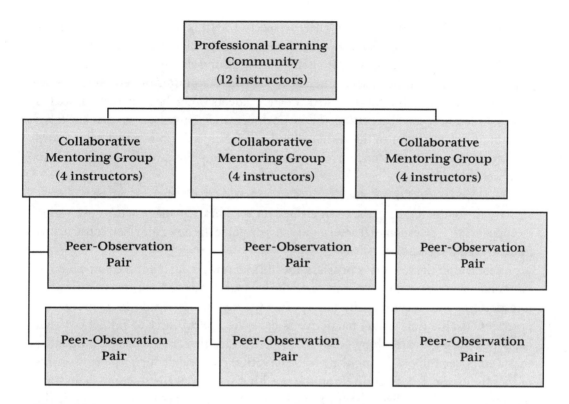

Figure 13.1
IDeA components

in consultation with the LMT, decided that observation partners and CMG configurations would be assigned each summer by the incoming IDeA facilitators, who serve as de facto program coordinators. While random assignments could potentially result in matches that wouldn't work due to differing work schedules or in repeats of previous years, IDeA leaders recognized the value of the option to trade partners with other colleagues and therefore built in the option for librarians to request to observe or to be observed by any other IDeA librarian in addition to their assigned partner. The option to trade allowed for the benefit of librarians choosing one's observer in order to work with someone they trust and respect; however, by intentionally creating the formal program pairs, facilitators also encouraged more interaction between campuses by pairing librarians from different campuses as well as those with differing backgrounds, training, and experience.

OBSERVATION PROTOCOL

All observations, regardless of type, follow the same observation protocol, which consists of three separate components, as described in most of the literature on the topic of peer observation of instruction.

Prior to the session, the two librarians meet for a *pre-observation conference*, in which they engage in a conversation to determine where the teaching librarian would like the observer to focus. This could be an area in which the teaching librarian is struggling or curious, or on which they would like a new perspective. During this conference, the participants agree upon a feedback format, and the teaching librarian may also communicate other information, such as specific limitations, extenuating circumstances, or instructor requests.[16] The role of the observer needs to be defined, in terms of determining how much interaction with the course instructor and students would be acceptable, as well as agreement on how the observation will be documented.[17] This discussion ideally takes place in person just prior to the session, but the program is flexible in that participants can decide to engage via e-mail or videoconference at any time within a week prior to the observation.[18]

The second stage of the protocol is the *observation*. As mentioned earlier, peer observers have the option of using the form created for the library management's observation (see appendix). It gives some structure and can help guide the observer when constructing feedback about the session.

As soon after the session as possible, the librarians meet again for the *post-observation conference*, so the observer can share the feedback and the two can work together to process how to meaningfully incorporate the observations into their individual practices. In this final stage, participants have the opportunity to reflect on what happened during the teaching session. It is important that the focus and guidelines that were agreed upon during the pre-observation conference form the constraints of the discussion.[19] Reflection upon the teaching session needs to come from both the observer and the observee. It can be helpful for the observed party to guide the discussion by sharing their own perceptions of the session, and for the observer to describe rather than evaluate.[20] The idea is to describe the instruction session from another point of view.

The observation protocol is intended to be formative in nature, rather than summative. There are plenty of examples of both types in the literature, but as previously discussed, the former was deemed a better fit for IDeA. In designing the program to incorporate formative observations, rather than the more rigid summative observation protocols, the librarians were able to build in flexibility that maximized the benefits and reduced unnecessary constraints.

Framing Feedback

If feedback, whether provided in the context of peer observation or not, is to influence teaching practice, instructors must engage in reflective practice. The instructor must be able to accept and act upon feedback received. The evaluation of one's teaching practice is a highly personal process, and the emotional aspect cannot be overstated. It is important that all participants keep in mind that

> reflective practice involves the process of teaching and the thinking behind it, rather than simply evaluating the teaching itself. It is, therefore, addressing the question of why as opposed to how and, most important, it is about learning from this process.[21]

Individual instructors can present the same material in very different ways, so it is important to focus on the reasoning behind decisions made in the classroom. This consideration of the reasoning is at the heart of IDeA's three-part structure: the observations provide the data to talk about, and the conversations in pairs, small groups, and large groups are what lead to growth and improvement in each librarian's practice.

During the PLC portion of the IDeA program, much attention has been given to best practices for framing feedback. Indeed, the focus of the first year was on this topic, and since then it has become a recurring theme. For further reading on the practice of giving and receiving feedback the IDeA team recommends these articles: "The Practice of Giving Feedback to Improve Feedback: What Is effective?" by Brinko, and "Criticism Is Not a Four-Letter Word: Best Practices for Constructive Feedback in the Peer Review of Teaching" by Alabi and Weare. Both articles could serve as recommended reading or to guide workshops for training observers, and content from both has been featured in IDeA's PLCs over the past year.[22]

Overview of the IDeA Program Creation Process and Benefits

The assessment team worked through a very organic process to develop this program. Figure 13.2 illustrates the time line and process. While the creation process started with a literature review and surveys of peer and aspirational institutions, and included frequent check-ins with the LMT, the most important feedback came from the librarian group. What has resulted is a program in which each participant has equal footing and ownership of the process.

After the first full year of implementation, IDeA facilitators solicited feedback to evaluate program efficacy and make adjustments for the next year. Of the eleven instruction librarians who participated in IDeA during year one, ten responded to the survey; of those, 100 percent reported that it was time well spent in that they benefitted from being observed and from the PLC activities. All who were able to observe their partner teach (nine out of ten) found that beneficial as well. Also, they all felt their instruction had improved as a result of their participation in IDeA. Specific comments highlight some of the benefits:

- "It was good for me to hear and see how another librarian taught similar content in a different way. I also appreciated the feedback from the librarian who observed me. It was beneficial to have some time one-on-one to talk about teaching one-shot classes and the issues related to it. I enjoyed the discussion";
- "The feedback I received was detailed, specific, and helped me identify areas of my practice that I can improve (as well as areas that are already working well)";
- "I found that PLC time gave me an opportunity to slow down and reflect on big-picture issues surrounding instruction in a way that rarely happens during my standard teaching preparations."

While the feedback was quite positive overall, some comments brought to light specific ways the program could be improved. For example, the original program design required each librarian to observe all others in their CMG twice, once in the fall semester and once in the spring semester. Since these groups consisted of three to four librarians, most participants noted that it was difficult to schedule that many required observations. This led IDeA facilitators to recommend modifying the observation protocol so that two people are paired within the CMG and expected to observe one another at least once throughout the whole academic year. Also, some reported a desire to observe peers other than their assigned partner and even outside their assigned CMG group, so IDeA facilitators reaffirmed that more observation is encouraged and does not need to be limited to just once and only with that one partner or another in their CMG. Finally, more than one respondent indicated a wish to see a more substantial reflection component built in; therefore, facilitators for the second year tried to provide more opportunities for reflection during the PLC time.

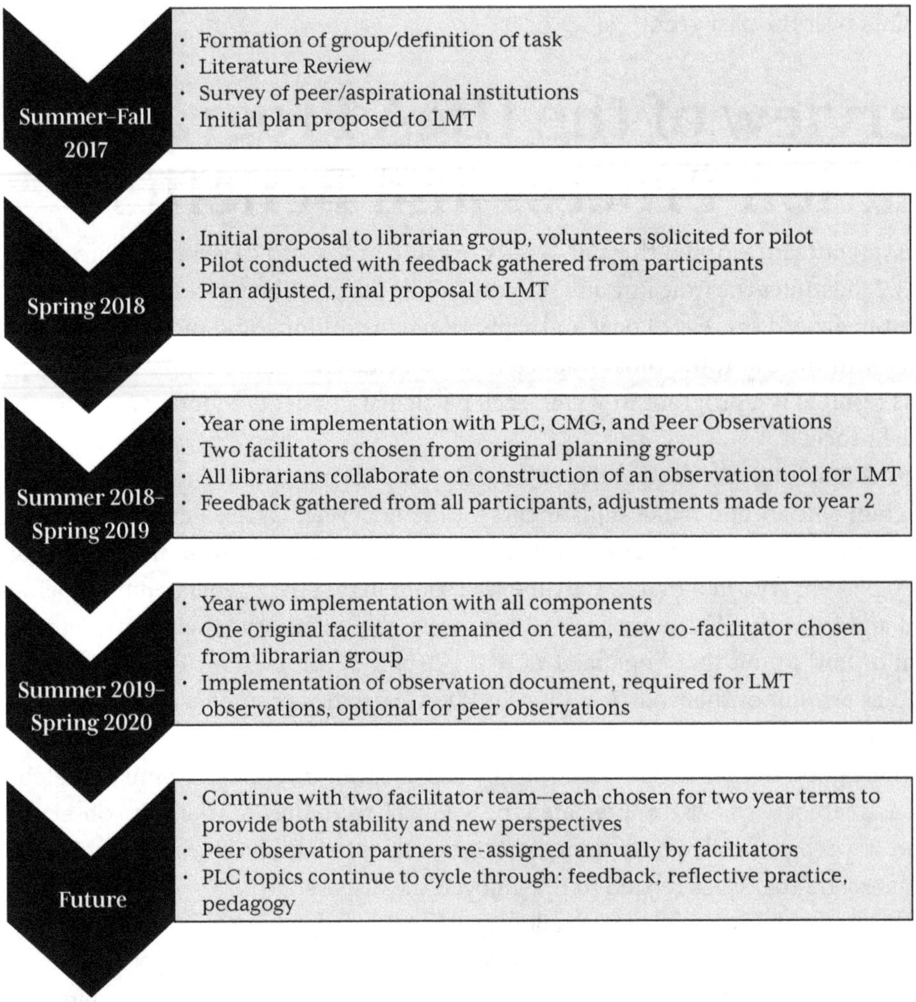

Summer–Fall 2017
- Formation of group/definition of task
- Literature Review
- Survey of peer/aspirational institutions
- Initial plan proposed to LMT

Spring 2018
- Initial proposal to librarian group, volunteers solicited for pilot
- Pilot conducted with feedback gathered from participants
- Plan adjusted, final proposal to LMT

Summer 2018– Spring 2019
- Year one implementation with PLC, CMG, and Peer Observations
- Two facilitators chosen from original planning group
- All librarians collaborate on construction of an observation tool for LMT
- Feedback gathered from all participants, adjustments made for year 2

Summer 2019– Spring 2020
- Year two implementation with all components
- One original facilitator remained on team, new co-facilitator chosen from librarian group
- Implementation of observation document, required for LMT observations, optional for peer observations

Future
- Continue with two facilitator team—each chosen for two year terms to provide both stability and new perspectives
- Peer observation partners re-assigned annually by facilitators
- PLC topics continue to cycle through: feedback, reflective practice, pedagogy

Figure 13.2
IDeA time line

Future Considerations

One of the most important aspects of IDeA is that, to the extent possible, it is managed by its participants. In keeping with that spirit, both the PLC topics and maintenance of the program are defined by the group as described below.

- IDeA participants overwhelmingly reported that they found a summer book study valuable, so the group will continue that practice. The facilitators will solicit book suggestions, and activities throughout the summer will focus on that reading.
- Facilitators will gather feedback from participants each spring and adjust the program based on that assessment.
- Facilitators will review the current and past CMG configurations and will assign new pairings.
- In the spring, a new facilitator will be chosen for a two-year term, and one of the original facilitators will move to the role of a participant.
- A LibGuide page houses all program documents, including an archive of all past PLC activities.[23]

Conclusion

It is difficult to take a program from one library and adopt it fully into another. Each library instruction program has its own needs and challenges. It is the goal of the authors that this chapter will empower the reader to assess those needs and challenges and then create something that works in their own teaching context. This could mean that a librarian from a small college will need to invite faculty from outside the library as part of their teaching and learning community. Conversely, at very large institutions, a similar program can be successful when participants join on a voluntary basis. Regardless of the resulting makeup of the program, it is important to be intentional. Put goals and structure in writing to ensure every participant knows the expectations. Monitor the program with frequent opportunities for participant feedback, and then take that feedback and adjust the program accordingly. In the end, if it creates opportunities to reflect and grow as an instructor, it will result in a better learning experience for students.

Appendix

IDeA Observation Form

Librarian: _____ Observer: _____ Date of session:_____

Pre-Observation Discussion:

Based on your plan for the session, comment below on the Information Literacy Frames you plan to cover within the context of TCC's Institutional Learning Outcomes. (*It's not necessary to address every frame in the session; objectives will be specific to the assignment and course instructor. This is meant as a conversation-starter, not a checklist or rubric.*)

Critical Thinking
Authority is Constructed & Contextual (e.g., Evaluating Sources, Information Cycle, where to look, etc.)
Searching as Strategic Exploration (e.g., Reference Databases, Looking for subject terms in results of a keyword search, etc.)
Research as Inquiry (e.g., Search strategies, research process, etc.)

Communication Skills	
Scholarship as Conversation (e.g., citation mining, publishing, licensing, information cycle, etc.)	Information Creation as a Process (e.g., publishing, peer review process, etc.)

Personal Responsibility	Social Responsibility
Information has Value (e.g., proper citation, avoiding plagiarism, access to information, etc.)	Scholarship as a Conversation (e.g., information cycle, popular vs. scholarly sources, core publications, etc.)

Other things to consider while observing the session (e.g., specific feedback requests, course information, students' prior knowledge, timing of instruction/assignment due date, etc.)

Observation Notes:

Consider the following observable behaviors:

Content/Organization:

- Session outcomes are clearly defined and communicated
- Session is well-organized, with topics presented in a logical sequence
- Relevance of content to student needs is clearly communicated

+	Δ

Presentation:

- Communicates clearly and defines unfamiliar terms and concepts, including library jargon
- Librarian is confident and engaged
- Matches content to the level of the class and/or instruction need
- Librarian paces lesson appropriately and uses class time well

+	Δ

Instructional Materials:

- Instructional materials have clear content and are well-organized
- Instructional materials can be clearly read/heard and are accessible to all students
- Librarian includes historically underrepresented groups in materials and activities when appropriate

+	Δ

Interaction:

- Incorporates active learning where appropriate
- Monitors student understanding and adapts instruction accordingly
- Encourages all students to participate
- Acknowledges multiple perspectives and respects diverse points of view

+	Δ

OTHER OBSERVATIONS:

Post Observation Discussion

Observer's Reflection:

What were the instruction librarian's major strengths, as noted in this observation?

What do you identify as the instruction librarian's potential areas for growth?

Librarian's Action Plan:

What are some next steps you plan to take to incorporate this feedback in your instruction practice?

Notes

1.   Ned Fielden and Mira Foster, "Crossing the Rubricon: Evaluating the Information Literacy Instructor," *Journal of Information Literacy* 4, no. 2 (December 2010): 78–90, https://doi.org/10.11645/4.2.1511; Cheryl Middleton, "Evolution of Peer Evaluation of Library Instruction at Oregon State University Libraries," portal: *Libraries and the Academy* 2, no. 1 (January 2002): 69–78, https://doi.org/10.1353/pla.2002.0019.
2.   Linda Hammersley-Fletcher and Paul Orsmond, "Reflecting on Reflective Practices within Peer Observation," *Studies in Higher Education* 30, no. 2 (2005): 214, https://doi.org/10.1080/03075070500043358.
3.   Jaena Alabi and William H. Weare Jr., "Peer Review of Teaching: Best Practices for a Non-programmatic Approach," *Communications in Information Literacy* 8, no. 2 (2014), https://10.15760/comminfolit.2014.8.2.171.
4.   Alabi and Weare, "Peer Review of Teaching"; Sue Samson and Donna E. McCrea, "Using Peer Review to Foster Good Teaching," *Reference Services Review* 36, no. 1 (2008): 61–70, https://doi.org/10.1108/00907320810852032.
5.   Janet L. Goosney, Becky Smith, and Shannon Gordon, "Reflective Peer Mentoring: Evolution of a Professional Development Program for Academic Librarians," *Partnership: The Canadian Journal of Library and Information Practice and Research* 9, no. 1 (2014), https://journal.lib.uoguelph.ca/index.php/perj/article/view/2966.

6. Mary Jo Bona, Jane Rinehart, and Rose Mary Volbrecht, "Show Me How to Do Like You: Co-mentoring as Feminist Pedagogy," *Feminist Teacher* 9, no. 3 (1995): 116–24; Goosney, Smith, and Gordon, "Reflective Peer Mentoring."
7. Goosney, Smith, and Gordon, "Reflective Peer Mentoring," 8.
8. Goosney, Smith, and Gordon, "Reflective Peer Mentoring"; Vidmar, "Reflective Peer Coaching."
9. Association of College and Research Libraries, *Framework for Information Literacy for Higher Education* (Chicago: Association of College and Research Libraries, 2016), https://www.ala.org/acrl/standards/ilframework.
10. Samson and McCrea, "Using Peer Review"; Fielden and Foster, "Crossing the Rubicon"; Middleton, "Evolution of Peer Evaluation "; Sarah R. Gewirtz, "Evaluating an Instruction Program with Various Assessment Measures," *Reference Services Review* 42, no. 1 (2014): 16–33, https://doi.org/10.1108/RSR-03-2013-0019.
11. Alabi and Weare, "Peer Review of Teaching."
12. Goosney, Smith, and Gordon, "Reflective Peer Mentoring," 3–4.
13. Gewirtz, "Evaluating an Instruction Program."
14. Alabi and Weare, "Peer Review of Teaching"; Lee-Allison Levine and Polly Frank, "Peer Coaching: Professional Growth and Development for Instruction Librarians," *Reference Services Review* 21, no. 3 (1993): 35–42.
15. Hammersley-Fletcher and Orsmond, "Reflecting on Reflective Practices."
16. Alabi and Weare, "Peer Review of Teaching."
17. Alabi and Weare, "Peer Review of Teaching; Levine and Frank, "Peer Coaching."
18. Gewirtz, "Evaluating an Instruction Program."
19. Levine and Frank, "Peer Coaching."
20. Levine and Frank, "Peer Coaching."
21. Hammersley-Fletcher and Orsmond, "Reflecting on Reflective Practices," 214.
22. Kathleen T. Brinko, "The Practice of Giving Feedback to Improve Teaching: What Is Effective?" *Journal of Higher Education* 64, no. 5 (1993): 574–93, https://doi.org/10.2307/2959994; Jaena Alabi and William H. Weare Jr., "Criticism Is Not a Four-Letter Word: Best Practices for Constructive Feedback in the Peer Review of Teaching," in *Energize! Accelerate! Transform! Fortieth National LOEX Library Instruction Conference Proceedings, Columbus, Ohio, May 3–5, 2012,* ed. Brad Sietz, Randal E. Baier, Susann DeVries, Sarah Fabian, Sara Memmott, and Robert Anthony Stevens (Ypsilanti: University Library, Eastern Michigan University, 2014).
23. Adam Brennan et al., "ACRL Framework Toolbox: Home," LibGuide, Tulsa Community College Library, last updated November 4, 2020, https://guides.library.tulsacc.edu/c.php?g=969735&p=7007492.

Bibliography and Additional Resources

Alabi, Jaena, and William H. Weare Jr. "Criticism Is Not a Four-Letter Word: Best Practices for Constructive Feedback in the Peer Review of Teaching." In *Energize! Accelerate! Transform! Fortieth National LOEX Library Instruction Conference Proceedings, Columbus, Ohio, May 3–5, 2012.* Edited by Brad Sietz, Randal E. Baier, Susann DeVries, Sarah Fabian, Sara Memmott, and Robert Anthony Stevens. Ypsilanti: University Library, Eastern Michigan University, 2014.

———. "Peer Review of Teaching: Best Practices for a Non-programmatic Approach." *Communications in Information Literacy* 8, no. 2 (2014). https://10.15760/comminfolit.2014.8.2.171.

Association of College and Research Libraries. *Framework for Information Literacy for Higher Education.* Chicago: Association of College and Research Libraries, 2016. https://www.ala.org/acrl/standards/ilframework.

Bona, Mary Jo, Jane Rinehart, and Rose Mary Volbrecht. "Show Me How to Do Like You: Co-mentoring as Feminist Pedagogy." *Feminist Teacher* 9, no. 3 (1995): 116–24.

Brennan, Adam, Jamie Holmes, Amy Lagers, and Marianne Myers. "ACRL Framework Toolbox: Home." LibGuide, Tulsa Community College Library. Last updated November 4, 2020. https://guides.library.tulsacc.edu/c.php?g=969735&p=7007492.

Brinko, Kathleen T. "The Practice of Giving Feedback to Improve Teaching: What Is Effective?" *Journal of Higher Education* 64, no. 5 (1993): 574–93. https://doi.org/10.2307/2959994.

Fielden, Ned, and Mira Foster. "Crossing the Rubricon: Evaluating the Information Literacy Instructor." *Journal of Information Literacy* 4, no. 2 (December 2010): 78–90. https://doi.org/10.11645/4.2.1511.

Gewirtz, Sarah R. "Evaluating an Instruction Program with Various Assessment Measures." *Reference Services Review* 42, no. 1 (2014): 16–33. https://doi.org/10.1108/RSR-03-2013-0019.

Goosney, Janet L., Becky Smith, and Shannon Gordon. "Reflective Peer Mentoring: Evolution of a Professional Development Program for Academic Librarians." *Partnership: The Canadian Journal of Library and Information Practice and Research* 9, no. 1 (2014). https://journal.lib.uoguelph.ca/index.php/perj/article/view/2966.

Hammersley-Fletcher, Linda, and Paul Orsmond. "Reflecting on Reflective Practices within Peer Observation." *Studies in Higher Education* 30, no. 2 (2005): 213–24. https://doi.org/10.1080/03075070500043358.

Levine, Lee-Allison, and Polly Frank. "Peer Coaching: Professional Growth and Development for Instruction Librarians." *Reference Services Review* 21, no. 3 (1993): 35–42.

Middleton, Cheryl. "Evolution of Peer Evaluation of Library Instruction at Oregon State University Libraries." *portal: Libraries and the Academy* 2, no. 1 (January 2002): 69–78. https://doi.org/10.1353/pla.2002.0019.

Samson, Sue, and Donna E. McCrea. "Using Peer Review to Foster Good Teaching." *Reference Services Review* 36, no. 1 (2008): 61–70. https://doi.org/10.1108/00907320810852032.

Vidmar, Dale J. "Reflective Peer Coaching: Crafting Collaborative Self-Assessment in Teaching." *Research Strategies* 20, no. 3 (2005): 135–48.

Biographies

Series Editors

Kaela Casey

Kaela Casey is a librarian at the Evelyn and Howard Boroughs Library at Ventura College. Her journey to becoming a librarian began just after high school when she became a student at Ventura College. Although her plan was to become a graphic artist, her path changed after a serendipitous course of events. First, a friend encouraged her to take a career assessment test, which showed that her best career match was a librarian. Next, a library student assistant position became available, which she applied for and got. Her experience working at the library inspired her to change her plan and work toward becoming a librarian. Kaela received her BA in Art from California State University, Channel Islands, in 2007. She worked full-time as a Library Assistant at the John Spoor Broome Library at California State University, Channel Islands, while raising a family and working on her MLIS. She is a 2009 ALA Spectrum Scholar and received her MLIS from San José State University in 2012. As a librarian at Ventura College, Kaela leads outreach efforts, provides support for library systems and technical services, and advances the information literacy instruction program through collaboration with faculty and student support services and creating a greater library presence online and in Canvas. Kaela has published and presented on topics including library outreach and social media, cross-institutional collaboration, online information literacy instruction, and partnerships with student support services. When not working, Kaela enjoys doing arts and crafts with her children, playing video games, and hiking.

Janet Pinkley

Janet Pinkley is a long-time adjunct librarian at Evelyn and Howard Boroughs Library at Ventura College. She is also the Head of Access Services at California State University, Channel Islands, where she oversees circulation, equipment, reference services, and course reserves. Her part-time role at the community college provides a different level of engagement with a diverse group of students and informs her professional practice at both institutions. Janet received her BS in Communicative Disorders from California

State University, Fresno, in 2004 and her MLIS from San José State University in 2006. Janet's published and presented on topics including reference best practices, library and student affairs collaborations, integrating information literacy into online curriculum, and exploring collaborative opportunities between regional K–12, community colleges, and universities to improve advocacy for informational literacy at all levels of education. In her free time, Janet enjoys spending time with her family, doing activities with her children, couponing, and gardening.

About the Authors

ARYANA BATES

Aryana Bates has worked as a librarian in the Washington State Community College system since 2006. She's been serving her current educational community as Dean of the Library, eLearning, Teaching and Learning Center, and Student Media Center at North Seattle College since 2017. She holds advanced degrees in library science and in the ethics and anthropology of religion.

BRYAN CLARK

Bryan Clark began working at Illinois Central College as the Technical Services Librarian in 2014. He spent the previous six years on the public services side as a community college reference librarian in Illinois. He received a Master's Degree in Library and Information Sciences from the University of Illinois at Urbana-Champaign.

MELINDA MCCORMICK COSLOR

Melinda McCormick Coslor, Director of Library Services, Skagit Valley College, retired. Dr. Coslor holds a Master of Librarianship from the University of Washington and a PhD in Higher Education/Community College Leadership from Oregon State University.

ANGELA L. CREEL

Angela L. Creel has been the Director of Library Services at Arizona Western College since 2003. After receiving her MLS from Indiana University, she has served as a Reference Librarian, Distance Education Librarian, and Adjunct Faculty. She is committed to providing a welcome learning environment for the wide range of students at the community college and the community at large and to supporting their lifelong learning goals.

ERICA DIAS

Erica Dias is the Hawaiian Resources Librarian at Kapiʻolani Community College, where she is primarily responsible for instruction, reference, and management of the Hawaiian and Pacific Collections. She earned her MLISc from the University of Hawai'i at Mānoa.

JOSEPH ESHLEMAN

Joe Eshleman was Librarian Senior at Central Piedmont Community College in Charlotte, North Carolina. He was previously the Instruction Librarian at the Johnson and Wales University Library–Charlotte from 2008 to 2015 and was Head Librarian for two years at the JWU Providence library. He received his MLIS degree from the University of North Carolina at Greensboro in 2007. He has completed the Association of College and Research Libraries' Immersion Program, an intensive program of training and education for instruction librarians. Eshleman is a coauthor of *Fundamentals for the Academic Liaison* (2014), *The Mindful Librarian* (2016), and *The Dysfunctional Library: Challenges and Solutions to Workplace Relationships* (2017), and *Cultivating Civility: Practical Ways to Improve a Dysfunctional Library (2020). He is also a coauthor of Librarians and Instructional Designers: Innovation and Collaboration* (2016) and a contributor to *The Personal Librarian: Enhancing the Student Experience* (2014). He has presented at numerous conferences on instructional librarianship and other topics.

AMY GLASS

Amy Glass has been with Illinois Central College as an Information Services Librarian since 2005. Before that, she spent over fifteen years as a public librarian in Illinois. She received a Master's Degree in Library and Information Sciences from the University of Illinois at Urbana-Champaign and a Certificate of Advanced Studies from San José State University.

MARY ANN LUND GOODWIN

Following a long career as a faculty librarian and community college library director, Dr. Goodwin, EdD, currently serves as Director of the Institutional Research Department at Community Colleges of Spokane. During her career, Goodwin has been passionate about creating professional development opportunities for other educators. As part of that work, she led the team coordinating a two-year grant-funded program that encouraged Washington state community and technical college librarians to learn about and adopt assessment practices using action research strategies.

ELIZABETH GORDON

Elizabeth Gordon (she/they), Assessment and Evaluation Coordinator at the Community College of Philadelphia, collaborates with faculty and staff to implement and improve assessment practices with a focus on student equity and social justice. She holds an MSEd in Educational Leadership from Old Dominion University in Norfolk, Virginia, and believes in using assessment and quality improvement work as a starting point to foster community connections and break down barriers. Her interests are in the roles of professional helping skills and social-emotional aspects of assessment and continuous improvement work, as well as the role of assessment in the pursuit of a liberatory form of post-secondary education. They spend their free time organizing within their community in Philadelphia, traveling, baking, and cuddling with their sweet cat, Fennel.

Joseph Harris

Joseph Harris is a Research and Assessment Analyst in the Institutional Research and Assessment Department at Tulsa Community College. He earned a master's degree in Cognitive Psychology and a PhD in Human Resource Education from Louisiana State University in 2013 and 2018 respectively, and his doctoral dissertation focused on best practices for online education.

Wendy Hoag

Wendy Hoag is the Information Technology Librarian at Arizona Western College in Yuma, Arizona. Wendy received her Master of Library and Information Science at San José State University, and her Bachelor of Science, History at Chowan University. When not assisting students with their research and technology questions, she enjoys visiting national parks and monuments, reading science fiction, and acrylic painting.

Jamie Holmes

Jamie Holmes earned her master's degree in Library Science at the University of North Texas and currently serves as a Reference and Instruction Librarian at Tulsa Community College. Prior to that, she taught secondary English for ten years before starting her career as an academic librarian at a four-year regional university.

Gwetheldene Holzmann

Dr. Gwetheldene L. Holzmann is an Associate Professor of Higher Education Administration in the Graduate School of Education at Oral Roberts University (ORU). In over twenty years at the university, she has served in a number of roles, most recently including the Director of State Authorization. Her work on ORU's Institutional Effectiveness team encompassed the areas of accreditation, assessment, project data and statistics, and legal compliance, among others. She earned a BA in Chemistry at Malone College, an MA in Education (Curriculum) at Regent University, and an EdS and EdD in Higher Education Administration at the College of William and Mary. Current research interests include assessment and the scholarship of teaching and learning.

Robert Holzmann

Robert Holzmann is the Systems and Digital Technologies Librarian at Tulsa Community College. Since coming to TCC in 2007, Bob has supported library systems, technology, cloud-based services, electronic resources, and data collection and statistics for the TCC Libraries. Bob chaired the Library Services Assessment Plan Team, serves as the Library Technical Services Team Leader, serves on the Library Website and E-resources Team, and leads the TCC Library's study about library impact on student success. Over his forty-year career, Bob has also worked for the Virginia Beach Public Library and Regent University Library and held a variety of IT-related positions in corporate and small businesses. Bob earned his Bachelor of Music degree at the University of Cincinnati College-Conservatory of Music and his MBA at the University of Phoenix.

MICHAEL J. KRASULSKI

Michael J. Krasulski is Department Head of and Assistant Professor and Access Services Librarian in, the Library and Learning Resources Department at the Community College of Philadelphia. He earned his MSLIS from Drexel University and has an additional master's degree from Temple University. Michael serves as the book review editor for the *Journal of Access Services*. Together with Trevor A. Dawes, he edited *Twenty-First Century Access Services: On the Frontline of Academic Librarianship*, which was published by the Association of College and Research Libraries in 2013.

AMY LAGERS

Amy Lagers is a Reference and Instruction Librarian at Tulsa Community College. She holds a Master of Library and Information Studies degree from the University of Oklahoma and has over twenty years of teaching experience in both K–12 and higher education.

AMANDA M. LEFTWICH

Amanda M. Leftwich is the Student Success Librarian at Montgomery County Community College. She holds a Master of Science in Library Science from Clarion University of Pennsylvania. Her expertise and research interests include mindfulness, reflective practice, and communities of practice. She is the founder of *mindfulinlis*, a virtual space dedicated to mindful practice in librarianship.

JOY OEHLERS

Joy Oehlers is the Information Literacy Librarian at Kapiʻolani Community College. She received her MLIS from the University of Victoria in Wellington, New Zealand, in 1999.

KENDRA PERRY

Kendra Perry is the Coordinator of Library and Learning Support Services at Hagerstown Community College. She has an MA in English from Andrews University and an MLIS from the University of Wisconsin-Milwaukee. Over two decades of educational experience, she taught many subjects, ranging from third grade Language Arts to Business German for Engineers, before transitioning into librarianship. She is passionate about connecting students with resources for success.

COURTNEY RAEFORD

Courtney Raeford is the Director of Institutional Research & Assessment at SUNY Old Westbury, where she provides institutional data and supports campus-wide assessment efforts. She holds an MEd in Education Psychology from Temple University and is currently pursuing her EdD in Higher Education. Her professional interests include developing methods for the assessment of institutional effectiveness and critical inquiry in education research. She most enjoys the time spent traveling and sharing a meal in the company of her partner, family, and close friends.

JACQUELYN RAY

Jacquelyn Ray currently serves as Director of Library Services at Walla Walla Community College in Walla Walla, Washington. Jacquelyn is currently pursuing her EdD in Leadership for Educational Equity, Higher Education with the University of Colorado Denver. She earned her MLIS from the University of Washington, Seattle, and her MA in English from Southern New Hampshire University. She has worked in a variety of Academic Libraries for over twenty years, and her professional passion is creating effective collaborations within her community to advocate for and support student success from Information Literacy to OER.

SAM SUBER

Sam Suber is currently the Electronic Resources Coordinator at the Moraine Valley Community College Library, where he manages assessment, electronic resources, budgets, periodicals, and government documents. Sam earned his MS in Library and Information Science from the University of Illinois at Urbana-Champaign and BA in English from the University of Minnesota, Twin Cities. For fun, Sam enjoys running and training for marathons and other long-distance events.

JOANNA THOMPSON

Joanna Thompson is an Adjunct Reference and Open Educational Resources Librarian at the Borough of Manhattan Community College and the New York City College of Technology at the City University of New York. She holds an MS in Library and Information Science from Pratt Institute, an MA in Visual and Media Anthropology from the Free University of Berlin, and a BA in Cultural Anthropology from the University of Louisville. Her research areas include qualitative research in libraries, anthropology of education, and open knowledge initiatives.

JOYCE TOKUDA

Joyce Tokuda is the Learning Resources Librarian at the Kapiʻolani Community College Library, where her primary areas of focus are instruction, reference, and collection management. She received her MLISc from the University of Hawaiʻi Mānoa.

SHARELL WALKER

Sharell Walker is the Student Outreach and Instruction Librarian at the Borough of Manhattan Community College, City University of New York. She holds an MS in Library Sciences and an MA in English Literature. Her research areas include outreach to diverse populations with an emphasis on minority community college students.

MELINDA (MINDY) WILMOT

Melinda (Mindy) Wilmot is a Professor and Reference Librarian at Bakersfield College, where she has worked since 2014. She received her MLIS from San José State University and has served on the college's Curriculum, Assessment, and Program Review Committees.